Teaching Multi‹
Literature in a I

MW00823839

This textbook is a comprehensive resource for teaching multicultural children's literature. Providing foundational information on how and why to integrate diverse children's literature into the classroom, this book presents a necessary historical perspective on cultural groups in the United States and context for how to teach children's literature in a way that reflects and sustains students' rich cultural backgrounds. The historical insights and context on diverse cultural groups at the heart of the book allow readers to deepen their understanding of why teaching about cultural diversity is necessary for effective and inclusive education. Part I offers foundational information on how to teach children's literature in a diverse society, and Part II overviews pedagogy, resources, and guidance for teaching specific culturally and linguistically marginalized groups. Each chapter contains book recommendations, discussion questions, and additional resources for teachers.

With authentic strategies and crucial background knowledge embedded in each chapter, this text is essential reading for pre-service and in-service teachers and is ideal for courses in children's literature, literacy methods instruction, and multicultural education.

AnnMarie Alberton Gunn is an Associate Professor of Literacy at the University of South Florida, U.S.A.

Susan V. Bennett is an Associate Professor of Literacy at the University of South Florida, U.S.A.

Teaching Multicultural Children's Literature in a Diverse Society

From a Historical Perspective to Instructional Practice

Edited by
AnnMarie Alberton Gunn
and Susan V. Bennett

NEW YORK AND LONDON

First published 2023
by Routledge
605 Third Avenue, New York, NY 10158

and by Routledge
4 Park Square, Milton Park, Abingdon, Oxon, OX14 4RN

Routledge is an imprint of the Taylor & Francis Group, an informa business

ISBN: 978-1-032-34398-3 (hbk)
ISBN: 978-1-032-32576-7 (pbk)
ISBN: 978-1-003-32194-1 (ebk)

DOI: 10.4324/9781003321941

Typeset in Goudy
by Taylor & Francis Books

Contents

PART II
Diverse and Marginalized Groups of People   93

Illustrations

Figures

Tables

Contributors

David Allsopp is Professor of special education and teacher education. His research and writing is focused on implementing effective instructional practices for students with exceptionalities and teacher education that enhances teachers' knowledge and skills to effectively serve students with exceptionalities.

Sohyun An is a Professor of social studies education, with research and teaching interests in anti-racist social studies education, critical war studies, and Asian American studies. She was a former high school social studies teacher in South Korea.

Susan V. Bennett is an Associate Professor in literacy studies and is a regional director for the National Association for Multicultural Education. Her research focuses on issues such as culturally sustaining pedagogy, multicultural literature, and community literacies, which includes working in correctional institutions and an afterschool and summer center.

Stephanie Branson is a visiting instructor in the literacy department at the University of South Florida. Her research areas include teacher professional development and exploring effective practices for developing literacy pedagogical content knowledge. She was a former elementary grades teacher in Georgia and Florida.

Tanya Christ is a Literacy Professor and Reading Clinic Director. Her research focuses on early childhood vocabulary, comprehension, and digital literacies learning; issues of educational access, equity, and social justice; and teacher education. She was formerly a teacher for NYC public schools.

Shanetia P. Clark is a former middle school English teacher, and is currently an Associate Professor of Literacy. She teaches courses in children's literature, elementary literacy methods, and aesthetic education. Her research interests include children's and young adult literature and the teaching of writing.

Elizabeth A. Cutrer-Párraga has enjoyed a long career as a general, special education and literacy teacher. Currently, she teaches literacy methods, multi-cultural and academic intervention courses to pre-service special education teachers. She researches how the use of children's books can support the social and emotional wellbeing of children.

Grace Enriquez is Professor of Language and Literacy at Lesley University. Her scholarship focuses on children's literature for social justice; critical literacies; reader response; intersections of literacies and embodiment; and writing instruction. She is a recipient of the Children's Literature Association Diversity Research Grant and the Children's Literature Assembly Research Award.

Aimee Frier is an Assistant Teaching Professor at Florida State University where she teaches literacy methods. Her research interests include digital literacies, pre-service teacher education, and students with reading difficulties.

Kristin Valle Geren is a doctoral student in literacy studies and a former elementary school ELA teacher, reading specialist, and literacy coach. Her research interests focus on the intersections of literacy policy, place, and equity.

Connie R. Green is a Professor Emerita from Appalachian State University where she taught children's literature, early childhood education, and language arts. She has had a long interest in religious diversity and spirituality.

AnnMarie Alberton Gunn is an Associate Professor in Literacy Studies. Dr. Gunn has numerous international, and national publications and conference presentations. Her passion is to support teachers and prepare future teachers to teach all children in a prek-12th grade classroom and serve the larger community.

Melissa A. Heath is a retired School Psychology Professor. She specializes in bibliotherapy to support children's social emotional learning, children's grief, youth suicide prevention, and school-based crisis intervention.

Katharine Hull is a doctoral student in Literacy Studies. She previously provided reading interventions to students of all ages, as well as delivered professional development to reading specialists and classroom teachers. Her research interests include critical literacy, the intersections of literacy and labor movements, teacher advocacy, and qualitative methodologies.

Margaret Krause, Ph.D. is a faculty member in the Literacy Studies Program at the University of South Florida. Her research focuses on pre-service teachers' developing literacy identities, multimodal literacy practices for children with reading differences, and the facilitation of inclusive literacy pedagogical practices for pre-service teachers in diverse educational settings.

Emily McConnaughy is a former elementary ELA teacher and currently a doctoral student in Literacy Studies at the University of South Florida. Her research interests are focused on community based literacies, multicultural literacies, and multimodal forms of composing.

Csaba Osvath is a visiting professor at the University of South Florida, pursuing literacy studies with a special focus on qualitative methods, extended reality (XR), and arts-based research. Prior to his graduate studies in the United States, Csaba studied theology and horticulture in Hungary and Wales.

Alexandra Panos is a former middle grades ELA teacher and currently works as an Assistant Professor of Literacy Studies at the University of South Florida. She centers her research on studying and working with communities on critical literacies and inquiry approaches for understandings and actions around complex and intractable challenges such as school equity, climate change, and spatial injustice.

Barbara J. Peterson is a Language and Literacy Consultant whose work focuses on design and implementation of afterschool/summer literacy and enrichment programming within diverse, low-income communities in the Tampa Bay region. Her research interests include multicultural literature, community-based literacies, and social-emotional learning through literacy instruction.

Donna Sabis-Burns (Mohawk) is a Supervisory Program Specialist at the U.S. Department of Education's Office of Indian Education in Washington, D.C. Dr. Sabis-Burns is an enrolled citizen of the Haudenosaunee-St. Regis Mohawk tribe. She is currently serving as a Board Member for the Children's Literature Assembly, and her research interests include Indigenous representation in literature for children and young adults.

Jenifer Jasinski Schneider is a Professor in Literacy Studies at the University of South Florida, Tampa. Her research focuses on arts-based approaches to literacy education in which children's literature, process drama, and digital tools support youth's symbolic development and meaning-making strategies.

Sue Ann Sharma is an Associate Professor and Chair of Graduate Education, Director of Early Childhood Education and Literacy Education programs. Her research and teaching interests focuses on early childhood and culturally responsive pedagogies; digital curation; and online teaching and learning. She was formerly a curriculum director, literacy coach, and teacher.

Lynn Atkinson Smolen is Professor Emerita of literacy education and teaching English as a second language. She is the co-editor of *Multicultural literature and response: Affirming diverse voices*. Her research focuses on multicultural literature and teaching English learners. She has been the Project Investigator for two U.S. Department of Education five-year grants.

Allison N. Symulevich (she/her) is an assistant librarian at USF Libraries. She manages the institutional repository at USF, Digital Commons @ USF. In addition, she is the liaison librarian to political science and criminology. Her research interests include open access and innovative digital archiving techniques.

Jessica N. Szempruch (she/her) is a faculty librarian at USF Libraries where she is liaison to multiple departments, focusing most passionately on the social and behavioral sciences. Her research combines aspects of information literacy, student success, interdisciplinary collaboration, emerging and virtual technologies, and educational innovation.

Kaya van Beynen is the Associate Dean of Research & Instruction at the University of South Florida Libraries. Her research has focused on interdisciplinary topics linking library science, education, and environmental studies. She has published articles in *College & Research Libraries*, *Journal of Academic Librarianship*, *International Journal of Science Education, Part B*, and *Early Childhood Education Journal*. In 2021, she was awarded the ACRL, EBSS Distinguished Education & Behavioral Sciences Librarian.

Ellie L. Young is a Professor and Department Chair in the Counseling Psychology and Special Education Department at Brigham Young University. As a school psychologist and professor, she has worked to address the social-emotional well-being of youth in school settings.

Foreword

I believe that it is appropriate to begin this narrative with the words of Seidel and Rokne (2011) who said, "Teaching in rapidly and ever-changing diversified learning communities in the context of global political, economic, and ecological strain and presents special questions and challenges for teachers who may feel anxiety about content, material, and language and literacy development" (p. 246). The message in this quote has broad implications for both teachers and students in schools today.

The ease of adaptability of children to a changing multicultural world is dependent upon opportunities to understand and develop respect for different cultures (Evans, 2010). The openness of educators to discussing and responding positively to issues of diversity, equity, and inclusion must be an educational priority. Teachers' beliefs about diversity influences their decisions about what and how they teach and their choices of the resources they will use to promote students' understanding. Anxiety about what to teach and how to teach students across all forms of diversity has been further complicated by the advent of the COVID-19 pandemic and the disparities in student access to instructional tools and materials and the social emotional repercussion associated with virtual learning. It requires pursuing a "new vision of what it means to educate all students" (Ladson-Billings, 2021, p. 170).

The editors of this text, Ann Marie Alberton Gunn and Susan V. Bennett, wholeheartedly embrace the need for and acknowledge the value of multicultural education to guide teachers in creating students who are change agents. Their commitment to diversity is reflected in their individual and collaborative research, writings, and teaching of both graduate and undergraduate students and their on-going reflection about culturally sustaining literacy practices through their long-term participation in the *Culturally Sustaining Literacy Pedagogy* Study Group of the Literacy Research Association (LRA).

This book, which features the research and writings of established scholars in the field of literacy, provides teachers with children's literature and resources that can expand their understanding of the cultural diversity of the learners in their classrooms. The authors believe that teachers must be guided by a rationale for learning about cultural diversity and understand the importance cultural markers have on student learning. They also believe that teachers must understand the historical perspective of the different cultural groups in the United States and promote student understanding of these issues by integrating literature about issues of diversity and equity and promoting reflection and discussion of these issues. To improve the academic achievement and social emotional needs of students across all forms of diversity, they must engage in culturally responsive teaching.

Literature serves a social function in the lives of children by providing them with opportunities to understand, affirm, or negotiate social relationships among peers, family members, and community members, as well as raise and develop their awareness of significant social issues and social problems (McGinley & Kamberelis, 1996). Creating opportunities for students to engage in critical conversation in digital spaces and classroom environments is essential. Literature can promote understanding of diversity, generate empathy for others, provide ways to respond to crises, and take actions about issues regardless of whether or not the experiences depicted have been experienced personally or vicariously (Johnson, Koss, & Martinez, 2018; Nikolajeva, 2013; Sipe, 2008). Children's picture books and young adult literature have been used to address topics with controversial political and socially controversial topics (Dunkerly-Bean & Bean, 2014; McCardle, 2017). Multicultural literature can promote critical inquiry about oneself and others through the presentation of multiple perspectives about critical issues (Taylor, 2000).

The International Literacy Association (ILA) specifies that "children have the right to read texts that mirror their experiences and languages, provide *windows* into the lives of others, and open *doors* into our diverse world" (International Literacy Association, 2018, p.10). Teachers must understand cultural diversity and how cultural markers influence the development of students' identities. Through their instruction, they must help students to recognize and value the beliefs and practices inherent in their individual cultural heritage while helping students acquire information about the greater cultural world and develop sociopolitical consciousness or to recognize, understand, and evaluate social inequities. When students perceive that their teachers are supportive of their engagement in reading about significant social issues, their attitudes toward and interests in reading about them become more positive, and when teachers use culturally responsive teaching practices, student engagement is increased (Aronson & Laughter, 2016).

Teachers' beliefs about diversity influences their decisions about what and how they teach and their choices of the resources they will use to promote students' understanding. Trends in immigration patterns and economic and social issues related to marginalization of children impacted by economic, gender, religious, and social issues point to a need for teachers to be prepared to implement a culturally responsive curriculum using culturally and linguistically responsive practices (Goodwin, 2017). Culturally responsive teachers who incorporate stories about "diverse experiences into the curriculum" can make the difference in exploring issues and engaging students in reflection and critical conversations about these issues. Selecting appropriate books requires that both pre-service and in-service teachers understand these cultural groups. This understanding of the complexities of communities and cultures come from both multicultural coursework and experiences in multicultural school settings (Ladson-Billings, 2021).

The issue of teacher predispositions about cultural diversity is important when teaching children across all forms of diversity since most teachers are White, middle-class, female, and Native English speakers. The U.S. teaching force does not reflect the cultural diversity of the students in today's classrooms (King, et al., 2016), nor does it share the values, cultures, and experiences of their students (Kahn, et al., 2014).

Teacher's beliefs about diversity impact the expectations, behaviors, instructional decisions, and their responses to students (Liang & Zhang, 2009; Walker-Dalhouse & Dalhouse, 2006). Therefore, it is important that "teachers examine their own culture and beliefs, have high expectations for their students; learn about and appreciate the cultures of their students, families, and communities to inform instruction" (International Literacy Association, 2018, p. 80). These "beliefs are formed early in a teacher's career (even before and during pre-service training) and are extremely difficult to change" (Gay, 2018, p. 64). Dispositional factors influence the likelihood that pre-service teachers will develop multicultural awareness and sensitivity in teaching education programs toward teaching diverse groups of students. Garmon (2004) identified three dispositional factors needed as **openness** (being receptive to new information, different types of diversity; or arguments), **self-awareness** (being aware of one's beliefs and attitudes), and **self-reflectiveness** (having the ability and willingness to think critically about oneself) as well as having a commitment to social justice. Multicultural understandings and sensitivity toward diversity are greater when pre-service teachers possess such knowledge and dispositions (Lee, 2016). The educational experiences and personal histories of not being exposed to critical content in their K-12 grade school experiences and a fear of making mistakes by introducing critical issues focused on racial and cultural diversity and power differences in society are factors that must be considered in explaining the resistance to introducing critical issues focused on racial and cultural diversity and power differences in society (Riley & Crawford-Garrett, 2016).

Equity and social justice are values advocated by many teacher preparation programs and assessed through teacher dispositions and practices used for responding to learners in the classroom and individuals in society. Opportunities to reflect upon perceptions and beliefs about diversity can result in an increased understanding of others (Barnes, 2006), and the impact that such beliefs can have on the academic performance of diverse students (Major & Brock, 2003). However, teacher education programs have been found to have limited to moderate impact on the cultural responsiveness of teachers (Cochran-Smith, et al., 2004). It is important that teachers strive to be culturally relevant educators who use critical literacy practices to examine and rethink oppressive practices and attitudes to become more multicultural in their perspectives (DeMulder, Stribling, & Day, 2014). However, "No single course or set of field experiences is capable of preparing pre-service students to meet the needs of diverse learners" (Ladson-Billings, 2000, p. 209).

Teacher education programs must develop teachers who are prepared to meet the needs of the diversity of students in today's schools. The International Literacy Association's *Standards for the Preparation of Literacy Professionals 2017*, as noted in Standard 4: *Diversity & Equity*, states there is "the need to prepare teachers to develop and engage their students in a curriculum that places value on the diversity that exists in society" (International Literacy Association, 2018, p. 14). Some potential avenues for achieving this goal include reexamining course work, examining teacher education admission procedures, and restructuring field experiences (Ladson-Billings, 2021).

Regardless of the procedures used to re-envision the ways to better prepare teachers for working with students across all forms of diversity, it is essential teachers have culturally relevant conceptions of knowledge and an awareness and acceptance of different ways of knowing (Gay, 1993). Additionally, teachers should not discount standards or larger cultural expectations, nor consider them to be above students' "ways of knowing" (Ladson-Billings, 1991). They believe that knowledge is continuously being re-created, recycled, or changed and shared. The use of literature is a means to achieve the goal of exploring sociopolitical issues and people in "otherworlds" in ways that challenge students' thinking, advocate for change, and ultimately serve to meet the educational and social emotional needs of all students because all children should have an equal right to succeed as readers and writers (Walker-Dalhouse & Risko, 2016).

Doris Walker-Dalhouse, Ph.D.
Professor of Literacy
Marquette University

References

Aronson, B. & Laughter, J. (2016). The theory and practice of culturally relevant education: A synthesis pf research across content areas. *Review of Educational Research*, 86(1), 163–206.

Barnes, C. J. (2006). Preparing pre-service teachers to teach in a culturally responsive way. *Negro Educational Review*, 57(1/2), 85–100.

Cochran-Smith, M., Davis, D., & Fries, K. (2004). *Multicultural teacher education: Research, practice, and policy*. Jossey-Bass.

DeMulder, E. K., Stribling, S. M., & Day, M. (2014). Examining the immigrant experience: helping teachers develop as critical educators. *Teaching Education*, 25(1),43–64.

Dunkerly-Bean, J. M., & Bean, T.W. (2014). *Using critical literacy to promote human rights and civic engagement*. International Literacy Association.

Evans, S. (2010). The role of multicultural literature interactive read-alouds on student perspectives toward diversity. *Journal of Research in Innovative Teaching*, 3(1), 92–99.

Garmon, M. A. (2004). Changing pre-service teachers' attitudes/beliefs about diversity. What are the critical factors? *Journal of Teacher Education*, 55(3), 201–213.

Gay, G. (1993). Building cultural bridges: A bold proposal for teacher education. *Education and Urban Society*, 25, 285–289.

Gay, G. (2018). *Culturally Responsive teaching* (3rd ed.). New York: Teachers College Press.

Goodwin, A.L. (2017). Who is in the classroom now? Teacher preparation and the education of immigrant children. *Educational Studies*, 53(5), 433–449.

International Literacy Association (2018). *Standards for the preparation of literacy professionals 2017*. Newark, DE: International Literacy Association.

Johnson, N. J., Koss, M. D., & Martinez, M. (2018). Through the sliding glass door: #EmpowerTheReader. *The Reading Teacher*, 71(5), 569–577.

Kahn, L., Lindstrom, L., & Murray, C. (2014). Factors contributing to pre-service teachers' beliefs about diversity. *Teacher Education Quarterly*, 41(4), 53–70.

King, J. B., McIntosh, A., & Bell-Ellwanger, J. (2016). *The state of racial diversity in the educator workforce*. U.S. Department of Education, Office of Planning, Evaluation and Policy Development, Policy and Program Studies Service.

Ladson-Billings, G. (1991). Beyond multicultural literacy. *The Journal of Negro Education*, 60, 147–157.

Ladson-Billings, G. (2000). Preparing teacher for diversity: Historical perspectives, current trends, and future directions. In L. Darling-Hammond & G. Sykes (Eds.), *Teaching as the learning profession: Handbook of policy and practice*, pp. 86–87. Jossey Bass.

Ladson-Billings, G. (2021). *Culturally relevant pedagogy: Asking a different question*. New York: Teachers College Press.

Lee, C. (2016). Teaching multiple literacies and critical literacy to pre-service teachers through children's literature-based engagements. *Journal of Language and Literacy*, 12(1), 39–52.

Liang, X., & Zhang, G. (2009). Indicators to evaluate pre-service teachers' cultural competence. *Evaluation & Research in Education*, 22(1), 17–31.

Major, E. M. & Brock, C.H. (2003). Fostering positive dispositions toward diversity: Dialogical explorations of a moral dilemma. *Teacher Education Quarterly*, 30, 7–26.

McCardle, T. (2017). "The horror" of structural racism: Helping students take a critical stance using classic literature. *Multicultural Perspectives*, 19(2)l, 98–102.

McGinley, W., & Kamberelis, G. (1996). Maniac Magee and Ragtime Trumpie: Children negotiating self and world through reading and writing. *Research in the Teaching of English*, 30, 75–113.

Nikolajeva, M. (2013). Picturebooks, and emotional literacy. *The Reading Teacher*, 67, 249–254.

Riley, K., & Crawford-Garrett, K. (2016). Critical texts in literacy teacher education: Living inquiries into racial justice and immigration. *Language Arts*, 94(2), 94–107.

Seidel, J., & Rokne, A. (2011). Picture books for engaging peace and social justice with children. *Diaspora, Indigenous, and Minority Education*, 5, 245–359.

Sipe, L. R. (2008). Talking back and taking over. Young children's expressive engagement. *The Reading Teacher*, 55(5), 476–483.

Taylor, S.V. (2000). Multicultural is who we are: Literature as a reflection of ourselves. *Teaching Exceptional Children*, 32(3), 24–29.

Walker-Dalhouse, D, & Dalhouse. A.D. (2006). Investigating white pre-service teachers' beliefs about teaching in culturally diverse classrooms. *The Negro Educational Review*, 58(1–2),69–79.

Walker-Dalhouse, D. & Risko, V.J. (2016). Culturally responsive literacy instruction. In A. Swan Dagen & R. M. Bean (Eds.), *Best practices of literacy leaders*, pp. 304–322. New York: The Guilford Press.

Preface

Many cultural and diverse topics are controversial in schools. Teachers have been ridiculed for reading children's books that feature such topics as religion, LGBTQ+, poverty, and immigration. Teachers also face confusion with curriculum, censorship, and laws that either support or oppose teaching these topics. Contemporary U.S. classrooms represent a mosaic of racial, ethnic, cultural, linguistic, and religious diversity, and as of 2018, more than 50% of the U.S. population, younger than 15 years of age, are from diverse backgrounds or non-White (Frey, 2019). The abundant and rich diversity observed in our classrooms—especially early childhood and elementary classrooms—continues to grow. This solicits the question: are our educational systems serving students in ways that embrace social and academic success for all children and their families?

We recognize how important it is for teachers to understand the content of a diverse world, and it is imperative that teacher education programs provide a space to develop this knowledge and insight into this diverse world. It is essential for children to engage with literature that is age-appropriate and culturally relevant to their lives and interests, which can facilitate an increase in literacy achievement and motivation to read (White et al., 2014). One way to accomplish this is to provide children with multicultural literature. Multicultural literature offers "mirrors" for children to affirm their identities and importance; multicultural literature also provides "windows" for children to learn about others' similarities and differences from ones represented in their own community (Bennett et al., 2021b; Bishop, 1990, 2012; Gunn et al., 2014, 2020a, 2020b, 2022). Even though we understand the significance multicultural literature plays in children's reading motivation, engagement and success, there has been a staggering lack of diversity in much of the literature available to children in schools and in their communities (Bennett et al., 2021a; Crisp et al., 2016).

Editors and Authors

We are middle-age, White, cisgender women from working-class backgrounds, AnnMarie of Polish heritage and Susan of Anglo-Celtic heritage. We chose education as our profession because of our commitment to advancing and advocating for equity for all children. We dedicated ourselves to literacy and teacher education with our vision to support children, families, and teachers for educational equity. Susan taught elementary school for six years in urban areas and on the Navajo Reservation, and AnnMarie taught elementary school in various counties in Florida for nine years in highly diverse schools. We recognize the significance of how cultural backgrounds impact teaching and learning, and we continue to reflect, expand, and cultivate our knowledge and thoughts. Therefore, we knew the importance of inviting authors from diverse backgrounds. We appreciate the internationally recognized scholars who contributed their expertise and their vast cultural identities which include such backgrounds as, but not limited to, gender, sexual orientation, age, race, ethnicity, social class, and religion.

Cover of the Book

In 2019, we developed a partnership with Heather Robb, executive director of a nonprofit afterschool center, which serves children and families. She asked us to help design an academic program to support the children; a majority were below grade level expectations. We then began volunteering at this center, and at this time, we counted 58 books on a bookshelf. Our mission instantaneously became to build a robust literacy program and increase children's access to high-quality, multicultural books. Considering the pandemic and social justice crises, we wanted to ensure children at this center had access to quality multicultural books that positively affirmed their cultural identities, sense of belonging, and connection to the center and their community.

The photograph on the cover represents the children from the center and the current library of multicultural literature, which now has over 5,500 books. From our time at this center, we witnessed the children engaging with these multicultural books, and it reinforced the importance of book selection that provides "windows and mirrors" for children to affirm their identities and see others in these books (Bishop, 1990). Since our partnership began, we have been able to achieve our goal and set forth more goals for the center, which include parent-family engagement, increasing books at home, social emotional based reading groups, creative arts integration, and small group and one on one academic support.

We appreciate the University of South Florida, our colleagues, private and public donations, and local organizations for supporting these initiatives. We are most thankful for the parents, caregivers, and children who welcomed us to work and play together in developing this literacy program.

Overview of this Book

Based on our experiences in education and multicultural literature, we wanted to present teachers and future teachers with authentic strategies and accurate content for their diverse classrooms. Our purpose in writing this book is to afford information, recommend children's literature, and suggest resources for teachers and future teachers to help children understand cultural diversity. The chapters in this book provide:

- a rationale for why teachers and children should learn about cultural diversity and the role of cultural markers;
- information for teachers to understand how to integrate children's literature into the classroom and navigate the difficult conversations that may arise;
- a historical perspective of cultural groups in the United States and then a context for how the integration of specific information about these groups has been received in schools and society;
- reflection questions in each chapter that can be used for self-reflection or classroom instruction/discussion;
- recommended children's literature that can be used to discuss and highlight specific cultural groups; and
- resources for pre-service and in-service teachers to learn more about these diverse cultural groups.

We divided the book into two sections, and we invited leading scholars and experts in/outside the field of literacy education to offer pre-service education and in-service teachers background knowledge to learn how to successfully navigate difficult conversations.

The first section includes chapters that offer teachers and future teachers the foundations of pedagogy they need to learn and teach about cultural diversity through children's literature. This section begins with connections between multicultural education and children's literature. It is our hope that these chapters can provide teachers and pre-service teachers the background knowledge, pedagogy, and strategies to navigate working in diverse classrooms using a multicultural framework. For example, in this section we have chapters about digital tools and state and national standards. In addition, we invited authors outside the field of literacy education to provide their expertise to foster discussion focused on these classroom topics. For example, professionals in the field of special education/school psychology wrote a chapter on bibliotherapy and university librarians wrote the chapter on censorship.

The second section consists of chapters specific to populations who have been marginalized in the United States, and we highlighted cultural groups rarely discussed in other books, such as children with a parent who is incarcerated or diverse religious groups. We carefully selected authors who offer an "insider" perspective or have the extensive knowledge working and learning with specific groups of people. This section provides chapters about immigrants and refugees, gender and LGBTQ+, social class, disabilities and the special child, African Americans, Latinos, Southeast Asians, and Indigenous people.

This book is designed to be read in any order. We carefully selected the two separate sections and the placement of each chapter. It is our goal that this book could be used for pre-service and in-service teachers' education to further develop their knowledge, understandings, and pedagogy to educate all children in their classrooms.

References

Bennett, S. V., Gunn, A. A., & Peterson, B. (2021a) Access to multicultural children's literature during COVID-19. *The Reading Teacher*, 74(6), 785–796. doi:10.1002/trtr.2003.

Bennett, S. V., Gunn, A. A., van Beynen, K., & Morton, M. L. (2021b). Religiously diverse multicultural literature for early childhood. *Early Childhood Education Journal*, 50, 663–673. doi:10.1007/s10643-021-01180-7.

Bishop, R. S. (1990). Mirrors, windows, and sliding glass doors. *Perspectives: Choosing and Using Books for the Classroom*, 6(3), ix–xi. Retrieved from https://scenicregional.org/wp-content/uploads/2017/08/Mirrors-Windows-and-Sliding-Glass-Doors.pdf.

Bishop, R. S. (2012). Reflections on the development of African American children's literature. *Journal of Children's Literature*, 38(2), 5–13.

Crisp, T., Knezek, S. M., Quinn, M., Bingham, G. E., Girardeau, K., & Starks, F. (2016). What's on our bookshelves? The diversity of children's literature in early childhood classroom libraries. *Journal of Children's Literature*, 42(2), 29–42.

Frey, W. H. (2019). Less than half of U.S. children under 15 are white, census shows. Retrieved from www.brookings.edu/research/less-than-half-of-us-children-under-15-are-white-census-shows/.

Gunn, A. A., Bennett, S. V., Alley, K. M., Barrera, E. S., Cantrell, S. C., Moore, L., & Welsh, J. W. (2020a). Revisiting culturally responsive teaching in an early childhood setting. *Journal of Early Childhood Teacher Education*, 42(3), 265–280.

Gunn, A. A., Bennett, S. V., & Leung, C. L. (2014). Pre-service teachers' "revelations and connections": Fostering deep conversations while reading multicultural literature. *Journal of Contemporary Research in Education*, 3(1/2), 37–52.

Gunn. A. A., Bennett. S. V., & Peterson, B. (2022). "She looks like me": Putting high-quality multicultural literature in children's hands during COVID-19. *Journal of Research in Childhood Education*, 36(3) 363–380. doi:10.1080/02568543.2021.1991532.

Gunn, A. A., & Bennett, S. V., van Beynen, K. (2020b). Talking about religious diversity: Using multicultural literature as a tool. *Social Studies and the Young Learner*, 33(1), 10–16.

White, T. G., Kim, J. S., Kingston, H. C., & Foster, L. F. (2014). Replicating the effects of a teacher scaffolded voluntary summer reading program: The role of poverty. *Reading Research Quarterly*, 49(1): 5–30. doi:10.1002/rrq.62.

Part I

Multicultural Education within Classroom Teaching

1 Creating Spaces of Freedom
Multicultural Education and Children's Literature

Sue Ann Sharma and Tanya Christ

Rationale and Historical Perspectives: Creating Spaces

Spaces for minoritized children to be seen in literacy have been historically quite limited. While White middle-class children are privileged to be seen in the books read in school, marginalized children are rarely seen in authentic ways across classroom libraries and read-alouds (Currie, 2013). This is problematic because "learners do not develop knowledge and literacy exclusive of their social histories, cultures, and immediate contest for using knowledge" (Gadsden, 1993, p. 358). Therefore, it is essential for all children to see their social histories and cultures through the selection of culturally sustaining text (Sharma & Christ, 2017) and to be seen by peers via these books that provide windows into other cultures (Sims-Bishop, 1990).

Spaces for children to be heard have also been historically quite limited. Predominantly, teachers maintain tight control over read-aloud conversations using a teacher-initiation then student-response pattern (Hindman et al., 2019). This leaves almost no space for children to insert their knowledge, interests, or expertise by expanding or initiating content during read-aloud discussions. Creating spaces for children to be heard can decenter whiteness by providing children from minoritized backgrounds opportunities to use their cultural and linguistic knowledge to support their participation (Pauly et al., 2019). Through this participation, children are empowered by ownership over their learning and simultaneously create opportunities for others to develop cultural competence (Meacham, et al., 2019; Ward & Warren, 2019). Creating spaces to be heard perpetuates, fosters, and sustains "linguistic, literate, and cultural pluralism" (Alim & Paris, 2017, p. 1).

Spaces of joy to celebrate minoritized children have been hindered by the historical dearth of books that reflect their triumphs and strengths. Further, the use of such books is limited by the knowledge of those of us who are selecting the books. That is, teachers need to understand the importance of selecting books that portray cultural joy and know where to find those books. We can change this trajectory

DOI: 10.4324/9781003321941-2

by investing time and resources into becoming knowledgeable about books that lionize children's culture by showing their triumphs and strengths, buying and reading these books, and thus increasing the publication demand for them. Finally, it is important to focus on the triumphs and strengths portrayed in these books when discussing them with children.

This chapter provides a step toward addressing each of these issues. In the following sections, we present how you can use read-aloud discussions to create spaces to be seen, spaces to be heard, and spaces to celebrate cultural joy.

Creating Spaces for Children to Be Seen

Creating spaces for children to be seen transcends the use of melting pot books, which perpetuate the discourse of culture as an amalgamation. St. John de Crèvecoeur (1782) coined the term *melting pot* when he described Americans as "melted into a new race of men" (p. 4). This idea aligns with what Reynolds and Kendi (2020) refer to as *assimilationist* thinking–the idea that everyone should assimilate to the culture of power. This is rooted in a deficit model: "to advance socially and economically in the United States, immigrants need to 'become American' in order to overcome their deficits in the new language and culture" (National Academies of Sciences, Engineering, and Medicine, 1996, p. 28). Assimilation forces minoritized children to diminish their home culture. Aligned with this, melting pot books present a facade of being seen, but not in one's wholeness or as one's true self. *The Snowy Day* written by Erza Jack Keats (1962) is a classic example of a melting pot book. It features a Black family from the perspective of a White male author; but it does not represent Black culture, language, or identity (Paul, 2011). Thus, we do not recommend using melting pot books if you want your minoritized children to be seen.

Instead, we promote the use of culturally sustaining books, in which minoritized children can see their lives, languages, cultures, and identities (Sharma & Christ, 2017). Further, through these books, others can be provided with windows into these worlds to expand their cultural competence (Ladson-Billings, 1995; Sims-Bishop, 1990). This approach aligns with Reynolds and Kendi's (2020) anti-racist perspective, in which people are celebrated for being exactly who they are. Importantly, when books align with children's culture, their literacy participation and performance are better (Christ & Cho, 2022; Christ et al., 2018). This is critically important given that children in U.S. schools are increasingly diverse (see Figure 1.1). We suggest three steps to shift your practice toward the use of more culturally sustaining books, to create spaces for children to be seen in your classroom.

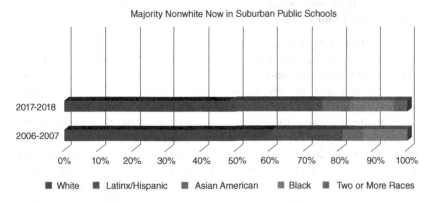

Figure 1.1 Shifting demographics in suburban public schools (Chen et al., 2021, n.p.).

Step 1: Recognize the Need for Culturally Sustaining Books and Books that Provide Windows into Other Cultures to Build Cultural Competence

Recognizing the need for culturally sustaining books that will allow a child to be seen in the classroom is important. Sometimes classroom events spark these needs. For example, Mrs. Locke noticed that Yasmin, a young Muslim girl in her class, was not eating lunch during Ramadan, and the other children were whispering about it. So, she read the class the book *Laila's Lunchbox: A Ramadan Story* (Faruqi, 2015) and discussed fasting during Ramadam and its significance in the Muslim community. This culturally sustaining book helped Yasmin's culture be seen in the classroom and provided the opportunity for other children to build more cultural competence.

It is also important to recognize the need for books that provide windows into other cultures, to help these cultures be seen, even if they are not represented in your classroom. For example, Mr. Kendall, who teaches in a school that serves predominantly White middle-class children, heard his children speaking about immigration in ways that were dehumanizing. He decided to engage in a read-aloud unit that would provide windows to make the experiences of immigrants seen and help his children gain new perspectives. He read books, such as *From North to South* (Laínez, 2013) and *Brothers in Hope* (Williams & Christie, 2005), and discussed the reasons for immigration and the conditions that people endured to make the journey.

Some ways to recognize the need for culturally sustaining and window books include (1) listening to children's conversations, (2) noticing cultural misunderstandings, and (3) noticing opportunities to learn about a culture related to your children's experiences or current events. Also, learning about your children's cultures more deeply may provide additional ideas (for guidance on how to learn more about your children's cultures, see Sharma & Christ, 2017).

Step 2: Search for and Select Diverse Books that Authentically Represent your Children's and Others' Cultures

It can be challenging for teachers to select books that address the multiplicities of readers' cultural identities (Tatum, 2009). Both using search engines and book award lists are helpful strategies. For example, Mrs. Locke might have searched for "picture books about Ramadan" in order to find the book *Laila's Lunchbox*. Of course, in addition to finding books via a search engine, it is also important to search to learn about their authenticity. For example, search for the answers to questions such as these (Sims-Bishop, 1991; Walters, 1998): Was the book written by a person who represents that culture? Has the book received favorable reviews from people from the culture being represented in the book? This additional searching to determine the authenticity of the book will help you avoid melting pot books or books that misrepresent a culture or perpetuate stereotypes.

Further, book award lists are an excellent way to find books that authentically represent cultures. Here are some of our favorites:

- Coretta Scott King Book Awards (depict the African American experience)—e.g. *Brown Girl Dreaming* (Woodson, 2016)
- Carter G. Woodson Book Award (depict themes of social justice and equity)—e.g. *The Power of Her Pen* (Cline-Ransome, 2020)
- Tomás Rivera Mexican American Children's Book Award (depict the Mexican American experience)—e.g. *They Call Me Güero* (Bowels, 2021)
- Sydney Taylor Manuscript Award (depict the Jewish experience)—e.g. *The Passover Guest* (Kusel, 2021)

Finally, to determine whether a book might be culturally sustaining for a particular child in your class, consider the following questions (Christ et al., 2018; Ebe, 2010):

1. *Cultural identities*: Do your children share the same cultural identities (race, ethnicity, religion, etc.) as the main character?
2. *Age and gender identity*: Do your children share the same age and gender as the main character?
3. *Dialect*: Do your children talk like the main characters?
4. *Places*: Do your children spend time in places that are like those in the settings of the book?
5. *Experiences*: Do your children have experiences similar to those in the book?

When Mrs. Locke chose *Laila's Lunchbox* to read to the class, she recognized that Laila in the book and Yasmin in her class shared a religious identity (being Muslim), were of similar age and gender, spent time in similar places (school) and had similar experiences (fasting at school during Ramadan). This book met most of the five selection criteria above, so it was very culturally relevant. It would have been slightly less culturally relevant for an older male child or one who is Muslim but does not fast for Ramadan. How culturally relevant a text is can be assessed as gradations from very relevant to not very relevant and is distinct for each child–even amongst children who share a cultural background (Christ & Cho, 2021; Christ et al., 2018).

Step 3: Integrate and Effectively Facilitate Book Discussions that Address Culture, Language, and Power

Imagine viewing every read aloud as an invitation to learn more about literacy and ourselves. We recommend selecting culturally sustaining and window books as artifacts that allow worlds to be seen, and, in turn, can be used for comprehension and language development.

Ms. Martin plans to do this with the book *Dear Primo: A Letter to My Cousin* (Tonatiuh, 2010). This book features two cousins, Carlitos and Charlie, who send each other letters about their respective lives in Mexico and the U.S. Ms. Martin chooses this book because it is culturally sustaining for her student, Pablo, who has family in Mexico with whom he maintains regular international communication. She also chooses it as a window for many of the White middle-class children in the class who do not have family in other countries to provide an opportunity for them to build their cultural competence.

Before Ms. Martin reads the book, she asks the children some questions based on the cover: What two cultures could this story be about? What do you notice about the languages used for the title; what are those languages? Does it look like the boys live in similar or different places? These questions act to center the focus on language and culture in the book discussion.

During the read-aloud, Ms. Martin asks the children about the author's devices: How does the author help us to know what the Spanish words mean without having to look up the English definitions? Again, this centers on the importance of the bilingual nature of the book and draws attention to the languages in the text.

After reading, Ms. Martin guides the class in a discussion of cross-cultural comparisons, using a Venn Diagram. They compare the activities, favorite foods, words used, etc. across Carlitos and Charlie. They discuss both the boys' similarities and differences.

As a follow up activity, Ms. Martin fosters further cultural identity and competence by engaging the children in making Carlitos' favorite food (quesadillas) in the classroom for lunch. Pablo's mother comes to the school to help with this activity.

Finally, for homework, Ms. Martin asks all the children to write down their own favorite family recipe. They will share these with the class the next day and discuss how they are related to each child's identity or culture.

Creating Spaces for Children to be Heard

Spaces for children to be heard during classroom read-alouds are created by teachers who thoughtfully follow principles of culturally sustaining pedagogy. Some of the most relevant principles related to creating spaces for children to be heard include using children's strengths as instructional starting points, creating nurturing and cooperative environments, reshaping the prescribed curriculum to decenter Whiteness, and sharing power in the classroom (Christ & Cho, 2021; Ladson-Billings, 1995). These principles create spaces intended to "perpetuate and foster–to sustain–linguistic, literate, and cultural pluralism as part of schooling" (Alim & Paris, 2017, p. 1).

While spaces to be heard can be crafted during any read-aloud, choosing books that are culturally and linguistically relevant for children from minoritized backgrounds provides important opportunities for them to use their strengths as starting points because the books align with their lived experiences, making it easier for them to connect and make meaning with these books (Christ et al., 2018; Ebe, 2010). Using children's strengths as instructional starting points also empowers children's ownership over their learning, develops their confidence, especially for the emergent multilingual children whose experiences are often marginalized in schools, and supports their positive literacy outcomes (Kim & Song, 2019; Meacham, et al., 2019).

Further, integrating culturally diverse books serves to reshape the prescribed curriculum to decenter Whiteness, offering new spaces in which children can construct understandings of the world from diverse perspectives. Decentering Whiteness changes the classroom dynamics by providing children from minoritized backgrounds the opportunity to use their cultural and linguistic knowledge as strengths to support their participation (Pauly et al., 2019). Also, decentering Whiteness provides opportunities for all classroom members to develop cultural competence (Meacham, et al., 2019; Pauly et al., 2019), which inspires new ways of being heard in a pluralistic society.

Regardless of book choice, in order for children to have space to be heard during read-alouds, teachers need to (1) create nurturing and cooperative environments in which children feel comfortable participating, (2) share power in the classroom to create space for this participation in ways that are truly collaborative (DiGiacomo, 2020), and (3) position children as "knowers" (Pappas et al., 2002, p. 441).

Nurturing and cooperative environments are created by developing deep and authentic relationships with children (Kim & Song, 2019), creating opportunities for children to collaborate with one another (Polleck & Spence-Davis, 2020), and supporting children's expressions of their ideas and feelings (Houchen, 2013).

Sharing power is accomplished by teachers who allow children to co-construct conversations with them (Christ & Cho, 2021). Sharing power with children improves their participation and opportunities to be heard (Christ & Cho, 2021; DiGiacomo, 2020). When these occur during read-alouds, children initiate topics during book discussions, support one another cognitively and linguistically, use their linguistic repertoires to identify vocabulary, harness cultural knowledge to make spontaneous inferences, predict, observe, connect, evaluate, clarify, question, and co-construct meaning (Christ & Cho, 2021; Pantaleo, 200717).

Positioning children as "knowers" assumes they have important knowledge to contribute to the group's learning (Pappas et al., 2002, p. 441). It requires creating space for and valuing these contributions.

The following vignette illustrates how a second-grade teacher, Ms. Mason, follows these principles to create spaces for her children to be heard during a read-aloud discussion (the transcript is from actual classroom data—see Christ & Cho, 2022; Christ, Cho, & Liu, 2022; Cho & Christ, 2021; Christ & Cho, 2021—all names are pseudonyms). In this excerpt, Ms. Mason and her children are discussing the book, *My Friend Jamal* (McQuinn & Frey, 2008), which is about a Somali-American boy, Jamal, and his friend Joseph. It highlights many aspects of Somali and Muslim culture and language. It is particularly culturally relevant for two children in the class, Bashiir and Fawzia, who are Muslim and whose parents immigrated to the U.S. as refugees from Somalia.

[1] MS. MASON:	[reading the book aloud] Sometimes when I'm at Jamal's house, his mom goes in her bedroom and prays.
[2] FAWZIA:	[interjects, making a spontaneous connection] Yeah, I pray.
[3] MS. MASON:	[to Fawzia] Is it the same?
[4] BASHIIR:	[looking at the illustration of the Qur'an] Hey, I can read that [Qur'an], but I can only read it at home ... I can see all the surahs.
[5] MS. MASON:	The letters? What's the surahs?
[6] BASHIIR:	No, the surahs are these [pointing to the Arabic script at the top of the illustration of the Qur'an]. These things.
[7] MS. MASON:	What are those?
[8] BASHIIR:	Those are surahs.
[9] MS. MASON:	I know, but what does that mean? I know you are saying surahs. But what does that mean? Do you know in English what that means?
[10] BASHIIR:	No.

[11] FAWZIA: I know. [looking closely at the illustration of the
                    Qur'an] I don't know what it says [exactly], but it's
                    one two threes.
[12] MS. MASON: Numbers?
[13] FAWZIA: Yes, numbers [surahs are chapters in the Qur'an, and
                    they are numbered 1–114].

The selection of the book *Jamal* reshaped the prescribed curriculum
to decenter Whiteness. It shifted from the predominant norm of
reading books that represents White, middle-class, Christian norms—
even in classrooms in which all children come from minoritized
backgrounds (Currie, 2013)–to centering book reading on a character
who is Muslim and has a Somali-American immigrant family background. This book selection opened space for Fawzia and Bashirr to
use their cultural and linguistic knowledge about the Qur'an to participate in the read-aloud discussion and to build others' cultural competence by teaching others about the surahs [lines 4, 6, 8, 11, 13]. This
book selection used Bashiir and Fawzia's strengths, such as knowledge
about the Muslim culture, and specifically the Qur'an, as an instructional
starting point. The book *Jamal* directly connected with their lived experiences of reading the Qur'an, which offered them an opportunity to initiate
content and develop ownership in the read-aloud discussion.

The vignette suggested that Ms. Mason created a nurturing and
cooperative environment and shared power in the classroom because
the children were comfortable interjecting during the discussion without being called upon to participate [lines 2, 4]. This created a truly
collaborative conversation in which children co-constructed meaning
with Ms. Mason [lines 5–6, 7–8, 9–10, 12–13] and one another [e.g.
lines 10, 11]. Further, Ms. Mason positioned children as "knowers"
when they initiated topics in the discussion by asking them follow-up
questions to learn more [lines 3, 5, 7, 9, 12].

The principles that Ms. Mason used during this discussion—i.e.,
reshaping the curriculum to de-centering Whiteness, using children's
strengths as instructional starting points, creating a nurturing and cooperative environment, sharing power in the classroom, and positioning
children as "knowers"—yielded several opportunities for children to
meaningfully participate and shape the read-aloud discussion, such as
harnessing cultural knowledge to make spontaneous connections [line 2],
initiating topics [lines 2, 4], using their linguistic repertoires to identify
vocabulary [lines 4, 6, 8, 11, 13], and supporting one another [line 11].

Creating Spaces of Cultural Joy

We present examples of how to lionize children's identities through
themes of cultural joy and strength. Children's author and illustrator

Christopher Myers (2014) argues that the "apartheid of children's literature", other than historical books about civil rights or slavery, has resulted in a dearth of books that affirm minoritized readers' identities and power, and thus create spaces for joy (np). Myers (2014) claims that "it's necessary to provide boys and girls like him with a more expansive landscape upon which to dream" (np) to counter the negative stereotypes often depicted in the media. Books of joy are fodder for building such a landscape. They also provide important counter-narratives from which non-minoritized children can learn. In the following subsections, we present some examples of how teachers have lionized cultural joy through stories of triumph and strength.

Lionizing Children's Black Identities

In Mr. Myers's class, Black children express concern about how the media framed a recent event in the community concerning Black male youth. Mr. Myers selects the book *I Can Write the World* (Sanders, 2019) to open a conversation with the children about how the power of stories is in the hands of those who are writing them. In the book, eight-year-old Ava Murray decides that she wants to become a journalist to write her world and make visible the beauty that has been hidden by the news media about her beloved Bronx neighborhood. Mr. Myers and his class discuss how they can use their own writing about community events to shift the narrative, and embark on dictating or writing editorial pieces for the school and local newspapers.

Further, Mr. Myers also reads Black *Boy Joy: 17 Stories Celebrating Black Boyhood* by Kwame Mbalie (2021) to celebrate Black boys' triumphs and counter the negative media messages that Black boys receive in a racist society. Mr. Myers opens discussions with the class about the book, specifically focusing on the counter narrative of the book as compared with the media, and asks children to question who writes each and why the stories are so different.

Lionizing Children's Latinx Identities

Mr. Brandt teaches in a predominantly White middle-class suburb of San Diego. He wants to uplift his students' knowledge of the contributions of the surrounding the Latinx community. First, he reads, *Be Bold! Be Brave!* (Reynoso, 2019). This book consists of biographic stories about 11 Latinas who came to the United States and their journeys to excel in a wide range of fields (e.g., medicine, science, sports, art, and politics). It highlights Latina women such as the first female Surgeon General of the United States, Supreme Court Justice, Oscar winner, and astronaut and provides a positive lens for viewing women and Latinx culture. Mr. Brandt discusses with his children the characteristics of the women in the book and the impact on our society of their accomplishments.

Mr. Brandt also reads *The Spirit of Chicano Park/El Espiritu del Parque Chicano* (Zamora, 2021), which is a bilingual picture book that tells the story of a Chicano/Mexican-American community's creation of a park in response to residents being displaced through eminent domain to build a public freeway and bridge. Then, he organizes a field trip to Chicano Park for his children to experience the living legacy of the history of the park and its Chicano community. Culture is everywhere in the park from murals painted by local artists to community activities, dance ceremonials, and political gatherings. After the trip, Mr. Brandt discusses the cultural, historic, and political importance of the park with his students. They also investigate other incidents in which minoritized communities are displaced by eminent domain and discuss issues of power and equity related to these.

Lionizing Children's Bicultural Identities

Ms. Krill acknowledges that "children from two different cultural backgrounds can sometimes feel as if they lie in 'two different worlds'" (Lara, 2020, n.p.). To celebrate her student Omar's biracial identity and lived experiences, she reads her class *Mixed Me* (Diggs, 2015). Then, she shares infographics about the increase in biracial families and individuals and information about famous biracial people, such as Mariah Carey, Hines Ward, and Kimora Lee Simmons. Finally, Ms. Krill guides the children in a discussion considering how being biracial can be an asset.

Likewise, Ms. Krill celebrates her student Lupita's bicultural experience by reading *The Heart of Mi Familia* (Lara, 2020). This book portrays a bicultural girl's experiences through her observations of the cultural differences between her grandmother's home and her Abuela's home and how she sees both of these two worlds in her own joyful home. After reading this book, Ms. Krill asks the children to consider how being bicultural is an asset in this book as well. Then, to promote cultural identity awareness, Ms. Krill has all the children make a list of ways they would describe their own cultural identities.

Lionizing Children's Muslim Identities

Mr. Devon teaches in a community that includes many Muslim families. To celebrate Muslim culture, he reads the book The *Crescent Moons and Pointed Minarets: A Muslim Book of Shapes* (Khan, 2018). The book shares that many everyday shapes, such as a crescent moon, square, and octagon, stem from Islam. This celebration of the origin of the origins of these shapes creates a space of joy to uplift the contributions of Islam.

Additionally, Mr. Devon reads *Proudest Blue: A Story of Hijab and Family* to celebrate the important and joyful moment at which a young girl begins to wear a hijab. Mr. Devon uses this book as a platform for having his class discuss how people's religious traditions make them feel, and related to these feelings, why it is important to respect one another's religious traditions.

Lionizing Children's Strength of Border Crossings

Mrs. Hernandez teaches in a predominantly Mexican-American community. She wants to celebrate the different kinds of border crossings that children in her classroom have experienced, or that are part of their heritage. First, she chooses the Pura Belpré winning book *Dreamers* (Morales, 2018). It is an autobiographical story of Yuyi Morales and her infant son's journey from Xalapa, Mexico to the United States. Mrs. Hernandez knows that some of her children will see themselves and their families in this story and be inspired by how Yuyi and her son found their place in a new country. Mrs. Hernandez facilitates a class discussion about the gifts that immigrants bring with them to their new country (e.g., strength, stories, talents, and passions).

Further, Mrs. Hernandez wants to celebrate her children whose families may have had more difficult journeys to the U.S. She reads *La Frontera: El Viaje Con Papa /My Journey with Papa* (Alva & Mills, 2018). This story portrays the difficult journey of a boy and his father from Mexico to Texas. Mrs. Hernandez leads a class discussion about the personal characteristics needed to make a similar journey, such as courage, resilience, and resourcefulness.

Reflection Questions

1. Inventory your classroom library. Create stacks of books that represent different cultures. Check each book for its authenticity, and make piles for books that authentically represent a particular culture vs. those that do not. How representative is your classroom library of the children in your class? How representative is it of the U.S. and world?
2. What are some specific steps that you can take to address the aspects of creating space to develop children's criticality during read-aloud discussions that are more difficult for you?
3. What aspects of creating spaces of joy to celebrate children from diverse cultures and identities do you find easy versus difficult?

Recommended Children's Literature

Book Information	Summary
Title: *I Can Write the World.* **Author and Illustrator:** Joshunda Sanders (Author), Charly Palmer (Illustrator) **Awards:** *N/A* **Grade Level Band:** K-3	**Summary:** This is a story about an eight-year-old girl, Ava, who values her positive way of seeing her neighborhood. She decides to become a journalist to tell the world about her Bronx neighborhood.
Title: *Brothers in hope: The story of the lost boys of Sudan.* **Author and Illustrator:** Mary William (Author), R. Gregory Christie (Illustrator) **Awards:** Corretta Scott King **Grade Level Band:** 2–5	**Summary:** This is a story about thousands of orphaned Sudanese boys and their journey to a refugee camp in another county.
Title: *Chocolate Me* **Author and Illustrator:** Taye Diggs (Author), Shane Evans (Illustrator) **Awards:** Parents' Choice Gold Award **Grade Level Band:** K-3	**Summary:** This is a book about racial bullying, and how a mother helps her son develop racial pride.
Title: *The Proudest Blue.* **Author and Illustrator:** Joshunda Sanders with S.K. Ali (Author), Hatem Aly (Illustrator) **Awards:** *Goodreads Choice* **Grade Level Band:** K-3	**Summary:** This book tells the story of Faizah's first hijab.
Title: *Black Boy Joy: 17 Stories Celebrating Black Boyhood.* **Author and Illustrator:** Kwame Mbalia **Awards:** Editors' Pick; #1 New York Times Bestseller **Grade Level Band:** 3–5	**Summary:** This book contains 17 stories that celebrate Black boyhood: loss, grief, and joy in finding one's voice.
Title: *Crescent Moons and pointed minarets: A Muslim book of shapes.* **Author and Illustrator:** Hena Khan (Author) Mehrodokht Amini (Illustrator) **Awards:** N/A **Grade Level Band:** K-3	**Summary:** This beautiful book explores shapes that stem from Muslim culture.

Book Information	Summary
Title: *From North to South/Del Norte al Sur* **Author and Illustrator:** René Laínez (Author), Joe Cepeda (Illustrator) **Awards:** N/A **Grade Level Band:** K-3	**Summary:** This is a story about Jose who traveled to the U.S. from Mexico, and misses his mother who was deported back to Mexico.
Title: *Dear primo: A letter to my cousin.* **Author and Illustrator:** Duncan Tonatiuh **Awards:** Pura Belpré **Grade Level Band:** K-3	**Summary:** In this book, two cousins share their lives and cultural traditions across the U.S. and Mexico.

Resources: Spaces to Learn

- Christ, T., & Cho, H. (2021). Sharing power in read-alouds with emergent bilingual students. *The Reading Teacher, 75*(3), 269–278.
- Sharma, S. A., & Christ, T. (2017). Five steps toward selection and integration of culturally relevant texts. *Reading Teacher, 71*(3), 295–307.

References

Alim, H.S., & Paris, D. (2017). What is culturally sustaining pedagogy and why does it matter? In D. Paris & H.S. Alim (Eds.), *Culturally sustaining pedagogies* (pp. 1–24). Teachers College Press.

Chen, X., Furuya, A., Harwin, A., & Herold, B. (2021). The 'dramatic' demographic shifts reshaping suburban schools: 7 key data points to know. *EducationWeek*. Retrieved from www.edweek.org/leadership/the-dramatic-demographic-shifts-re shaping-suburban-schools-7-key-data-points-to-know/2021/03.

Cho, H., & Christ, T. (2021). How two emergent bilingual students from refugee families make inferences with more and less culturally relevant texts during read-alouds. *TESOL Quarterly, 56*(4), 1112–1135.

Cho, H., Christ, T., & Liu, Y. (2022). Recognizing emergent bilingual parent-child dyads' funds of identity through their discussions about culturally relevant text. *Journal of* Christ, T., Chiu, M. M., Rider, S., Kitson, D., Hanser, K., McConnell, E., Dipzinski, R., and Mayernik, H. (2018). Cultural relevance and informal reading inventory performance: African-American primary and middle school students. *Literacy Research and Instruction, 57*(2), 117–134.

Christ, T., & Cho, H. (2021). Sharing power in read-alouds with emergent bilingual students. *The Reading Teacher, 75*(3), 269–278.

Language, Identity & Education. Online ahead of print. doi:10.1080/15348458.2021. 2004893

Christ, T., & Cho, H. (2022). Emergent bilingual students' small group read-aloud discussions. *Literacy Research and Instruction*. Online ahead of print. doi:10.1080/19388071.2022.2085637

Cline-Ransome, L. (2020). *The power of her pen: The story of groundbreaking journalist Ethel L. Payne*. Simon & Schuster/Paula Wiseman Books.

Crèvecoeur, J. (1782). *What is an American? Letter III of letters from an American farmer.* National Humanities Center. Retrieved from https://americainclass.org/sources/makingrevolution/independence/text6/crevecoeuramerican.pdf.

Currie, A. R. (2013). Truth be told: African American children's literature in two fourth-grade classrooms. Doctoral dissertation, Oakland University. Retrieved from www.proquest.com/dissertations-theses/truth-be-told-african-american-chil drens/docview/1857454203/se-2

DiGiacomo, D.K. (2020). Supporting interests and sharing power: Insights from a Scottish youth program. *Journal of Youth Development*, 15(5), 68–92.

Ebe, A. E. (2010). Culturally relevant texts and reading assessment for English language learners. *Reading Horizons*, 50(3), 193–210.

Gadsden, V.L. (1993). Literacy, education, and identity among African- Americans: The communal nature of learning. *Urban Education*, 27(4), 352–369. https://doi.org/10.1177/0042085993027004003.

Hindman, A. H., Wasik, B. A., & Bradley, D. E. (2019). How classroom conversations unfold: Exploring teacher–child exchanges during shared book reading. *Early Education and Development*, 30(4), 478–495. doi:10.1080/10409289.2018.1556009.

Houchen, D. (2013). "Stakes is high": Culturally relevant practitioner inquiry with African American students struggling to pass secondary reading exit exams. *Urban Education*, 48(1) 92–115. doi:10.1177/004208.

Kim, S., & Song, K. H. (2019). Designing a community translanguaging space within a family literacy project. *The Reading Teacher*, 73(3), 267–279. doi:10.1002/trtr.1820.

Ladson-Billings, G. (1995). Toward a theory of culturally relevant pedagogy. *American Educational Research Journal*, 32(3), 465–491.

Meacham, S. J., Meacham, S., Thompson, M., & Graves, H. (2019). Hip-Hop early literacy in K–1 classrooms. *The Reading Teacher*, 73(1), 29–37. doi:10.1002/trtr.1809.

Myers, C. (2014). The apartheid of children's literature. Retrieved from www.nytimes.com/2014/03/16/opinion/sunday/the-apartheid-of-childrens-literature.html.

National Academies of Sciences, Engineering, and Medicine (1996). *Statistics on U. S. immigration: An assessment of data needs for future research.* Washington, DC: The National Academies Press. https://doi.org/10.17226/4942.

Pantaleo, S. (2007). Interthinking: Young children using language to think collectively during interactive read-alouds. *Early Childhood Education Journal*, 34(6), 439–447.

Pappas, C. C., Varelas, M., Barry, A., & Rife, A. (2002). Dialogic inquiry around information texts: The role of intertextuality in constructing scientific understandings in urban primary classrooms. *Linguistics and Education*, 13(4), 435–482.

Pauly, N., Kingsley, K. V., & Baker, A. (2019). Culturally sustaining pedagogy through arts-based learning: Preservice teachers engage emergent bilinguals. *LEARNing Landscapes*, 12(1), 205–221. doi:10.36510/learnland.v12i1.988.

Paul, P. (2011). "The snowy day" celebrates 50 years. *ArtsBeat*, August 18. Retrieved from https://artsbeat.blogs.nytimes.com/2011/08/18/the-snowy-da y-celebrates-50-years/.

Polleck, J., & Spence-Davis, T. (2020). Centering# BlackLivesMatter to confront injustice, inspire advocacy, and develop literacies. *English Journal*, 109(4), 87–94.

Sharma, S. A., & Christ, T. (2017). Five steps toward selection and integration of culturally relevant texts. *Reading Teacher*, 71(3), 295–307.

Sims-Bishop, R. (1990). Mirrors, windows, and sliding glass doors. *Perspectives*, 6(3), pp. 9–12.

Sims-Bishop, R. (1991). Evaluating books by and about African- Americans. In M.V. Lindgren (Ed.), *The multicolored mirror: Cultural substance in literature for children and young adults* (pp. 31–34). Fort Atkinson, WI: Highsmith.

Tatum, A.W. (2009). *Reading for their life: (Re)building the textual lineages of African American adolescent males*. Portsmouth, NH: Heinemann.

Walters, T. (1998). The language of a literate classroom: Rethinking comprehension dimensions. Retrieved from ERIC database. (ED418430).

Ward, A. & Warren, N. (2019). Equitable education for English learners through a pedagogy of multiliteracies. *Kappa Delta Pi Record*, 55(2), 89–94.

Children's Literature Cited

Alva, A. & Mills, D. (2018). *La Frontera: El viaje con papa /My journey with papa*. Barefoot Books.

Bowles, D. (2021). *They call me Güero: A border kid's poems*. New York: Kokila.

Diggs, T. (2015). *Mixed me!*New York: Feiwel & Friends.

Doyon, S. (2020). *Magnificent homespun brown: A celebration*. Thomaston, ME: Tilbury House Publishers.

Faruqi, R. (2015). *Laila's lunchbox: A ramadan story*. Tilbury House.

Hoffman, S. (2020). *Jacob's new dress*. Park Ridge IL: Albert Whitman & Company.

Keats, E. J. (1962) *The snowy day*. London: Puffin Books.

Khan, H. (2018). *Crescent moons and pointed minarets: A Muslim book of shapes*. San Francisco, CA: Chronicle books.

Kusel S. (2021). *The Passover guest*. New York: Neal Porter Books

Laniez, R. (2013). *From north to south/Del norte al sur*. Children's Book Press.

Laniez, R., & Cepeda, J. (2013). *From north to south/Del norte al sur*. Highland Park, IL: Children's Book Press.

Lara, C. (2020). *The heart of mi familia*. Washington, DC: Magination Press.

Mbalie, K. (2021). *Black boy joy: 17 stories celebrating Black boyhood*. New York: Delacorte Press.

McQuinn, A. & Frey, B. (2008). *My friend Jamal*. Alanna Books.

Morales, Y. (2018). *Dreamers*. New York: Neal Porter Books.

Muhammad, I. & Ali, S. K. (2019). *The proudest blue*. New York: Little, Brown Books for Young Readers.

Reynolds, J. & Kendi I. (2020). *Stamped: Racism, antiracism and you*. New York: Little Brown and Company.

Reynoso, N. (2019). *Be bold! Be brave!*Con Todo Press.

Sanders, J. (2019). *I can write the world*. Houston, TX: Six Foot Press.

Tonatiuh, A. (2010) *Dear primo: A letter to my cousin*. New York: Abrams.

Williams, M., & Christie, G. (2005). *Brothers in hope: The story of the lost boys of Sudan*. New York: Lee & Low Books.

Woodson, J. (2016). *Brown girl dreaming*. New York: Nancy Paulsen Books.

Zamora, B. (2021). *Spirit of Chicano Park*. Tolteca Press.

Appendix: Foundational Teaching Tips

Creating Spaces for Children to Be Seen

1. Create text sets of books that authentically represent the cultures that reflect the children in your class, and that provide windows into other identity groups.
2. Discuss language, culture, connections, and disconnections across books in each text set.
3. Ask your children for feedback about how culturally sustaining they think particular texts are, and why. To guide this discussion, use the guiding questions about cultural identities, age and gender identity, dialect, places, and experiences.

Creating Spaces for Children to Be Heard

1. Create space for children to interject and initiate new topics during book discussions—without you asking a question or calling on them. This will increase their participation and opportunities to be heard. Also, respond and follow up when children interject and initiate new topics—this demonstrates that you value their contributions and position them as "knowers". These are part of creating a nurturing and cooperative environment.
2. Choose culturally relevant books that represent the backgrounds of children in your classroom who are from minoritized groups. Make sure the books have experiences and language that mirror those of these children (Christ et al., under review; Christ & Sharma, 2018; Ebe, 2010; see Sharma & Christ, 2017 for more guidance on book selection). This will support these children's participation and opportunities to be heard during read-aloud discussions. Also, choose books that represent culturally and linguistically diverse groups and are written by authors who are part of those cultures, even if your children are all from similar backgrounds, to provide opportunities for diverse groups to be heard through the text during read-aloud discussions. This can decenter Whiteness and build children's cultural competence.

Creating Spaces for Joy

1. Select read-alouds that create spaces to celebrate children's cultural joy, and center the book discussions on the characters' triumphs and strengths.
2. Find spaces within your community that celebrate your children's cultures. Visit, read and write about these spaces with your children.
3. Invite families to share their celebrations of cultural joy in the classroom.
4. Have children write, or audio- or video-record stories about their own personal triumphs and strengths. Collect these in a class anthology. Have a public reading of these to celebrate your children's joys.

2 Classroom Bibliotherapy to Support Social Emotional Learning

Increasing Inclusion, Kindness, and Understanding of Diversity

Melissa A. Heath, Elizabeth A. Cutrer-Párraga, and Ellie L. Young

In this chapter, we discuss the importance of expanding academic education to include children's social and emotional learning (SEL). Without this educational expansion, Fredericks warned:

> People know all too well what smarts without social skills looks like in kids. It can look like individuals who are obsessed with their own success and status but are indifferent to the plight of others. It can look like youth who are unable to sustain employment because they cannot get along with their coworkers. It can look like the many young people who resort to an array of self-destructive behaviors because they are unable to communicate their pain and grief and confusion to anyone else.
>
> (Fredericks, 2003, pp. 3–4)

We recommend using stories—carefully selected children's books—to assist teachers in supporting social skills that are integrally linked with children's SEL. In particular, our information is intended to support students' understanding of and appreciation for personal differences. We expect students to respectfully interact with and include others and to show kindness.

As we prepared this chapter, we started with facts and statistics. Then as we polished the chapter, we impulsively altered the academic introduction. We opted to start with Jacqueline Woodson's insights. In *A Velocity of Being: Letters to a Young Reader* (Popova & Bedrick, 2018), the book's first letter is written by Jacqueline Woodson. She creates amazing stories that ring true and draw us into a world where we learn of and identify with others' feelings and perspectives. Her letter discusses her reading a book with her seven-year-old son, in which all, including the king, despise and are cruel to a troll. "'I don't know why the king is so mean,' my son says. 'That's not kindness, right Mommy?'" She describes this moment as "the two of us inside one story ... this perfect moment,

DOI: 10.4324/9781003321941-3

called Now" (Popova & Bedrick, 2018, p. 16). She also says she prefers to share books with her children, "where their young brown selves were/are represented on the page …" (p. 16).

Historical Perspectives of Diversity Portrayed in Children's Literature

Historically, children of color (Larrick, 1965), children with disabilities (Dyches et al., 2006), and other populations from diverse backgrounds (Botelho, 2021) have been either absent, underrepresented, or misrepresented in children's literature. In the 1960s, not long after the *Brown versus the Board of Education* Supreme Court ruling and subsequent school desegregation, Larrick (1965) noted only White children were portrayed in the books that helped children learn to read; Black children were absent from those books. Larrick (1965) noted children were being "brought up on gentle doses of racism through their books" (p. 63). She also described a five-year-old Black student who, while looking at a picture book in her school, asked, "Why are they always *white* children?" (p. 63).

Educating All Children Now?

Schools face many challenges as families and communities become more diverse and schools' educational responsibilities expand beyond academic achievement to include children's physical health and social and emotional wellbeing. As school-related hot topics and political issues escalate, schools continue to hold primary responsibility to educate and prepare all children for the future, which includes an increasingly diverse population. In fall 2018, according to the latest available public K–12 school data, the ethnic breakdown of America's 50.7 million students was described as 47% White; the majority (53%) of students were from a variety of other ethnic/racial backgrounds (National Center for Education Statistics, 2021a). In addition to ethnic diversity, based on the U.S. 2020 census, languages other than English are spoken in 21.5% of homes with individuals five years and older (National Center for Education Statistics, 2021b; United States Census Bureau, 2021); and 13.5% of the U.S. population reported being born outside of the U.S. (United States Census Bureau, 2021).

Furthermore, schools are required to educate *all* children, regardless of their parents' citizenship and legal documentation. Although difficult to verify, Culbertson et al. (2021) estimate that in 2020, approximately 491,000 undocumented children from Mexico, Guatemala, Honduras, and El Salvador entered the U.S., and 321,000 of these children were subsequently enrolled in U.S. public schools (K–12). Additionally, these numbers have drastically increased over the past year (American Immigration Council, 2022). When serving these children, schools are challenged in providing adequate educational services and struggle to communicate effectively with parents and caregivers. Indeed, welcoming all children and creating classrooms and schools that are inclusive requires extra funding, creativity, and dedicated effort (Bennett et al., 2018; Culbertson et al., 2021; Osorio, 2018).

Another educational concern, based on data collected across the past several years, mental health disorders in children are increasing at an "alarming rate" and identified as a "substantial public health concern" (Bitsko et al., 2022, p. 1). Data from the Centers for Disease Control and Prevention (CDC) indicate that annually 20% of all children meet criteria for a mental health disorder, and prior to age 18, 40% of all children will at one time or another have met these criteria (Bitsko et al., 2022; Shim et al., 2022). In particular, the CDC's data indicate increasing rates of mental health disorders in young children (Shim et al., 2022).

Schools have increasingly taken on the responsibility of providing mental health support for youth (Ali et al., 2019), with the majority of children's mental health services offered in schools (Burns & Hoagwood, 2002). Even so, youth living in poverty and from diverse backgrounds continue to be at high risk for mental health and behavioral disorders and rarely seek or accept mental health support from mental health professionals, whether in school or in the community (Kazdin, 2019). One barrier is parents' distrust in the existing health care system (Lazar & Davenport, 2018). Other barriers include lack of money and insurance to pay for services and perceived stigma and embarrassment surrounding the need for mental health support (Radez et al., 2021).

Social Emotional Learning and Tier 1 Interventions

To more fully meet the mental health needs of all students, Tier 1 school-wide interventions are being provided in classrooms (Gueldner et al., 2020). One example of such an effort is classroom-based bibliotherapy, reading books that support students' SEL (Heath et al., 2017; Prater et al., 2006). Reflecting the core of the Collaborative for Academic, Social, and Emotional Learning (CASEL) model, Weissberg defines SEL in the following way:

> the processes through which children and adults acquire and effectively apply the knowledge, attitudes, and skills necessary to understand and manage emotions, set and achieve positive goals, feel and show empathy for others, establish and maintain positive relationships, and make responsible decisions.
>
> (Weissberg, 2015, p. 185)

This description of SEL arose from many years of collaboration among educators, researchers, advocates, and practitioners. They recognized the dual nature of education, importance of preparing students academically and socially, and effectiveness of schools prioritize both aspects of learning. However, given the complex nature of today's schools—the diversity of students and political climate—embedding SEL in the fiber of schooling is not an easy task.

When SEL curriculum is a school-wide effort, pre-implementation planning must consider how to incorporate the community values and integrate respect for diverse and marginalized groups (Jones et al., 2018). Culturally sensitive SEL helps youth develop a deeper understanding of themselves and of others who may appear physically different or may think and act in unfamiliar ways.

Teachers and parents play a large part in teaching students to feel and demonstrate care and empathy for others. Students who are mastering SEL skills, such as including others who may be marginalized, showing kindness to others, and understanding diversity, will then be able to make and follow through with responsible and caring decisions (CASEL, 2022a). Inclusion is fostered when students are emotionally aware of their own feelings and of others' feelings and when this increased awareness leads to behaviors that enhance unity and cooperation rather than divisiveness.

Schonert-Reichl (2017) states, "Teachers are the engine that drives social and emotional learning (SEL) programs and practices in schools and classrooms" (p. 137). When teachers proactively share children's books that target SEL, they create a culture and language and thinking that integrates SEL into the classroom. In addition to teachers reading in classrooms, Tier 1 interventions extend across all school settings to include all students, teachers, support personnel, staff, and administrators. All are taught and prompted to use the targeted skills. For example, if the school sets a goal for all students to be inclusive of others, stories read in the classroom might include *Each Kindness* (Woodson, 2012), *The Invisible Boy* (Ludwig, 2013), *Yoon and the Jade Bracelet* (Recorvits, 2008), and *The Other Side* (Woodson, 2001). These stories are carefully selected to match the targeted skill and to fit the diverse needs of students and the school community. Then on the playground, a variety of activities might be planned to involve all children. All students and school adults practice what to say and what to do (expected language and expected behaviors), then follow through when someone is being left out, bullied, or marginalized. To reiterate, *everyone* knows what is expected of them. Peers and adults promote and prompt identified skills as needed. Across the school year, teachers and staff meaningfully reinforce inclusion strategies. This preventative approach may seem time consuming and distracting from traditional academic instruction; however, school wide SEL is an investment in the future, an alternative to the reactive, *putting out fires* approach. SEL infused throughout the school yields benefits that optimally extend beyond the school doors and into communities. Additionally—a motivation for educators, Durlak et al. (2011) found, when school wide SEL is promoted, students' levels of academic achievement increased.

CASEL Model

The CASEL Model is divided into five major areas: self-awareness, self-management, responsible decision making, relationship skills, and social awareness (CASEL, 2022a). In their 2020 updated graphic of SEL, these major areas are set within the context of classrooms, schools, families and caregivers, and communities (for additional details, refer to the CASEL website at https://casel.org). CASEL also included the following information on their website, indicating their dedication to educational equity, serving all children, expanding their vision beyond the school and into the community, and focusing on supportive collaboration between students, teachers, parents, and community:

> SEL advances educational equity and excellence through authentic school-family-community partnerships to establish learning environments and experiences that feature trusting and collaborative relationships, rigorous and meaningful curriculum and instruction, and ongoing evaluation. SEL can help address various forms of inequity and empower young people and adults to co-create thriving schools and contribute to safe, healthy, and just communities.
>
> (CASEL, 2022b)

Multicultural Books to Address SEL

At the heart of bibliotherapy is selecting the right book, a story that sends an "arrow to the heart" (Colville, 1990, p. 35). Noting the importance of drawing readers into stories, Rudine Sills Bishop's (1990) metaphors describe the levels of engagement, how multicultural literature may reflect as a mirror, where children see themselves in the story and see their own perspective; provide an opportunity to see outside of oneself, as looking through a window; or invite children to enter into another's world through a sliding glass door, using one's imagination to become part of a world outside their own (McNair & Edwards, 2021).

When selecting books for bibliotherapy, one must consider books that align with specifically identified SEL goals. Another important consideration, the prioritized goals should match the needs of the children and the diversity of the school and community. We included suggested books that are sensitive to human diversity in Table 1 and Table 2. The following website provides a free lesson plan for each of the books in Table 2, sponsored by Brigham Young University: [*https://education.byu.edu/buildingsocialskills*]. Additionally, websites that describe literary awards for children's literature that promote various aspects of human diversity, award-winning children's books, and booklists for consideration are in Appendix A. Another suggestion to consider is consulting the school librarian and community children's librarian when selecting books for bibliotherapy.

Examples of Books and Activities That Promote SEL

The following three books (*Henry and the Kite Dragon*, *Each Kindness*, and *Something Beautiful*) were selected because the authors are from diverse backgrounds. The books include characters that represent ethnic diversity, the illustrations beautifully portray the story's characters and context, and the story in each of the books is well written and provides thoughtful insights. We believe these books offer students an opportunity to ponder and gain new insights regarding inclusion of others, the importance of kindness, and an increased understanding of diversity. Additional information about these three books and awards honoring these books are listed in Table 2.1.

Henry and the Kite Dragon

Bruce Edward Hall (2004), a fourth-generation Chinese American, authored *Henry and the Kite Dragon*, a children's picture book. The story is based on events that actually happened in New York City's Chinatown and Little Italy. The story takes place the 1920's, and the story's major character, eight-year-old Henry Chu lives in Chinatown. An older man, Mr. Chin, who the boys refer to as "Grandfather," makes and flies beautiful kites from the roof of his tall apartment building. When the kites fly over the nearby park, Tony and a group of boys from "Little Italy" throw rocks at the kites because the kites scare their pet pigeons. After the damaged kites crash to the ground, the boys from Little Italy destroy the kites. As you might imagine, the children from Little Italy and the children from Chinatown do not get along. Avoiding fights, Henry never goes to the park when the rival group is there. This story is about how these two groups of children learn about each other and about Chinatown's kites and Little Italy's pet pigeons. Once they understand each other's concerns, the children work through their disagreements and find ways to reduce the conflict.

Teachers can use this book as a springboard for teaching about inclusion and resolving differences with those from different backgrounds. This story helps children develop a broader understanding of barriers that separate groups and threaten civility between groups. Teachers might consider the following strategies to expand student learning:

Table 2.1 Multicultural literature for elementary aged classrooms.

Book Information	Summary
Title: *Henry and the Kite Dragon* Author and Illustrator: Bruce Edward Hall (Author), William Low (Illustrator) Awards: *Irma Simonton Black and James H. Black Award, Jane Addams Children's Book Award, Notable Books for a Global Society Award,* and *Book Links' Lasting Connections Award* Grade Level Band: K-4 CASEL: Social Awareness: This book helps children understand and respect others' perspectives.	The story is based on events that occurred in NYC's Chinatown and Little Italy during the 1920's. With the help of an older man, a group of Chinatown boys make and fly beautiful kites from an apartment building's rooftop. When the kites fly over the nearby park, a group of boys from "Little Italy" throw rocks and destroy the kites that are scaring their pet pigeons. Once they understand each other's concerns, the children find ways to reduce conflict.
Title: *Each Kindness* Author and Illustrator: Jacqueline Woodson (Author), E. B. Lewis (Illustrator) Awards: *The School Library Journal Best Book of the Year Award, Notable Children's Books Award, Coretta Scott King Honor Award,* and *Jane Addams Peace Award* Grade Level Band: K–4 CASEL: (a) Social Awareness: This book helps children understand and respect others' perspectives. (b) Relationship Skills: This book helps children understand the importance of friendship and being kind.	This story is about a new girl (Maya) who comes to school wearing old and tattered clothing. The classmates move away from her, exclude her, ignore her, and tease her. Over time, the cruelty continues. One day Maya's desk is empty, and she does not return to school. One girl regrets how unkind she was to Maya and wishes she had behaved differently toward Maya.
Title: *Something Beautiful* Author and Illustrator: Sharon Dennis Wyeth (Author), Chris K. Soentpiet (Illustrator) Awards: *Parents Magazine Best Children's Books of the Year; National Parenting Publication Award Honor Book, Selectors' Choice; The National Council for Social Studies-Children's Book Council Award for Notable Trade Book in Field of Social Studies;* and *The International Reading Association Notable Book for a Global Society Award.* Grade Level Band: K–4 CASEL: Self-Awareness: This book promotes resilience and encourages students to consider how thoughts and emotions affect behavior.	A young girl walking to school notices harsh and discouraging details in her environment. Her teacher writes "beautiful" on the chalkboard. He asks students to find something beautiful in their life. She finds wonderful people and beautiful things around her. As she arrives home, she scrubs the word "die" off her front door. The girl asks her mother, "What is *something beautiful?*" Her mother says that her daughter is her *something beautiful.*

- Encourage students to notice underlying details in the story that might be overlooked or not fully understood.
- Encourage readers to reflect on where this story takes place, which cultures are represented in the story, and some background details about this time in history and these specific communities within New York City.
- Encourage classroom discussion to assist students in making comparisons and contrasts between this story and their own life and today's culture.

  a. Draw two circles. In one circle list the story's details that portray the culture and time period. In the other circle, list details about current day similarities and contrasts. Draw connecting lines between the two circles to show similarities.

  b. Discuss the differences. Make connections with conflict that currently arises between student groups at school and in the community. Identify possible misunderstandings people have when they are from different backgrounds and how these misunderstandings might lead to conflict if not carefully negotiated between the groups.

- Discuss new vocabulary and concepts, including *immigration, assimilation, enculturation, perspectives, power, bias, conflict*, and *conflict resolution*.

Each Kindness

Jacqueline Woodson (2012), an award-winning Black writer, authored *Each Kindness. Each Kindness*, a children's picture book, is about a new girl (Maya) who comes to school wearing old and tattered clothing. Although Maya seems to be a friendly girl and smiles at other students, the students move away from her and ignore her. At recess Maya wants to join in with the other girls' play. However, they do not want her joining in with them. When Maya invites others to join her in play, they refuse. Other students tease and call Maya names because of her old clothing. One day Maya's desk is empty, and she does not return to school. One girl feels bad about her cruel behavior toward Maya. She regrets how unkind she was to Maya and wishes she had behaved differently. In the classroom, the teacher explains the ripple effect of kindness. She then asks each student to drop a small pebble into a container of water and observe the rippling water. As they drop the pebble, the teacher asks students to think of a kind deed they have done for others. The book ends with one girl feeling sad and wishing she had another chance to be kind to Maya.

After reading the book with students, teachers might ask questions such as, "How do you think Maya felt when she heard others calling her names?" "How did she feel when others did not include her in their activities?" "If Maya were to come to our school, how would you treat her?" "What can we do to include other students in our activities?"

After a discussion, teachers and students might continue to talk about how things could be different if Maya came back to school. Teachers could help students consider how they might help Maya feel included. For a post-reading activity, teachers could instruct students to write a letter to Maya. This letter would include students' apologies and perceptions of what happened and what could be done differently if Maya came back to school or what students would say and do to help Maya feel included in the classroom. After students finish writing their letters, teachers could encourage the students to come back together and discuss the letters in *pair and share* dyads. This would allow each student an opportunity to talk about their letter.

For closure, teachers could remind their students about the importance of helping each person feel welcomed and included. Teachers could reiterate about how sorry the classmate in *Each Kindness* felt for what she had said and done to Maya. To remind students about the importance of kindness and inclusion, teachers might also help students write an alternate ending to the story so that story ends on a positive note. Additionally, teachers could post an inspirational quote in their classroom. The following quotes are provided as examples:

- "Kindness is a language which the deaf can hear and the blind can see." *Mark Twain*
- "No act of kindness, no matter how small, is ever wasted." *Aesop*
- "It's nice to be important, but it's more important to be nice." *Author unknown*
- "Do unto others as you would have them do unto you." *The Golden Rule*
- "When you are kind to others it not only changes you, it changes the world." *Harold Kushner*
- "A warm smile is the universal language of kindness." *William Arthur Ward*

Something Beautiful

Something Beautiful is a children's picture book authored by Sharon Dennis Wyeth (1998), a Black writer. This story tells of a young girl who sees her world as a harsh environment. As she leaves for school in the morning, she notices that someone has written the word "die" on her front door. On the way to school, she sees litter, broken glass, and a person sleeping alongside the street. In school, her teacher writes *beautiful* on the chalkboard and asks students to find something beautiful in their life. From this point forward, she begins to look at her world in a very different way. Where she once saw terrible things, she now sees positive things. She thinks about the meaning of the word *beautiful*, "something that when you have it, your heart is happy." After school, as she walks home, she finds wonderful people and beautiful things all around her. As she arrives home, she gets a bucket of water and scrubs the word "die" off her front door. When her mother arrives home from work, she asks her mother, "what is *something beautiful?*" Her mother says that her daughter is her *something beautiful*. The book ends with a happy and hopeful feeling.

After treading the story with students, teachers might ask the following questions, "What is different about this girl's walk to school, as compared to her walk home?" "What *beautiful* things does this girl discover on her way home from school? "How does finding *something beautiful* help us face our challenges and tough times?" Teachers could explain that when we look for beautiful things around us, we will be much happier, even when things are not perfect. Teachers could also explain that each person has the power to do something—even something very small—that will make our life more beautiful.

For a post-reading activity, teachers might consider the following activity.

- Allow a few minutes for students to consider what is beautiful in their life.
- Pass out a blank white sheet of paper and several markers/crayons for each student.
- Ask students to draw (for younger children) or write (for older children) about something beautiful in their life.
- Explain that *something beautiful* helps us stay positive during hard times.
- After completing this activity, ask students to describe their "something beautiful" and why this person or thing is beautiful to them.

Teachers might consider reading the following quote from the author, Sharon Dennis Wyeth. This quote is included in the back cover of the book, *Something Beautiful*:

> When I was eight years old, I asked my mother, whose name is Evon, for 'something beautiful.' She gave me one of her wedding gifts: a small white china pitcher with a golden handle and a golden rose embossed on it. I put the pitcher on my windowsill so I wouldn't have to look at the alley outside. I called the pitcher my something beautiful. When Mommy gave me the gift, she cautioned me not to forget that I already had something even more beautiful— the something beautiful I had inside. I still have the little pitcher. I keep it next to my bed. It helps keep alive the memory of childhood and my mother's love.

For closure, teachers are encouraged to remind their students that everyone has *something beautiful* in their life. Teachers could explain the importance of finding and remembering beautiful things. Additionally, teachers should stress the importance of finding *something beautiful* in the people and things in our environment. Reflecting on the following list of inspirational quotes, teachers could select and post a quote to remind students about finding *something beautiful*.

- "The best and most beautiful things in the world cannot be seen or touched, but just felt in the heart." *Helen Keller*
- "Every time you smile at someone, it is an action of love, a gift to that person, a beautiful thing." *Mother Teresa*
- "Beauty in things exists in the mind which contemplates them." *David Hume*
- "Everything has beauty, but not everyone sees it." *Confucius*
- "Though we travel the world over to find the beautiful, we must carry it with us or we find it not." *Ralph Waldo Emerson*

Reflection Questions for Pre-Service Teachers

1. Has a children's story ever stuck with you and changed your way of thinking?

   a. What details about that particular story were influential on changing your perspective?

2. As you expand student's academic learning to include SEL, which stories would you consider reading to your students?

3. After exploring the resources in the Appendix *Resources and Book Lists to Strengthen Children's Sensitivity to Diversity*, which specific resources would help you select a story to expand students' understanding of cultural diversity?

Resources

In 2016, with the help of several professors and many student research assistants, Brigham Young University (BYU) created a bibliotherapy website, *Building Social Skills with Books*. This website (https://education. byu.edu/buildingsocialskills) includes teacher-ready lesson plans and activities that are based on carefully selected children's picture books, each addressing a specific social skill aligned with one of the five CASEL SEL categories. For this book chapter, we only provide the lesson plans related to the following three important topics: (a) appreciating personal differences, (b) respectfully interacting with and including others from a variety of backgrounds, and (c) showing kindness to others. Table 2.1 includes the book titles that are linked to lesson plans on the BYU website. Table 2.1 also shows the organization of how the books, lesson plans, and associated social skills are organized on the website. For each lesson plan, we organize the information as outlined in the following section. This lesson plan format was developed after consulting teachers, parents, and considering recommendations from those who have expertise in bibliotherapy. We also considered schools' time constraints, making the lesson plans simple and easy to follow with minimal preparation. Teachers or parent volunteers can be given the responsibility to read the stories and follow the lesson plans.

Bibliotherapy Lesson Plan

Each lesson has a primary objective. In one or two sentences, the basic goal for the bibliotherapy lesson is defined. Then in the *Lesson Materials and Advance Preparation* section, the lesson plan specifies materials needed for the bibliotherapy lesson and describes advance preparation (if any). In the section, *Key Vocabulary and Concepts*, we review book's vocabulary and concepts that might be unfamiliar to the students.

Next, the *Pre-Reading Activity* involves asking students one or more questions and typically showing the front cover of the book to pique students' interest and prepare them to listen to the story. Then, the teacher or parent reads the book to the children. When reading to a classroom of children, we find that having the book projected onto a screen helps all children to see the pictures.

After reading the book, we recommend having a *Post Reading Discussion*. A few engaging questions will elicit discussion. When asking for students' insights, the adult might refer to a specific picture in the book or a specific statement.

After a short discussion, we recommend a *Post Reading Activity*. This is an extension to the story that involves the children in an engaging activity. This activity extends learning into practical application. Select activities that are fun, brief, and easily managed in the classroom.

Finally, we recommend the final section, *Closure*. This will wrap up the lesson with a few statements fortifying the lesson's objectives. The adult can challenge students to set a goal related to the lesson's objective. During the week, the adult can check in with students to monitor progress towards meeting their goal. In the classroom, the adult can post a visible reminder of the lesson's main objective, such as a poster, inspirational statement, or an object that ties back to the story.

The BYU *Building Social Skills with Books* website has lesson plans that are already prepared and follow the described lesson plan format. Selected books (that relate to diversity) are shown in Table 2.1 and Table 2.2. Each of the book titles in Table 2.2 has an accompanying lesson plan on the BYU website (https://education.byu.edu/buildingso cialskills).

Table 2.2 Building social skills with books: selected books with lesson plans aligned with SEL.

CASEL: SOCIAL AWARENESS: Helping students understand others' perspectives and being thoughtful of others' feelings, even when others disagree and have differing opinions

Perspective Taking

- *My Friend is Sad*
- *Wait*
- *Windows*
- *Duck! Rabbit!*

Appreciating Diversity

- *Rosa*
- *It's Okay to be Different*
- *Separate is Never Equal*
- *Alma and How She Got Her Name*

CASEL: RELATIONSHIP SKILLS: Helping students form friendships and positive interactions across the lifespan

Working Together

- *The Lion and The Mouse: A Fable by Aesop*
- *Anansi the Spider: A Tale from the Ashanti*
- *My Very Own Room*

Showing Appreciation

- *Gracias Thanks*

Being Kind

- *Should I Share my Ice Cream?*
- *Sidewalk Flowers*

Joining In & Inviting Others to Join In

- *Each Kindness*
- *Yoon and the Jade Bracelet*
- *The Other Side*
- *Can I Play Too?*
- *The Invisible Boy*
- *Ricky, The Rock That Couldn't Roll*

Making A Compromise

- *The Art Lesson*
- *Funny Bones*
- *First Day in Grapes*

CASEL: SELF-AWARENESS: Encouraging students to be mindful of one's own thoughts and emotions and how these affect their behavior

Being Optimistic

- *Gandhi: A March to the Sea*
- *Galimoto*
- *Coming on Home Soon*
- *The Gardener*
- *Beautiful Hands*
- *Stars*
- *Joseph Had a Little Overcoat*
- *The Road Home*

Being Resilient

- *Something Beautiful*
- *Beautiful Oops*
- *Harold and the Purple Crayon*

Note. Free lesson plans accompany these books on the BYU website: https://education.byu.edu/buildingsocialskills

References

Ali, M. M., West, K., Teich, J. L., Lynch, S., Mutter, R., & Dubenitz, J. (2019). Utilization of mental health services in educational setting by adolescents in the United States. *Journal of School Health*, 89(5), 393–401. https://doi.org/10.1111/josh.12753.

American Immigration Council. (2022, March). Rising border encounters in 2021: An overview and analysis (fact sheet). Author. www.americanimmigration council.org/rising-border-encounters-in-2021.

Bennett, S. V., Gunn, A. A., Gayle-Evans, G., Barrera, E. S., & Leung, C. B. (2018). Culturally responsive literacy practices in an early childhood community. *Early Childhood Education Journal*, 46(2), 241–248. https://doi.org/10.1007/s10643-017-0839-9.

Bishop, R. S. (1990). Mirrors, windows, and sliding glass doors. *Perspectives: Choosing and Using Books for the Classroom*, 6(3), ix–xi. https://scholar.google.com/scholar_lookup?title=Mirrors%2C%20windows%20and%20sliding%20glass%20doors.%20Perspectives&publication_year=1990&author=R.%20Sims%20Bishop.

Bitsko, R. H., Claussen, A. H., Lichtstein, J., Black, L.J., Everett Jones, S., Danielson, M. D., Hoenig, J. M., Davis Jack, S. P., Brody, D. J., Gyawali, S., Maenner, M. M., Warner, M., Holland, K. M., Perou, R., Crosby, A. E., Blumberg, S. J., Avenevoli, S., Kaminski, J. W., & Ghandour, R. M. (2022, February 25). Surveillance of children's mental health – United States, 2013–2019. *Morbidity and Mortality Weekly Report*, 71(2),1–42. www.ncbi.nlm.nih.gov/pmc/articles/PMC8890771/.

Botelho, M. J. (2021, Spring). Reframing mirrors, windows, and doors: A critical analysis of the metaphors for multicultural children's literature. *Journal of Children's Literature*, 47(1), 119–126. www.proquest.com/docview/2575546116/abstract/2AA0CA91B2AA48EDPQ/1?accountid=4488.

Burns, B. J., & Hoagwood, K. (2002). *Community-based treatment for youth: Evidence based interventions for severe emotional and behavioral disorders*. Oxford University Press.

Cahill, M., Ingram, E., & Joo, S. (2021). Storytime programs as mirrors, windows, and sliding glass doors? Addressing children's needs through diverse book selection. *The Library Quarterly*, 91(3), 269–284. https://doi.org/10.1086/714317.

CASEL. (2022a). About CASEL. Retrieved from https://casel.org/about-us/.

CASEL. (2022b). What is the CASEL framework? Retrieved from https://casel.org/fundamentals-of-sel/what-is-the-casel-framework/.

Colville, B. (1990, Fall). Magic mirrors. *Bookmark*, 35–36.

Culbertson, S., Kaufman, J. H., Kramer, J. W., & Phillips, B. (2021). *Undocumented and asylum-seeking children from Central America and Mexico: Where they are and how schools are doing*. RAND Corporation. Retrieved from www.rand.org/pubs/research_briefs/RBA1326-1.html.

Durlak, J. A., Weissberg, R. P., Dymnicki, A. B., Taylor, R. D. & Schellinger, K. B. (2011). The impact of enhancing students' social and emotional learning: A meta-analysis of school-based universal interventions. *Child Development*, 82(1): 405–432.

Dyches, T. T., Prater, M. A., & Jenson, J. (2006). Portrayal of disabilities in Caldecott books. *Teaching Exceptional Children Plus*, 2(5), Article 2. Retrieved from http://escholarship.bc.edu/education/tecplus/vol2/iss5/art2.

Fredericks, L. (2003, April). Making the case for social and emotional learning and service-learning. Retrieved from http://digitalcommons.unomaha.edu/slceslgen/1.

Gay, G. (2018). *Culturally responsive teaching: Theory, research, and practice* (3rd ed.). Teachers College Press.

Gueldner, B. A., Feuerborn, L. L., & Merrell, K. W. (2020). *Social and emotional learning in the classroom: Promoting mental health and academic success* (2nd ed.). Guilford Press.

Heath, M. A., Smith, K., & Young, E. (2017). Using children's literature to strengthen social and emotional learning. *School Psychology International*, 38, 541–561. https://doi.org/10.1177/0143034317710070.

Jones, S., Bailey, R., Brush, K., & Kahn, J. (2018). *Preparing for effective SEL implementation*. Harvard Graduate School of Education Easel Lab, Wallace Foundation. Retrieved from www.wallacefoundation.org/knowledgecenter/Documents/Preparing-for-Effective-SEL-Implementation.pdf.

Kazdin, A. E. (2019). Annual research review: Expanding mental health services through novel models of intervention delivery. *Journal of Child Psychology and Psychiatry*, 60(4), 455–472. https://doi.org/10.1111/jcpp.12937.

Larrick, N. (1965, September 11). The all-white world of children's books. *Saturday Review*, 63–65, 84–85.

Lazar, M., & Davenport, L. (2018). Barriers to health care access for low-income families: A review of literature. *Journal of Community Health Nursing*, 35(1), 28–37. https://doi.org/10.1080/07370016.2018.1404832.

McNair, J. C., & Edwards, P. A. (2021). The lasting legacy of Rudine Sims Bishop: Mirrors, windows, sliding glass doors, and more. *Literacy Research: Theory, Method, and Practice*, 70(1), 202–212. https://doi.org/10.1177/23813377211028256.

National Center for Education Statistics. (2021a). *Racial/ethnic enrollment in public schools. Condition of education*. U.S. Department of Education, Institute of Education Sciences. Retrieved from https://nces.ed.gov/programs/coe/indicator/cge.

National Center for Education Statistics. (2021b). *English language learners in public schools. Condition of education*. U.S. Department of Education, Institute of Education Sciences. Retrieved from https://nces.ed.gov/programs/coe/indicator/cgf.

Osorio, S. L. (2018). Multicultural literature as a classroom tool. *Multicultural Perspectives*, 20(1), 47–52. https://doi.org/10.1080/15210960.2018.1408348.

Popova, M., & Bedrick, C. Z. (Eds.). (2018). *A velocity of being: Letters to a young reader*. Enchanted Lion Books.

Prater, M. A., Johnstun, M. L., Dyches, T. T., & Johnstun, M. R. (2006). Using children's books as bibliotherapy for at-risk students: A guide for teachers. *Preventing School Failure: Alternative Education for Children and Youth*, 50(4), 5–10. https://doi.org/10.3200/PSFL.50.4.5-10.

Radez, J., Reardon, T., Creswell, C., Lawrence, P. T., Evdoka-Burton, G., & Waite, P. (2021). Why do children and adolescents (not) seek and access professional help for their mental health problems? A systematic review of quantitative and qualitative studies. *European Child & Adolescent Psychiatry*, 30, 183–211 (2021). https://doi.org/10.1007/s00787-019-01469-4.

Schonert-Reichl, K. A. (2017, Spring). Social and emotional learning and teachers. *The Future of Children*, 7(1), 137–155. https://files.eric.ed.gov/fulltext/EJ1145076.pdf.

Shim, R., Szilagyi, M., & Perrin, J. M. (prepublication release, 2022). Epidemic rates of child and adolescent mental health disorders require an urgent response. *Pediatrics*. https://doi.org/10.1542/peds.2022-056611.

Taylor, R. D., Oberle, E., Durlak, J. A., & Weissberg, R. P. (2017). Promoting positive youth development through school-based social and emotional learning interventions: A meta-analysis of follow-up effects. *Child Development*, 88(4), 11561171. https://doi.org/10.1111/cdev.12864.

United States Census Bureau. (2021, July 1). Quickfacts: United States. www.census.gov/quickfacts/fact/table/US#.

Weissberg, R. P. (2015). Education to promote all students' social, emotional, and academic competence. In M. J. Feuer, A. I. Berman, & R. C. Atkinson (Eds.), *Past as prologue: The National Academy of Education at 50. Members reflect* (pp. 185–210). National Academy of Education. https://naeducation.org/wp-content/uploads/2016/11/NAEd-50th-anniversary-bookmarks-11-18-15.pdf.

Children's Literature Cited

Baumgarten, B. (2015). *Beautiful hands*. Blue Dot Press.

Cotton, K. (2017). *The road home*. Abrams Books for Young Readers.

Denos, J. (2021). *Windows*. Candlewick.

dePaola, T. (1978). *The art lesson*. G. P. Putnam's Sons.

Giovanni, N. (2007). *Rosa*. Square Fish.

Hall. B. E. (2004). *Henry and the kite dragon*. Philomel.

Jay, M. (2018). *Ricky, the rock that couldn't roll*. Lyric and Stone.

Johnson, C. (2015). *Harold and the purple crayon*. HarperCollins.

Lawson, J. (2015). *Sidewalk flowers*. Groundwood Books.

Ludwig, T. (2013). *The invisible boy*. Knopf Books for Young Readers.

Martinez-Neal, J. (2018). *Alma and how she got her name*. Candlewick.

McDermott, G. (1987). *Anansi the spider: A tale from the Ashanti*. Henry Holt and Company.

McGinty, A. B. (2013). *Gandhi: A march to the sea*. Two Lions.

Mora, P. (2009). *Gracias thanks*. Lee & Low Books.

Parr, T. (2009). *It's okay to be different*. Little, Brown Books for Young Readers.

Perez, A. I. (2008). *My very own room*. Children's Book Press.

Perez, L. K. (2014). *First day in grapes*. Lee & Low Books.

Pinkney, J. (2009). *The lion and the mouse*. Little, Brown Books for Young Readers.

Portis, A. (2015). *Wait*. Roaring Brook Press.

Ray, M. L. (2011). *Stars*. Beach Lane Books.

Recorvits, H. (2008). *Yoon and the jade bracelet*. Farrar, Straus and Giroux.

Rosenthal. A. K. (2014). *Duck! Rabbit!*Chronicle Books.

Saltzberg, B. (2010). *Beautiful oops!*Workman Publishing Company.

Stewart, S. (2007). *The gardener*. Square Fish.

Taback, S. (2021). *Joseph had a little overcoat*. Viking Books for Young Readers.

Tonatiuh, D. (2014). *Separate is never equal*. Harry N. Abrams.

Tonatiuh, D. (2015). *Funny bones*. Harry N. Abrams.

Willems, M. (2007). *My friend is sad*. Hyperion Books for Children.

Willems, M. (2010). *Can I play too?*Hyperion Books for Children.

Willems, M. (2011). *Should I share my ice cream?*Hyperion Books for Children.

Williams, K. L. (1991). *Galimoto*. HarperCollins.

Woodson, J. (2001). *The other side*. Nancy Paulsen Books.

Woodson, J. (2004). *Coming on home soon*. Nancy Paulsen Books.

Woodson, J. (2012). *Each kindness*. Nancy Paulsen Books.

Wyeth, S. D. (1998). *Something beautiful*. Bantam Doubleday Dell Publishing Group.

Appendix: Foundational Teaching Tips

Table 2A.1. Resources and book lists to strengthen children's sensitivity to diversity.

The American Library Association's Association to Library Service for Children
www.ala.org/alsc/awardsgrants/bookmedia/childrens-book-awards-other-organizations
This Internet site includes information about numerous children's literature awards related to many aspects of human diversity.

Internet Site: We Need Diverse Books
https://diversebooks.org/resources-for-race-equity-and-inclusion/
We Need Diverse Books, a non-profit grassroots group, advocates essential changes in the publishing industry to produce and promote children's literature that reflects and honors the lives of all young people. One section of this site, Resources for Race, Equity, Anti-Racism, and Inclusion, includes book recommendations and resources for further reading and educational resources.

Internet Site: Library of Congress: Aesop's Fables
https://read.gov/aesop/001.html
This Library of Congress website contains over 100 Aesop's Fables, stories designed to teach universally accepted values, such as hard work, kindness, respect, etc. Supposedly originally told by a slave, a Greek storyteller— about 600 BC—these fables are known all around the world and are translated into many languages.

Internet Site: A World of Difference® Institute, Anti-Defamation League— Books Matter: Children's Literature
www.adl.org/education-and-resources/resources-for-educators-parents-families/children s-literature
For children, parents, and educators, this Internet site recommends multicultural and anti-bias books for children and youth. Includes a search option. Categories include Ability, Disability & Ableism; Bias, Discrimination & Hate; Bullying Awareness & Prevention; Gender & Sexism; Genocide & Holocaust; Jewish Culture & Anti-Semitism; LGBTQ People & Homophobia/Heterosexism; People, Identity & Culture; Race & Racism; Religion & Religious Bigotry; and Social Justice.

American Library Association's Notable Children's Books
www.ala.org/alsc/awardsgrants/notalists/ncb
Annually, the Association for Library Service to Children (ALSC) identifies "notable" books of commendable quality for children ages 2–14. This list of recommended books includes Newbery, Caldecott, Belpré, Sibert, Geisel, and Batchelder Award and Honor books.

Database of Award-Winning Children's Literature (DAWCL)
www.dawcl.com
This database includes a searchable book list of quality children's literature, including award winning children's literature. The list includes over 16,000 books and identifies 165 awards.

Colours of Us: All About Multicultural Children's Books
https://coloursofus.com/2022-ala-award-winning-multicultural-childrens-ya-books/
2022 ALA Award-Winning Multicultural Children's & YA Books. This site contains numerous literary awards representing multiple aspects of diversity portrayed in children's and young adults' literature.

Dolly Gray Children's Literature Award
www.dollygrayaward.com/
This award was initiated in 2000. The award recognizes authors, illustrators, and publishers of high-quality children's literature that authentically portray individuals with developmental disabilities (e.g., autism spectrum disorders, intellectual disabilities, and Down syndrome). Awarded every even year, this biennial award is presented to one or more authors and illustrators of a children's picture book, an intermediate book, and/or a young adult book. The website also includes the award-winning books from past years.

3 Children's Literature in Immersive Technologies

Stories as Magical Spaces for Diversity and Inclusion

Csaba Osvath and Jenifer Jasinski Schneider

Rationale

Storytelling devices from analog books to tablets to head-mounted displays (HMD) are tools that can change how we think (Vygotsky & Cole, 1981) and alter our lived experiences (van Manen, 1990). As Wolf (2018) indicates, "What we read, how we read, and why we read changes how we think" (p. 2).

Whereas previous generations needed books to engage with the stories in children's literature, today's youth can inhabit fictional worlds across multiple modes. Therefore, teachers must adapt to provide students with equitable access to digital spaces, and they also need to develop the skills for guiding students through other worlds. This is also true for stories appearing on screens (films and videogames) or through immersive technologies (gaming platforms and devices).

> Translation: the young reader can either develop all the multiple deep-reading processes that are currently embodied in the fully elaborated, expert reading brain; or the novice reading brain can become "short-circuited" in its development, or it can acquire whole new networks and in different circuits. There will be profound differences in how we read and how we think, depending on which processes dominate the formation of the young child's reading circuit.
>
> (Wolf, 2018, p. 8)

As we all know from the pervasive use of smartphones, reading extends beyond the pages of books into the realm of videogames and virtual experiences. In this chapter, we champion the ongoing cultivation and strengthening of the lived imagination (Lee & Patkin, 2016; Nachmanovitch, 1990) and multiple modes of reading (Jewitt, 2008; Rogowsky, et al., 2016) with a special focus on immersive and interactive narratives that expose more students to the transformative power of stories (Sims-Bishop, 1990).

DOI: 10.4324/9781003321941-4

Background Information: Technology Vocabulary

Books have evolved due to advances in technology, from 2D manipulated texts to 3D immersive experiences. Each of these forms changes the role of the reader, the role of text, and a level of immersion that can alter the ways students think and how they understand the world.

Interactive Analog Books

Interactive books have elements that require the reader to physically interact with the text through digital and analog features. These elements range from non-moving alternate endings and puzzle structures (e.g., escape rooms) to the 3D art of pop-up artists, such as Robert Sabuda and Matthew Reinhart. To see some of the intricacies in pop up books, watch this short video (Schneider & USF Media Innovation Team, 2016).

Game Books

Game books include options for readers to select plotlines or to follow secret paths using numbered paragraphs or alternate endings. Readers make their own decisions, and therefore, have agency in co-creating the plot and navigating the story world through their choices of what to read next. Examples include "Choose Your Own Adventure" books (www.cyoa.com).

Movable Parts and Paper Engineering

Many interactive books expand from a 2D reading experience to a 3D experience. Some of the common features of movable part books are lift-the-flap, transformations, volvelles, and pop-up books. For the history of moveable books, watch the talk by Rubin (2010) or visit the Movable Book Society website (https://movablebooksociety.org).

Interactive Digital Books

Commonly known as e-books, digital interactive books require actions and interactivity with technological elements. Features such as sounds, animations, music, and videos are embedded in the text. Readers can click, touch, or swipe the screen to activate these features that enhance the text or extend the text. The American Library Association creates a notable children's digital media list that includes dynamic and interactive media content for children 14 years of age and younger. Teachers can find curated collections that have been vetted by expert librarians (see www.ala.org/alsc/awardsgrants/notalists/ncdm).

Video Games

Video games are digitally based games typically played on personal computers or dedicated gaming devices, such as game consoles (e.g., Xbox, PlayStation) or handheld game devices (e.g., 3DS, Vita) (DaCosta et al., 2015). Video game lists are widely available, but we find recommendations from reputable educational sources. For example, *Edutopia* published a list of high-quality narrative games that support literacy instruction (Ham, 2021). And the National Literacy Trust created a website that compiles research and teaching suggestions for integrating video games into the literacy curriculum (National Literacy Trust, 2022a). They also compiled a family gaming database to support reading and writing (National Literacy Trust, 2022b).

Extended Reality

As the words suggest, *extended reality* (XR) refers to technology that adds a new layer to the physical reality we live in. Of course, there are many tools and inventions that extend reality, such as books or films, but in this context, XR is an umbrella term for immersive technologies including Augmented Reality, Virtual Reality, and Mixed Reality. See Table 3.1 for our recommended sources.

Augmented Reality

Augmented reality (AR) is an interactive experience in which objects in the real world are modified by computer-generated perceptual information. In other words, viewing the world through a device that alters what we see, hear, feel. Examples include *Pokemon Go*, projection mapping on Cinderella's castle, Snapchat face augmentation features, and virtual "trying on" experiences at Sephora, Rolex, or Warby Parker.

Virtual Reality

Virtual reality (VR) is a computer-generated environment that is perceived through headsets or helmets. The environment can be realistic or fictional. VR simulates experiences and has physical effects. Users can feel as if they are falling, flying, or touching the virtual objects around them.

Mixed Reality

In *mixed reality* (MR), the real world is not hidden entirely by the virtual environment as people can see and experience virtual elements placed within the real world. Using AR headsets, such as Microsoft's HoloLens,

Table 3.1 Recommended immersive texts for elementary aged classrooms.

CHILDREN'S BOOKS

Below, we recommend texts that mark the moment when children's literature leaves the pages of a book, and every student becomes "a child of books" (Jeffers, 2016) through interactive experiences with immersive stories.

Title: *Press Here*
Author and Illustrator: Herve Tullet
Publisher: Chronicle Books
Awards: ALA Notable Children's Book, 2012
Grade Level Band: PreK-1

Summary: Tullet creates an interactive text, asking readers to press dots, shake the book, and move pages, resulting in changes in illustrations that are the direct result of the reader's actions.

Title: *Choose Your Own Adventure Books*
Author and Illustrator: R.A. Montgomery
Publisher: www.cyoa.com/
Grade Level Band: Grades 2–4

Summary: From the Abominable Snowman to Minecraft, these series books provide opportunities for readers to follow their own paths across a variety of topics and different stories.

Title: *Encyclopedia Prehistorica Dinosaurs*
Author and Illustrator: Robert Sabuda and Matthew Reinhart
Publisher: London Walker
Awards: ALA Notable Children's Books 2006
Grade Level Band: Grades 3–6

Summary: The big dinosaurs lift off the page, with multiple interactive features to support the presentation of information.

VIDEO GAMES

We recommend classrooms to have at least one dedicated Gaming PC with a selection of video games that could be integrated into the curriculum and used during lessons. A gaming PC would also allow students to run game engines, such as Unity and Unreal Engine to create games, learn coding, and animation, etc. (Cost: $500.00—$700.00)

Title: *Journey (2020)*
Developer: *thatgamecompany*
Awards: *BAFTA Awards; Academy of Interactive Arts & Sciences; Annie Awards; Game Developers Choice Award, etc.*
Grade Level Band: K-5
Platform: Microsoft Windows, iOS, Playstation
Price: $14.99 (PC version on STEAM)

Summary: Journey is like an interactive wordless picture book or epic poem in the form of a video game. It is an evocative retelling of the hero's journey, exploring existential themes, and human emotions through music, movement, and stunning visual storytelling.

Title: *Walden, A Game* (2017)
Developer: USC Game Innovation Lab
Awards: *Best Overall Game; Best Educational Game at Intentional Play 2018; Game Academy Award at CAFA Beijing Serious Games Exhibit 2018; Game of the Year; Most Significant Impact at Games for Change 2017, etc.*
Platform: Microsoft Windows, iOS, XBox
Grade Level Band: 3 and up
Price: $9.99 (PC version on STEAM)

Summary: Through this open-world, interactive videogame, students can experience the life of Henry David Thoreau and his life at Walden Pond. Students can explore the natural environment around Walden Pond, practice observation skills, and wrestle with philosophical questions. Aiding educators, there is a downloadable curriculum guide developed by USC Innovation Lab.

Title: *Little Mouse's Encyclopedia (2019)*
Developer: Circus Atos
Awards: Hitomi Prize, Tokio, 2018
Platform: Microsoft Windows, iOS, Mobile
Grade Level Band: K-2
Price: $4.99 (PC version on Steam)

Summary: This educational game functions as an animated informational text or interactive encyclopedia. Players interested in botany and zoology can accompany Little Mouse on her adventures in various natural environments, learning about local flora and fauna.

Title: *Valiant Hearts: The Great War*
Developer: Ubisoft Montpellier
Awards: BAFTA Games Award for Original Property; The Game Award for Best Narrative; BAFTA Games Award for Artistic Achievement; The Game Award for Games for Change
Platform: Android, iOS, Nintendo Switch, PlayStation 4, Xbox One, PlayStation 3, Microsoft Windows, Xbox 360
Grade Level Band: 5–8
Price: $14.99 (PC version on Steam)

Summary: This interactive 2D platformer/puzzle game offers players a powerful learning experience about World War 1, taking on the lives of four characters and four different perspectives. Through collecting artifacts, students can learn about important historical facts related to the war. The game fosters perspective taking, empathy, and historical knowledge, reinforcing the reality that in war each side endures tremendous suffering and harm generated by politics and violence.

AUGMENTED REALITY BOOKS

We advocate for a special classroom library section dedicated to interactive books and AR books. Though AR glasses are not yet a mainstream technology, these experiences are best accessible via tablets and mobile phones. (Cost $200.00–$400.00)

Title: *An Elephant in our Garden*
Author and Illustrator: Patrick E. McLeod and Jeffrey M. Arnold
Grade Level Band: K-5

Summary: This picture book with AR integration allows readers to uncover the causes of a mysterious event in a family garden. By following Isabella and her father as they investigate the mystery, readers can utilize the AR features of their smartphones and tablets to learn about animals and their habitats. The animated sequences through AR technology also foster repeated readings.

Title: *Animal Kingdom Education Book*
Author and Illustrator: Ron Magill (photographer) and Interactive Art
Grade Level Band: K-5

Summary: Through this interactive book, students can read along, listen, learn, interact and explore the wildlife and their habitats. Using AR technology, the images of the book come to life through 3-D, animated scenes, enhancing the learning experience. The book also comes with a full set of interactive collectible cards.

Title: *Ernie's Wish Trail: A 3D Interactive Children's Picture Book*
Author and Illustrator: Maia Orion and Lauren Gallegos
Grade Level Band: K-3

Summary: Readers can follow Ernie, a piglet who wishes to be someone else—a butterfly, fish, a squirrel. Accessing AR features with a phone or tablet, Ernie's wishes become visible to readers through 3D animated scenes and sound effects. Ernie eventually rediscovers the simple pleasures and the joys of being himself.

Title: *Jurassic World: Where Dinosaurs Come to Life*
Author and Illustrator: Caroline Rowlands
Grade Level Band: K-5

Summary: This informative AR book explores the exhibits seen in the movie Jurassic World. The AR feature allows readers to see 3D renderings of the dinosaurs, as they come to life as animated AR objects. Readers can also manipulate the size, the motions, and the location of these majestic creatures, while also learning about them.

VIRTUAL REALITY EXPERIENCES

We recommend classrooms adopt VR headsets. Tethered VR experiences require a dedicated gaming computer to provide better quality VR experiences and a larger selection of apps and games. However, Meta's (formerly Facebook) stand-alone VR headsets the Quest 1 and 2 are excellent and affordable options to introduce VR into classrooms. ($300.00/per headset)

Title: *Henry* (2016)
Developer: Oculus
Awards: Emmy Award
Platform: Oculus Quest, Rift-S
Grade Level Band: K-5
Price: Free

Summary: Though this is a non-interactive VR experience, viewers step inside and witness the magical home of Henry, the hedgehog, who is about to start celebrating his birthday. As soon as Henry walks into the room, he makes and maintains eye contact with the viewer, creating an emotional bond. The story explores loneliness, friendship, and creative problem-solving. This short experience is ideal to introduce VR narratives to younger audiences.

Title: *Crow: The Legend* (2018)
Developer: Baobab Studios
Awards: Official selection of Cannes Le Marché du Film and Venice International Film Festival.
Platform: Oculus Quest, Rift-S
Grade Level Band: K-5
Price: Free

Summary: This interactive story places the reader/player into the role (body) of a faintly visible but always present spirit creature whose actions (movements) are instrumental in the unfolding of this mythical story about a group of animals. The story masterfully retells a Native American legend about the Crow who was the most admired animal in the forest. However, when the very first winter arrives, Crow will have to make personal sacrifices to save his friends and the natural environment.

Title: *Curious Alice* (2021)
Developer: Preloaded
Platform: Oculus Rift, PC VR
Grade Level Band: 3 and up
Price: Free

Summary: This immersive and interactive reimagining of Wonderland features the original artworks by Icelandic illustrator Kristjana S. Williams. Viewers take on the role of Alice as they are guided by the White Rabbit searching for missing objects and solving the caterpillar's mind-bending riddles from a first-person perspective.

Title: *Down the Rabbit Hole* (2020)
Developer: Cortopia Studios
Awards: Nominee 2021 VR Game of the Year
Platform: Oculus Rift, Oculus Quest, Playstation VR, PC VR
Grade Level Band: 3 and up
Price: $19.99 (Steam)

Summary: Through this story-rich VR puzzle and adventure game, players explore Wonderland. The player controls Alice as she descends further down towards Wonderland, holding onto tree roots, skillfully navigating the virtual space. The progression of the story is dependent on the player's ability to solve complex problems, which relies on close reading and close listening of the virtual environment and the words spoken by the characters.

Title: *Moss* (2018)
Developer: Polyarc
Awards: Best VR Game
Platform: Oculus Rift, Oculus Quest, PC VR, Playstation VR
Grade Level Band: 3 and up
Price: $29.99 (Steam PC version)

Summary: Players take on the role of mysterious creature possessing magical abilities. At the beginning of the game, they form a bond with Quill, the mouse, and guide her through breathtaking landscapes—exploring caves, ruins, searching for artifacts and fighting battles. Quill is aware of the player's presence and communicates with him/her via gestures and sign language. This immersive experience teaches players the principles of interdependence, collaboration, and problem-solving.

Title: *The Bond* (2018)
Developer: Axis Studios
Platform: PC VR
Grade Level Band: 3 and up
Price: Free (Steam PC version)

Summary: The Bond is a visually stunning, non-interactive VR experience about an indigenous healer and her connection with all living things. Players can experience an alien planet and its breathtaking flora and fauna, accompanying TiaMuati and her faithful animal companion to bring balance to the world by confronting destructive forces. This experience allows players to experience the world from multiple perspectives and become various creatures through the story.

Title: *The Raven*
Developer: Thomas Pasieka
Platform: Oculus Rift (PC VR)
Grade Level Band: 6 and up
Price: Free (Oculus Store)

Summary: The Raven is a pioneering example of immersive poetry in virtual reality. This experience transports readers/players into a digital recreation of a 19th-century parlor, creating a gothic atmosphere in which Edgar Allan Poe's poem, The Raven appears on the walls as flaming letters. The player can freely move around the room while enjoying the environment created by Thomas Pasieka, music by Jordan Rudess, and the reading of the poem by Barry Carl.

Title: *Arden's Wake*
Developer: Penrose
Awards: Lion for Best VR at Venice Film Festival; Best Storytelling in VR at Raindance Film Festival; Best Animated VR Feature at Tribeca FIlm Festival
Platform: PC VR
Grade Level Band: 3 and up
Price: $7.99 (Steam PC version)

Summary: This non-interactive, immersive Cli-Fi (climate fiction) story allows readers/players to witness the story of a family touched by tragedy and climate change, by becoming an omniscient, observer and a third-person perspective. Players follow Meena, a young woman who is searching for her father after he disappears into the forbidden, post-apocalyptic waters. This immersive story allows players to explore a volumetric story environment, and freely observe the unfolding drama from multiple vantage points while accompanying Meena on a journey of family history, climate change, and self-discovery.

Title: *Psychonauts in the Rhombus of Ruin*
Developer: Double Fine Productions, React Games
Awards: Nominated for Immersive Reality Game of the Year by DICE Awards
Platform: PC VR
Grade Level Band: 5 and up
Price: $19.99 (Steam PC version)

Summary: As the sequel of the popular 2005 platformer game, this interactive, virtual reality version of the Psychonauts universe picks up the story where the video game ended. Players will assume the role of a young psychic, Razlutin (Raz), a gifted young boy who is part of an elite group of international psychic secret agents. This unique VR experience allows users to try out psychic abilities, manipulate objects and solve puzzles in order to save a kidnapped prisoner from the heart of the Rhombus of Ruin—a mysterious part of the ocean.

Title: *Wolves in the Walls*
Developer: Fable Studio, Inc.
Awards: Winner of the 2019 Prime-time Emmy for Outstanding Innovation in Interactive Media.
Platform: PC VR, Oculus Quest
Grade Level Band: 6 and up
Price: $8.99 (Oculus)

Summary: This is one of the best examples of how a traditional children's picture book can be adapted for virtual reality. Based on Neil Gaiman's *Wolves in the Walls*, this immersive, interactive experience offers readers/players the opportunity to become a new, imaginary character created by Lucy. Through a functioning virtual avatar body, the player can accompany Lucy as her trusted friend to solve the great mystery afflicting Lucy's and her family's life and cherished home.

Title: *Nanite Fulcrum*
Developer: The Spiraloid Workshop Company
Awards: Winner of the 2019 Primetime Emmy for Outstanding Innovation in Interactive Media.
Platform: PC VR, Oculus Rift
Grade Level Band: 6 and up
Price: $4.99 (Oculus)

Summary: This virtual experience offers a glimpse into the future of graphic novels and demonstrates how immersive technology may shape this genre. This interactive, virtual graphic novel contains several interactive minigames, demonstrates how graphic novels can function in virtual environments, and gives the reader agency and an active role to shape or influence the outcomes of the story. There are some war images, but not violence.

Title: *SENS VR*
Developer: Red Corner
Awards: Emotional Games Awards 2016: VR category
Platform: PC VR, Oculus Rift
Grade Level Band: 6 and up
Price: Free (Oculus)

Summary: This VR adaptation of a graphic novel takes advantage of head tracking, creating a unique reading experience. This innovative game mechanic, unique to VR, allows the reader/player to control the actions and progression of the protagonist's movements by directing his or her gaze to certain objects. This virtual graphic novel calls for close reading and refined observational skills as the player must solve increasingly difficult environmental puzzles to escape a complicated maze.

Title: *Manifest 99*
Developer: Flight School Studio
Awards: Best Interactive Narrative VR Experience at Raindance Film Festival's VRX Awards
Platform: PC VR, Oculus Rift
Grade Level Band: 6 and up
Price: $5.99 (Steam PC version)

Summary: This immersive story similarly utilizes gaze or eye movements. In this story, the player not only traverses the virtual environment by directing his or her gaze toward environmental clues, but by looking at certain characters, the player/reader can witness the world from the perspective of those characters. This story explores themes of guilt, suffering, redemption, the interconnectedness of life, and the consequences of one's crime.

Title: *Coco VR*
Developer: Magnopus, Walt Disney Studios
Awards: Outstanding Original Interactive Program—2018
Platform: PC VR, Oculus Rift
Grade Level Band: 3 and up
Price: Free (Oculus)

Summary: This stunning VR adaptation of Pixar's movie, Coco, allows players to visit and experience several locations in the land of the dead. Players can travel by train or even take a magical gondola ride, flying above the city, or participate in the festivities by becoming a musician and performing in a street band. This game also has a multiplayer feature so players from different physical locations can join together to explore the city and learn about the celebration of Día de los Muertos. In addition, this experience includes a Spanish version, thus it can be incorporated into the language learning curriculum.

Title: *A Fisherman's Tale*
Developer: InnerspaceVR
Awards: VR Game of the Year (2019)
Platform: PC VR, Oculus Rift
Grade Level Band: 6 and up
Price: $14.99 (Steam PC version)

Summary: This mind-bending VR puzzle adventure game places players into the body of a wooden puppet, Bob, who lives alone in a tiny cabin. This story takes full advantage of the interactive features of VR, allowing players to use their hands to pick up and combine objects, to throw things, etc. This game requires complex interactions with the environment to progress the story.

Title: *Bonfire*
Developer: Baobab Studios, Inc.
Awards: VR Game of the Year (2019)
Platform: PC VR, Oculus Rift, Oculus Quest
Grade Level Band: 3 and up
Price: $4.99 (Oculus Store)

Summary: This interactive narrative places the player into the role of Space Scout 817 on a mission to discover a new home for the human race. In order to survive, the player has to interact with his or her trusted robot companion, tame a cute alien inhabitant, scare away a not-so-friendly creature, not to mention making an ethical decision about the fate of this new planet.

Title: *Doctor Who: The Runaway*
Developer: BBC Media Applications Technologies Ltd
Platform: PC VR,
Grade Level Band: 6 and up
Price: Free (Steam PC version)

Summary: This interactive VR experience offers players the opportunity to experience the world of *Doctor Who*. The story begins inside of Tardis where the player will be assisting the Doctor. As The Doctor's trusted assistant, the player is given a sonic screwdriver, fulfilling the dreams of many *Doctor Who* fans.

Title: *Paper Birds*
Developer: 3DAR
Platform: PC VR,
Grade Level Band: 6 and up
Price: $5.99 (Steam PC version)

Summary: From a third-person perspective, players can witness the story of Toto, the young musician who is searching for his sister while being confronted with a dark family secret involving his grandfather and origami paper birds. This experience utilizes Oculus's hand tracking technology and can be played without touch controllers. Players can use their physical hands to paint with light beams, create sound effects, and open portals into the land of darkness while assisting and guiding Toto throughout his adventures.

Title: *Baba Yaga*
Developer: Baobab Studios
Awards:
Platform: Oculus Quest
Grade Level Band: 3 and up
Price: $5.99 (Oculus Quest)

Summary: Players can enter and witness the stunning environments of a haunting fairytale world. As the children of a dying, sick mother they search for and confronted by the enigmatic witch, Baba Yaga. Based on the player's decisions throughout the story, this interactive tale has multiple endings.

allows seamless integration of computer-generated images with reality, making it hard to differentiate between the two. VR and AR are essential ingredients in mixed reality as MR is the blending of real and virtual worlds to produce new environments and visualizations (Lanier, 2017). A good example of Mixed Reality is the VOID franchise, a popular entertainment attraction, where visitors can freely explore and interact with virtual and physical settings.

Historical Perspectives

Good Trouble

Although many students have experienced the impact of technology on book reading (e.g., TV, Internet, Kindle, iPad), this is the first time in history when a new technology has delivered story content without a visual frame. In other words, immersive technologies have disrupted our experience of reading. A *disruptive technology* is an innovation that significantly alters the way consumers, industries, or businesses operate (Magana, 2017). Disruptive technologies sweep away the systems or habits of a culture and replace them with attributes that are perceived to be superior.

All previous storytelling mediums, including books, paintings, movies, television, video games, and even the theater, have presented text, narratives, ideas, or concepts inside an enclosed space or rectangular frame such as the pages of a book, the confines of a canvas, the borders of the screen, or the spatial parameters of the stage. However, new, immersive technologies (e.g., VR, AR) discard the limitations of framed content and extend reality for participants (XR).

By placing readers into seemingly boundless 3D spaces and virtual environments, readers are no longer required to follow a linear, statically unfolding story from a single point of view (like watching a movie or TV show or reading a book). Similar to an omniscient narrator, stories or narratives in XR often invite the participant-reader to take on a role, or even switch roles, within the narrative experience. Role taking creates the opportunity for readers to interact with the story and its environment, thus changing the outcome of the story by generating multiple endings. In these ways, XR platforms are disruptive technologies, and we must approach and treat these technologies as an entirely new interface for storytelling that provides readers with different capabilities for engagement. XR can generate a powerful sense of spatial and psychological presence because experiences in XR are perceived and interpreted by our brains as real experiences (Bailenson, 2018; Greengard, 2019; Rubin, 2018).

This is the first time in the history of literacy when a technological tool or storytelling device puts the reader somewhere else—not through imagination, but through physical sensations and interactions. Through XR applications, readers exist directly inside the story-world where they have agency over the story, its objects, and characters in real-time.

Given the power of these new mediums, and the agency students can experience, it is vital for educators, authors, publishers, parents, and scholars to actively engage with immersive technologies and to participate in the creation, development, and evaluation of stories and narratives accessible through multiple modes.

Facts and Trends

Although many literacy teachers and researchers recognize that the "digital divide" impedes technology integration because there is limited access to digital tools at home and in schools (Dolan, 2016; van Deursen & van Dijk, 2011), the reality is that all children, from all SES groups will experience digital tools as a pervasive part of life and work. For example, according to a recent Pew survey,

> In April 2021, about eight-in-ten parents of a child who was age 11 or younger at the time of the first interview (81%) said their kid ever used or interacted with a tablet computer—even if just to watch videos or listen to music—up from 68% in March 2020. About seven-in-ten (71%) said the same thing about their kid's use of a smartphone, up from 63% the year before. And 51% of parents with a young child said

their child used a game console or portable game device in 2021, up slightly from 2020.

(McClain, 2022)

In addition to youth using technology, adults extensively use gaming technologies.

- 69% of all heads of household play computer and video games.
- 40% of all gamers are women.
- 25% of gamers are over 50.
- The average game player is 35 years old and has been playing for 12 years.
- Most gamers expect to play games for the rest of their lives.

(McGonigal, 2011)

These survey findings demonstrate that technology is pervasive and to fully prepare all students with equitable access to fields of study and genres of power (Cope & Kalantzis, 1993; Luke, 2018), educators must learn how to creatively integrate technology and immersive experiences in spite of the lack of resources in schools. Failure to provide diverse students with XR experiences that allow them to develop imaginative solutions contributes to sustained inequities across their lifespans. For these reasons, in Table 3.1, we provided examples of interactive texts that are more freely available in libraries, and we curated a list of gaming resources that are financially accessible.

As literacy educators, teachers need to think about their role in providing students with equitable access to digital communities and their responsibility for developing students' skills and strategies for using digital tools. The digital divide requires teachers to creatively bridge the gap in their schools and districts even when the tools are not provided. And, in fact, providing access to new and engaging technologies is one of the ways teachers can actively engage in ensuring equity and access to multiple texts. Teachers do not need high-tech skills; they need expansive mindsets. According to the International Society for Technology in Education (2022), students need teachers who are learners, leaders, citizens, collaborators, designers, facilitators, and analysts. It's not about the tools; it's about the teacher's disposition to share creative learning (Jenkins, 2006).

Necessary Literacies

Often, parents and some teachers have mixed reactions to technology. Some view these texts as "playing" not reading, while others recognize the potential of digital enhancements. Along these lines, research indicates both positive and negative learning effects on young children's reading of digital picture books with results dependent upon the designs of the books and whether the digital features support or distract from the story (Furenes, et al., 2021). Most of this research focuses on young children's comprehension of text. We want to be clear, in this chapter, we are not addressing early reading instruction or the explicit processing of text. Instead, we are focused on students' engagement with stories and their access to immersive technologies that can expand their lived experiences, their orientation to the world, and their skills with digital tools.

Although the general public might perceive gaming as a purely recreational activity, engaging with immersive technologies requires academic and technical skills that correspond to the developmental level of the child. In addition, the primary function of school is to prepare students for the digital and literacy demands of the workplace (Greengard, 2019). From recent developments of Fintech (Bitcoin) to the creation of the Metaverse, the future of work is digitally oriented, and K-12 students must be prepared for these challenges. Specifically, the visual designs of video games and XR assets (e.g., camera shots and angles, video production, website construction, etc.) are necessary literacies (Schneider, 2015).

To participate in twenty-first-century culture, students need basic competencies with a range of digital devices as well as an understanding of how media-based texts work because AR, VR and MR have fundamentally changed the way we learn, shop, build, and interact. These technologies produce new ways of thinking by rewiring sensory processing (Greengard, 2019, pp. 120–121).

Solving academic and workplace problems, such as following technical specifications and project management, requires critical reading, deep thinking, and the ability to navigate analog and digital texts and data sources. To this end, playing immersive, virtual-reality games supports the development of these skills because participants take on embodied roles in simulation narratives to solve problems in the virtual world. VR enhances learning through embodied cognition because virtual reality games or experiences mobilize the user's full body and movement. This is why training in VR simulations is so effective: users are immersed in an actual experience, such as learning to fly in a flight simulator or practicing surgery skills on a virtual cadaver.

Immersive narratives require the reader/experiencer/player to discover clues, solve puzzles, and accomplish tasks through literacy skills and problem solving. The game mechanics have the potential to serve as learning spaces as they merge narrative engagement (borrowed from the themes and genres of children's literature) with relevant problem solving (involving critical and creative thinking) and the navigation of digital spaces.

Therefore, all students, especially those from marginalized communities and low-income families, need exposure to the elements of gaming that require users to experience embodied learning through role-play and problem-solving simulations. They also must understand how the games are developed and designed. In other words, students need experience with digital composing to leverage what psychologists call "embodied cognition" through muscle movements and other sensory experiences (Bailenson, 2018, p. 38).

However, there are potential downsides to experiencing stories through XR (especially in virtual reality). There is the potential problem of diminishing imagination, since VR readers are immersed in a fully functioning virtual world teaming with objects, characters, etc. Therefore, the use of role play becomes an essential element to foster imagination alongside and within XR experiences (Schneider & Jackson, 2000). Also, "reading the world" is not purely a function of comprehending text because XR experiences can be coded with gendered, racialized and ableist programming (Buolamwini, 2018; de Roock, 2020). Therefore, reading XR worlds requires critical reading and thinking. As always, the teacher is essential for selecting materials, introducing students to the experiences, and guiding students' learning from these new forms of text (Furenes, et al., 2021; Kozdras, et al., 2015).

Therefore, we advocate for XR experiences, not an escape from reading, but as an extension of reading activities that build from other types of interactive texts and exist inside and intimately merge with the curriculum. We also advocate for XR experiences because they provide students with culturally relevant experiences that are curated and carefully selected by teachers. Students can try on roles, experience competing perspectives, and engage as active agents in the metaverse (Osvath, 2018). Thus, when students take off their headsets and leave behind fantastic lands and wondrous encounters, they have additional lived experiences that transform into lived wisdom that can alter their points of view and the potential of their real lives.

Reflection Questions

1. How can you integrate immersive, imaginative literacy experiences with no technology? With some technology? With high technology?
2. Why do many adults lose the ability to play and imagine? Is imagination a critical skill of a teacher? What role should schools have in cultivating a child's imagination?
3. Systemic inequities happen in many ways. When students are more frequently placed in remedial programs, required to complete skill and drill activities, or restricted to reading leveled texts, while "gifted" or successful students receive the rewards of games, playtime, and digital texts, what happens to the imagination, the ability to immerse in a story, or to critically evaluate text? Now think about who is placed under curricular constraints at higher rates than others. How can you change opportunities for all students in your classroom?

Resources and Teaching Tips for Expansive Texts

Below, we explore how technological adaptations of stories shape the domain of literacy and children's literature. We outline storytelling, especially in XR spaces, presents new horizons and possibilities for engagement, research, and the creation of immersive and interactive children's literature.

Curating Classroom Libraries as Mini Media Centers

Classroom libraries are portals into expansive environments where students can learn. Beyond books, think about other resources and materials that will build your "media center."

- Analog Materials
    a. Books
    b. Performance Materials for Improvisational Theater
        - Scripts
        - Costumes
        - Props

    c. Simulation Experiences
        - Board Games
        - Role Playing Games (RPG) in tabletop form such as Dungeons & Dragons (D&D)

- Digital
    a. Mobile (handheld smartphones, tablets)
    b. Stationary (computers/laptops)
    c. Wearable (AR/VR)
    d. Hybrid (combination of the above)
    e. Web based Alternate Reality Games

Role Playing through Drama

Process drama is a method of teaching and learning in which students and teachers work in and out of roles to explore stories or content. The purpose of process drama is to engage students in imaginative roleplay, not a dramatic production. Children's literature can serve as the pretext for process drama, sparking opportunities for students to take on roles of main characters, side characters, or imagined characters in plotlines beyond the book. Through process drama, teachers can offer immersive, imaginative experiences prior to and alongside XR experiences with technology.

- **Arts on the Move** (www.artsonthemove.co.uk). Provides drama teaching resources such as scripts, books, and creative contacts.
- **Arts Online** (https://artsonline.tki.org.nz). Provides teaching and learning resources and planning tools for curriculum development.
- **Drama-Based Instruction– DBI Network:** (https://dbp.theatredance.utexas.edu). Provides videos, plans, and a searchable database to find games based on age, space needed, type of strategy and content area.

Immersive Gaming Corners

Teachers can create *Immersive Corners* by setting up a space for a gaming computer and a VR station for immersive experiences and coding. Connecting a gaming PC to a media projector can offer collaborative gaming sessions, where children can take turns playing games, but they can also watch and guide the player, thus turning gaming into a communal experience. VR content can also be projected to a screen, so students can see on the screen what an individual player is seeing and experiencing in VR.

- For more specific directions for Immersive Corners, read Kozdras, et al. (2015).
- For a list of games see Table 3.1.

References

Bailenson, J. N. (2018). *Experience on demand: What Virtual Reality is, how it works, and what it can do*. W. W. Norton.

Branscombe, M. (2015). Showing, not telling: Tableau as embodied text. *The Reading Teacher, 69*(3), 321–329. https://doi.org/10.1002/trtr.1375.

Buolamwini, J. (2018). When the robot doesn't see dark skin (Op-Ed). *New York Times*. www.nytimes.com/2018/06/21/opinion/facial-analysis-technology-bias.html.

Cope, B., & Kalantzis, M. (Eds.). (1993). *The powers of literacy: A genre approach to teaching writing*. University of Pittsburgh Press.

DaCosta, B., Seok, S., & Kinsell, C. (2015). Mobile games and learning. In Z. Yan (Ed.), *Encyclopedia of mobile phone behavior* (Vol. 1, pp. 46–60). IGI Global.

de Roock, R. S. (2020). On the material consequences of (digital) literacy: Digital writing with, for, and against racial capitalism, *Theory into Practice, 60*(2), 183–193. https://doi.org/10.1080/00405841.2020.1857128.

Dolan, J. E. (2016). Splicing the divide: A review of research on the evolving digital divide among K–12 students. *Journal of Research on Technology in Education, 48*(1), 16–37.

Furenes, M. I., Kucirkova, N., & Bus, A. G. (2021). A comparison of children's reading on paper versus screen: A Meta-Analysis. *Review of Educational Research, 91*(4), 483–517. https://doi.org/10.3102/0034654321998074.

Greengard, S. (2019). *Virtual reality*. The MIT Press.

Ham, H. (2021). *High-quality video games can rival good books*. Edutopia. www.edutopia.org/article/high-quality-video-games-can-rival-good-books.

International Society for Technology in Education (2022). *ISTE standards: Educators*. ISTE. www.iste.org/standards/iste-standards-for-teachers.

Jeffers, O. (2016). *A child of books*. (S. Winston, Illus.). Candlewick Press.

Jenkins, H. (with Clinton, K., Purushotma, R., Robison, A. J., & Weigel, M.). (2006). *Confronting the challenges of participatory culture: Media education for the 21st century*. MacArthur Foundation. www.macfound.org/media/article_pdfs/jenkins_white_paper.pdf.

Jewitt, C. (2008). Multimodality and literacy in school classrooms. *Review of Research in Education 32*(1), 241–267.

Kozdras, D., Joseph, C., & Schneider, J. J. (2015). Reading games: Close viewing and guided playing of multimedia texts. *The Reading Teacher*, 69(3), 331–338. https://doi.org/10.1002/trtr.1413.

Lanier, J. (2017). *The dawn of the new everything: Encounters with Virtual Reality*. Picador.

Lee, K. H. Y., & Patkin, J. (2016). Reading as experience: Literature, response, and imagination. *Changing English: Studies in Culture and Education*, 23(1), 67–76. https://doi.org/10.1080/1358684X.2015.1133764.

L'Engle M. (1980). *Walking on water; Reflections on faith and art*. North Point Press.

Luke, A. (2018). *Critical literacy, schooling, and social justice*. Routledge.

Magana, S. (2017). *Disruptive classroom technologies: A framework for innovation in education*. Corvin.

McClain, C. (2022). How parents' views of their kids' screen time, social media use changed during Covid-19. *Pew Research Center*. https://pewrsr.ch/3Koo0qU.

McGonigal, J. (2011). *Reality is broken: Why games make us better and how they can change the world*. Penguin.

Nachmanovitch, S. (1990). *Free Play: Improvisation in Life and Art*. Jeremy P. Tarcher/ Putnam.

National Literacy Trust. (2022a). Video games and literacy. https://literacytrust. org.uk/information/what-is-literacy/video-games-and-literacy/.

National Literacy Trust. (2022b). Family gaming database. www.taminggaming. com/search/category/Get+Children+Reading.

Osvath, Cs. (2018). Ready learner one: Creating an oasis for virtual/online education. *Journal of Language and Literacy Education*, 14(1), 1–20.

Rogowsky, B. A., Calhoun, B. M., & Tallal, P. (2016). Does modality matter? The effects of reading, listening, and dual modality on comprehension. *SAGE Open*, 6(3), https://doi.org/10.1177/2158244016669550.

Rubin, E. G. K. (2010). A history of pop-up and movable books: 700 years of paper engineering. [Video]. You Tube www.youtube.com/watch?v=2KuWxdQdyUY.

Rubin, P. (2018). *Future presence: How virtual reality is changing human connection, intimacy, and the limits of ordinary life*. HarperCollins.

Sabuda, R. & Reinhard, M. (2005). *Encyclopedia prehistorica dinosaurs*. Walker.

Schneider, J. J. (2015). itext, but idon't teach with it: An essay on i-literacy in teacher Education. *Action in Teacher Education*, 37(2), 120–137, https://doi.org/ 10.1080/01626620.2014.969850.

Schneider, J. J., & Jackson, S. A. W. (2000). Process drama: A special space and place for writing. *The Reading Teacher*, 54(1), 38–51.

Schneider, J. J., & USF Media Innovation Team. (2016). Look, touch, shake, and swipe: Pop up books and interactive ebooks. [Video]. www.kaltura.com/tiny/wlrn1.

Sims-Bishop, R. (1990). Mirrors, windows, and sliding glass doors. *Perspectives: Choosing and Using Books for the Classroom*, 6(3), 1–2.

Tullet, H. (2011). *Press Here*. Chronicle Books.

van Deursen, A., & van Dijk, J. (2011). Internet skills and the digital divide. *New Media & Society*, 13(6), 893–911.

van Manen, M. (1990). *Researching lived experience: Human science for an action sensitive pedagogy*. SUNY Press.

Vygotsky, L. S., & Cole, M. (1981). *Mind in society: The development of Higher Psychological Processes*. Harvard Univ. Press.

Wolf, M. (2018). *Reader, come home*. Harper.

4 Critical Equity Literacies for Moving Beyond State and National Standards

Alexandra Panos, Katharine Hull, and Kristin Valle Geren

Critical Equity Literacies for Moving Beyond State and National Standards

State and national standards and standards-driven curricular approaches are often found to conflict significantly with critically oriented, equity-focused, and justice-driven teaching and learning (Knoester & Au, 2017; Kohn, 2000). It is clear that many teaching practices dictated by standards-driven pedagogies in their current forms do not serve all children (Smith et al., 2022). Instead, policy across the United States (U.S.) has unevenly emphasized standardized pedagogy and created deficitizing classroom norms that damages, impacting minoritized children most deeply. In addition, across the U.S., states are leveraging new legislative actions, standards, and curricula that restrict teaching to best meet the needs of all children and work towards a civically engaged future for our diverse society. Indeed, there is an assault taking place on academic freedom through censorship of materials and pedagogical practices that have been proven to best support *all* children.

Teachers, who are majority White in the U.S., often struggle with developing literacy practices in the face of such restrictions and ingrained norms (Dutro, 2010). Teachers tend to recognize that standardized learning practices are damaging (Comber & Nixon, 2009). And yet, many teachers struggle to align the imperatives of social justice and culturally responsive and sustaining pedagogies with what they do and believe they are able to do in the classroom (Miller & Weilbacher, 2020; Paris & Winn, 2014). Importantly, minoritized teachers, such as Black, Indigenous, People of Color (BIPOC), LGBTQ+, immigrant, and/or disabled teachers among others, experience greater stressors and risk in terms of job security and safety, leading minoritized teachers to higher levels of burnout (Haberman, 2005). Teachers committed to serving every student in their classrooms must learn to effectively navigate a web of policy mandates, curricular demands, and localized expectations to create humanizing learning environments that meet the needs of diverse learners.

DOI: 10.4324/9781003321941-5

This chapter starts from the premise that standards-driven and censoring/restrictive approaches to curriculum and policy can cause damage to the children who schools are meant to serve *and* teachers can resist and reframe that damage. The chapter will outline the history of this damage, focusing on standards and standardized testing, and then offer reflection opportunities that support teachers in how to center equity and justice in the face of damaging norms. We believe teachers must take up the work of moving beyond standards and standardized ways of teaching through growing our own literacy practices, as a recursive process of understanding and action, in service of equity and justice for classrooms that serve all children and our collective future society.

In the first section, we focus on *understandings* necessary to think about standards and standards-driven teaching and learning. In the second section, we describe how critical equity literacies might frame our work as teachers and help us to *take action* by moving beyond these paradigms and nourish a teaching practice that values teaching all children, in particular those who have been historically marginalized and damaged by schooling.

Historical Framing of the Standards Movement: Understandings for Equity

> Business thinking has had a tremendous influence on American curriculum for at least 150 years.
>
> (Null, 2017, p. 51)

The argument over the "purpose of schooling" has been waged for over a century. However, for the past few generations, the dominant public education paradigm in the U.S. is that of human capital (Hawkins, 2007; Spring, 2011). Within this paradigm, the value of education and human worth is measured through economic growth, and present models of teaching and learning align to the idea that what is valued is that which can be measured. Evidence of this can be found through an emphasis on standardized testing and standards-based curricula as well as in evaluation of teaching performance based on standardized testing of students.

What led to this business model being applied to K-12 education? How did reliance on standardized curriculum and testing become the dominant model? Early in the twentieth century, educational leaders (e.g., John Franklin Bobbit, Werrett Wallace Charter) advocated that curriculum-making should serve communities in economic, pragmatic, and useful ways (Eisner, 1967; Null, 2017). There was also a goal to turn teaching into a scientific profession where teachers were technicians who implemented a curriculum system designed by curriculum experts (Null, 2017). This was followed by the Essentialist Movement in education during the late 1930s. William Bagley and others in the movement asserted states must develop curriculum standards for each of the core subjects that could be used to compare how successful schools taught these standards (Imig & Imig, 2006).

In the 1950s, the advent of federal categorical aid led to more cen-tralized educational control as the aid linked school policies to national policy objectives (Spring, 2011). Title I, a provision of the Elementary and Secondary Education Act (ESSA), was signed into law in the mid-1960s. While commonly associated with serving low-income children and communities, this legislation was also instrumental in the use of standardized test scores to hold schools accountable for student per-formance (Stein, 2004). The late 1970s saw an increased application of business techniques to curriculum and schooling: researchers, such as Fenwick English, brought business language and ideas, for instance, "curriculum auditing" to educational leadership and the public (Null, 2017).

After decades of shifting toward increased standards and account-ability, the 1983 report A Nation at Risk energized the movement (Stedman, 2010). The report argued the U.S. education system was far behind other nations and proposed "rigorous and measurable stan-dards" and standardized tests "at major transition points" to become more globally competitive (National Commission on Excellence in Education, 1983, pp. 70, 73). The education system responded, and districts required more testing programs. Congress expanded the National Assessment of Educational Progress (NAEP) to state testing and reporting, and professional organizations such as the National Council of Teachers of Mathematics issued explicit standards documents (Kendall & Marzano, 2004).

The 1990s and early 2000s saw an increased push toward standardiza-tion and accountability. Following is a list of educational reforms passed during that time:

- The Improving America's Schools Act of 1994 (IASA)

  - required states to develop standards and test students annually
  - introduced the adequate yearly progress benchmark (Dillon, 2019; Stedman, 2010).

- No Child Left Behind (NCLB), 2002

  - stressed "stronger accountability for results" (U.S. Department of Education, n.d.).
  - required all states that accepted Title 1 funds to test reading and math annually in grades 3–8 and once in 10–12 (Stedman, 2010).
  - set annual test-score targets for subgroups of students (Common Core State Standards, CCSS)

- developed by the National Governors Association (NGA) and the Council of Chief State School Officers (CCSSO)
- aimed to provide goals and expectations for the knowledge and skills students need to be college and career ready

- Race to the Top (2009)

  - States had to meet certain criteria such as:

    - adopting internationally benchmarked standards and assessments;
    - recruiting, developing, retaining, and rewarding effective teachers and principals;
    - building data systems that measure student success;
    - and turning around the lowest-performing schools (Spring, 2011; U.S. Department of Education, n.d.).

What has reform that centers on standardized curriculum and assessments meant for education? According to Null (2017), the primary goal of NCLB "was to prepare students to compete economically in the global marketplace" (p. 41). Similarly, the authors of CCSS offered the purpose of that curriculum was to strengthen the economy and prepare students for their role in the workforce through increased standardization (National Governors Association, 2011). Major critiques of the CCSS have been that local control over decisions about what courses and content are taught were taken over by more centralized government, politicians, and education entrepreneurs and researchers (Spring, 2011). Unfortunately, the quest for consistent standards across curriculum led to what has been called "egregious regulation" (Harrison et al., 2021, p. 3) of content through one-size-fits-all curricular approaches that negatively impact instruction, teachers, and students, particularly those students and families who have been historically marginalized.

From Standards to Legislated Content

In the current context, beyond this ongoing standardization of teaching and the complexity it creates for children and educators, teachers are also grappling with mandated curriculum more locally. From January 2021 to May 2022, 183 educational bills targeting classroom discussions of race, racism, gender, socio-emotional learning, and American history have been introduced in 40 different states (Friedman & Tager, 2021; Sachs et al., 2022). Of these, 19 became law, and 83 others wait to be signed as of May 2022 (Sachs et al., 2022). These bills, which ban "divisive" concepts, appear designed to control information under increasingly restrictive mandates (Parker, 2022). As Friedman and Tager (2021) note, the bills are effectively "educational gag orders" (p. 4). These kinds of curricular mandates fly in the face of best practice by excluding and damaging historically marginalized students (Gay, 1994; Grant & Sleeter, 2011).

Harrison et al. (2021) note bans on teaching concepts such as systemic racism, bias, privilege, and gender identity constrain how educators can address topics currently found within the curriculum. Compounding these concerns are the fact that many of the passed bills are sloppily written, "making basic factual errors, introducing contradictory language, and leaving important terms undefined" (Sachs, 2022, para 5). Furthermore, schools and teachers are often not provided with official guidance on what language and topics are included or excluded in the education laws, leaving teachers confused and frightened about the potential for disciplinary action (Pollock et al., 2022; Sachs et al., 2022). Perhaps of greatest concern is this legislated content essentially devalues and/or erases the lived experiences of anyone—which consists of children, teachers, and their families—existing outside dominant experiences, including those to do with race, ethnicity, sexual orientation, gender identity, ability, and nationality.

Impacts of Standardized Ways of Literacy Learning to Marginalized Students and Families

For decades, researchers (see Cramer et al., 2018; Darling-Hammond, 2004; Ravitch, 2010) have noted that marginalized and minoritized children (e.g., children of color, immigrants, LGBTQIA+ children, children from low socioeconomic backgrounds, children with disabilities) are being disproportionately damaged by these standardized approaches to teaching and learning. Cases such as *Mendez v. Westminster School District* (1947) and *Brown v. Board of Education* (1954) led to an attempt at desegregation of schools in America. However, U.S. schools remain deeply segregated, and generations of minoritized children have continued to experience unequal schooling (Fennimore, 2017). A critical issue with standardized measures is they are "calibrated on middle- and upper-middle-class (white) language usage, experience, and knowledge" (Anyon, 2014, p. 84). However, the U.S. student population is culturally, geographically, linguistically, and in *many* other ways, diverse. The funds of knowledge and fluency of language use - the many assets and ways of knowing - that students bring to the classroom are not captured by these standardized assessments (González, et al., 2006; Lee, 1998).

Research has also demonstrated standardized testing plays an important role in perpetuating a deficit perspective of children (Bower & Thomas, 2013; Harry & Anderson, 1994). This perspective designates "low-achievement" students, especially Black youth, as "problems to be solved" (Wun, 2014, p. 469) and contributes to students learning about themselves in school settings in ways that harm their self-worth and perceived value. For example, a 2011 joint position paper from Advancement Project and several other organizations focused on children's education, legal rights, and well-being, described how NCLB contributes to inequitable educational opportunities experienced by children living in poverty and children of color. They note NCLB's attachment of high-stakes consequences to the results of standardized tests creates enormous pressure for schools to produce results and actually incentivizes schools to remove lower-performing students (Darling-Hammond, 2007; Klehr, 2009). Drawing on research by Feierman et al. (2009), the authors also illustrate the role NCLB has played in expanding the school to prison pipeline for marginalized students. According to the study (as well as later research by Heitzeg, 2009 and Mallett, 2016), NCLB encouraged the referral of students to law enforcement for school-based behavior, which often contributes to the needless criminalization of children and youth.

Impacts to Literacy Instruction and Teachers

> We have come to believe that... the only way to measure a child's knowledge is through pre-packaged high-stakes state tests, the results of which undermine teachers' autonomy, deprofessionalize the teaching field, and leave dark children in the crosshairs of projected inferiority.
>
> (Love, 2019, p. 101)

Teachers have substantial concerns about the consequences of standardized teaching, learning, and testing. Research over decades has demonstrated, in addition to their fears regarding how students' low test scores might impact their job security (Kumashiro, 2012), teachers feel that testing programs substantially reduce the time available for instruction, narrow curricular offerings and modes of instruction (Crocco & Costigan, 2007; Smith & Kovacs, 2011) and have negative emotional impacts on students (Smith, 1991). Darling-Hammond (2004) references studies that found "that high-stakes tests can narrow the curriculum, pushing instruction toward lower order cognitive skills" (p. 1049). This narrowing of curriculum constrains the definition of literacy to a set of skills or knowledge to be acquired and measured (Botzakis, 2007).

Additionally, tying evaluation systems to rewards and sanctions undermines teacher morale, disincentivizes teacher collaboration, and contributes to inequities in education, as talented teachers may avoid high-needs students and schools (Nichols & Berliner, 2008; Baker et. al, 2010). These policies, which strip educators of pedagogic decision-making opportunities and de-intellectualize the field, lead to, as Kumashiro (2012) notes, "a deprofessionalizing and weakening of the teaching force" and this in turn leads to a more inequitable public school system (p. 9).

The demands of "teaching to the test" constrain educators from teaching in ways that foster creative thinking and intellectual and emotional growth (Smith & Kovacs, 2011). Measuring student achievement through standardized testing in particular seems antithetical in an education system that ostensibly aims to support student agency and democratic principles (Bower & Thomas, 2013). Teachers are understandably frustrated by these issues and recognize that they are in conflict with teaching that not only serves all children but also the kinds of classrooms that intentionally value and sustain the communities our schools serve.

Critical Equity Literacies: Acting Towards Equity

The historical and present context of standards-driven education helps to trace education's trajectory through standards-driven approaches. For teachers, these conditions can leave us feeling angry, helpless, and conflicted about how to go about our work. But a deep understanding of the policies that shape what happens in our classrooms can also be the ground from which we build more humane teaching practices to serve the children in our classrooms. We have found the framing of *critical equity literacies* incredibly helpful to make changes to our personal teaching practice. These changes include becoming better able to advocate effectively for teaching and learning that serve all of our students.

Critical equity literacies, for us, are defined as a deep understanding of an issue of equity (such as standards-driven teaching and learning or children's book selection) and then intentional actions that work towards more equitable and just conditions based on that knowledge. In this section, we unpack the idea of critical equity literacies and offer opportunities to reflexively (re)consider how to work towards equity-focused classroom environments.

Equity might best be defined, from Muhammad and Mosley (2021), as "fairness, access, and opportunity for all youth in schools" (p. 190). The context of standards-driven teaching and learning means many of our teaching practices are not aligned with this notion of equity. The idea of equity *literacy* (as recursive understanding and action) is used in a variety of education subfields (e.g., social sciences, foundations, leadership, literacy studies) and offers a framing for how to work towards being critically *literate* about equity issues in a given field (Swalwell, 2011). In this case, being literate means having necessary knowledge about equity issues and being able to enact teaching practices and stances to align with that knowledge. This kind of literacy is part of a recursive, but linear, *process* to build necessary understandings and confront damages to children directly (Gorski & Swalwell, 2015). Gorski (2016) offers a set of actions that help accomplish this work:

1. Recognize bias and inequity
2. Respond to inequities immediately
3. Redress inequities in the long term
4. Seek actionable outcomes to create and sustain equity

In other education subfields, steps have been taken by principals, parents, community members, and researchers to work towards equity in a variety of schooling conditions, such as revising curriculum, reframing leadership practices, and working towards equity conditions across different schools within a district (Gorski, 2016; Green, 2018; Panos, 2021; Wessel-Powell et al., 2021). Certainly, there is a long tradition of equity and justice focused literacy education initiatives that advocate for direct action and humanizing, sustaining, and justice-oriented pedagogies. For example, literacy education and research argues literacy teaching should include skill-sets in identifying issues of equity and working to address them as part of teachers' ways of knowing, being, and doing (Vasquez et al., 2019) located in each educators' specific teaching context (Comber, 2015). This means teachers must closely reflect on and examine their identities, skills, and critical orientations to their literacy teaching practice (Muhammad, 2020). The first step is for teachers to understand how historically we came to the conditions in which we teach today. This requires each teacher to learn about the history of education in the country, specifically in their region, at their school, and with their students. Teachers must have a clear mission of ensuring and sustaining equity and justice for each child, each school, and each community (Comber, 2015; Paris & Alim, 2017). This looks like teachers closely studying and learning *from* who and where they teach. Critical equity literacies look, feel, sound, and *are* materially, politically, and logistically unique and need to match our unique teaching contexts.

Invitation to Reflect: Using Critical Equity Literacies to Move Beyond and Resist State and National Standards

In this section, we draw on four opportunities for action as outlined by Gorski (2016) as recursive steps (meaning we can always return anew to each action step) teachers can use to consider their critical equity literacy practices and (re)think approaches to resisting and moving beyond state and national standards. We use Gorski's steps to offer opportunities to reflect and then act on what teachers might witness in their own pedagogical approaches, classrooms, schools, and districts. We orient to these opportunities for action as invitations to "collectively inquire into common interests and questions, utilizing [people's] lives and diverse textual, semiotic, and cultural resources" (van Sluys et al., 2006, p. 203). Reflection might begin for a teacher individually or in partnership with one colleague, for example, before turning into intentional actions within a personal sphere of influence (e.g., book selection, pedagogical practice, conversations with administration).

In particular, literacy teachers have opportunities for reflection and action on an almost daily basis through decisions about which stories they choose to share (or *not* share) with their students. The selection of children's literature can be viewed through a reflexive critical equity literacy lens when teachers reflect on how texts reinforce–or disrupt–bias and inequities. As teachers use their own critical equity literacy practices as a lens to (re)consider pedagogical decisions, intentional choices can be made about which books to include and how to engage with these texts in authentic and critical ways. For example, teachers might select books that demonstrate the unique ways we make sense of the world, books that explore histories and realities of inequities and injustice, or books that honor creative approaches to sharing what we know with those around us. This type of thoughtful book selection can provide a way for teachers to take action within their own classrooms as they find ways to move beyond and resist state and national standards.

As teachers, we must have deep knowledge of how inequities operate in our own classrooms and schools, and work to redress them in contextualized ways. This means working with our students and their families to understand the strengths and perspectives they add to our schools, along with those of our colleagues and administrators. Only then can we take action that has an impact. This is the real starting place for building coalitions advocating for equity and justice across schools, districts, states, regions, and our nation for educational policy and practice that resists damage to the most marginalized children we serve.

Recognizing Bias and Inequity

Gorski suggests recognition is a first step in an equity literacy practice and must include the skills needed to "reject deficit views that locate the sources of outcome inequalities (like test score disparities) as existing within the cultures or mindsets of people experiencing poverty [or other forms of marginalization] rather than as barriers and challenges pressing upon families" (Gorski, 2016, p. 21). As teachers, reflecting on biases and inequities present in schooling contexts and our teaching practices can be challenging and rewarding. It demands we orient ourselves as teachers engaged in *practice*, to be ceaseless learners who will continue to grow and change.

As teachers build their ability to recognize bias and inequity in their teaching, it might be helpful to consider the following questions:

- Who do I believe is responsible for testing outcomes?
- Do my curricular materials, including the children's literature I select, align with what I know about equity?

- How does my personal pedagogy align with my knowledge of how curricular and policy mandates operate, and how might my teaching choices impact different populations of students?
- What biases might I be personally and professionally navigating as I come to determine responsibility for testing outcomes?
- What norms and biases are present in the ways my colleagues and I teach at our school or schools where I taught, or attended, in the past?
- How do the teaching practices, curricular materials, and pedagogies most employed at my school affect the children I teach?
- Do my actions, the materials I select, and the practices at my school align with what I know about how standards-driven curriculum and policy operate, and who they harm?

Responding to Bias and Inequities Immediately

Following reflection to *recognize* bias and inequities, it is the responsibility of every educator to act with intention and specificity. This means educators must learn to "intervene effectively when we find biases or inequities in learning materials, school policies, or student interactions" (Gorski, 2016, p. 21). As teachers take action and respond, we suggest they be thoughtful about localized issues and work with understandings of how schools and colleagues operate as they refuse to ignore the biases and inequities present. When teachers respond immediately they might consider these questions:

- Who is being harmed, and how can we create space to alleviate the harm in the short term?
- How do those being harmed want me to address the issue?
- Can I describe with detail, using tools such as clear descriptions, equity audits, research, and/or expert guidance, the issue of bias or inequity present?
- Who is the best person to take this issue to, and why would they be the most effective person with whom to communicate my concerns immediately?
- What else do I need to understand, know, or do to be effective in my response?

Redressing Biases and Inequities in the Long Term

Beyond just responding to inequities in the moment, critical equity literacy requires teachers to consider how to redress inequities in the long term. As teachers consider the inequitable practices or biases that are reinforced within their own school context, they must "advocate against inequitable school practices ... and advocate for equitable school practices" (Gorski, 2016, p. 22). This may require resisting standards and policies that are harmful to students over time, rather than as a one-off issue. Similar to responding, this requires careful and considered action, but also demands additional planning, coordination, and collective response. It is impossible to redress issues in the long term without the buy-in of a larger group of people. These kinds of actions invite teachers to consider:

- Who can I collaborate with on this issue, and who can challenge my thinking?
- What do we know about the issue that needs to be redressed, and what do we not yet know but need to understand?
- Whose perspectives are missing from our collective understanding of this issue, and how might we best come to understand and center their experiences?
- How does the issue at hand impact different people differently?
- Who needs to hear this message?
- How can we communicate to all audiences who need to hear this message?

Create and Sustain Bias-Free and Equitable Learning Environment

This work is not accomplished by addressing one issue of equity or executing one attempt at advocacy. This is an ongoing component of teaching that continually invites us as educators to come to understand difficult issues through a lens of equity and then, in an ongoing way, create and sustain environments in which children experience equity (and satisfaction, joy, and power) in their learning. Indeed, critical equity literacy encourages teachers to seek meaningful and *long term* changes to create and sustain equitable learning environments. In order to do this, educators must "consider the interests of the most marginalized students and families in every aspect of our educational work" (Gorski, 2016, p. 22) and make lasting changes, again and again.

As outlined above, many teachers face various legislative mandates and standardized approaches to teaching which do not recognize (or even allow for) the teaching of children's literature that matches the diversity of experiences across the U.S. and within individual classrooms. It is important for teachers to approach their work with an understanding of their own teaching context, considering and contextualizing what these kinds of inequities and the damage they do means for their students and the communities they serve. Educators in other states or local contexts may encounter different standards or policy pressures as well as teach different students. We recognize there are many factors impacting the vulnerability and safety of teachers, particularly those from marginalized communities who are often most harmed by these standards and policies. Who we are and who we teach should be an essential part of what critical equity literacies means in our work as teachers.

Reflection Questions

1. What is a deficit ideology?

    a. What are some common deficit views regarding students?
    b. How do these relate to equity literacy?

2. What are the differences between "celebrating diversity" and cultivating equity literacy?

    a. How might activities like Multicultural Night contribute to students' and educators' existing stereotypes and biases?

3. What is an inequity that you have observed in your classroom or school?

    a. Who is experiencing this inequity?
    b. What steps, if any, have been taken to address this inequity?
    c. What role might you play in helping others to recognize it, respond to the issue, redress it in the long term, and create more sustainable equitable conditions?

Children's Literature

Table 4.1 Recommended children's literature

Book Information	Summary
Title: *Separate is Never Equal: Sylvia Mendez & Her Family's Fight for Desegregation* Author and Illustrator: Duncan Tonatiuh Awards: *Pura Belpré Award; Jane Addams Award* Grade Level Band: 1–4	This nonfiction picture book spotlights an often overlooked chapter of American civil rights. In 1940s California, Sylvia and her brothers are sent to a school designated for Mexicans, although they are American citizens. The inspiring story of the Mendez family's fight for the desegregation of California schools is brought to life by Tonatiuh's unique illustrations and use of interviews and information from court files and news accounts.
Title: *The Undefeated* Author and Illustrator: Kwame Alexander (Author) & Kadir Nelson (Illustrator) Awards: *Carter G. Woodson Book Award; Coretta Scott King Book Award; John Newberry Medal; Randolph Caldecott Medal* Grade Level Band: 3–8	Kwame Alexander's poem is a tribute to the adversity and beauty of Black life and history in America and a call to action for those who continue to persevere and dream. In this picture book version of the poem, the powerful illustrations of Kadir Nelson depict historical moments, significant figures, and present-day scenes of Black life. The author's note provides valuable information to teachers about the historical figures and events featured in the book.

Book Information	Summary
Title: *We Rise, We Resist, We Raise Our Voices* Author and Illustrator: Wade Hudson & Cheryl Willis Hudson (Editors) Awards: *Jane Addams Children's Book Award; International Latino Book Award* Grade Level Band: 3–8	This book is a collection of essays, poems, artwork, and letters from 50 children's authors and illustrators aimed at answering the question: *"In this divisive world, what shall we tell our children?"* The editors, Wade Hudson & Cheryl Willis Hudson, compiled this anthology with the purpose of providing hope to children in the face of harmful rhetoric and inequities in today's society. It offers multiple perspectives and diverse voices and can be used to empower students (and teachers) to take action and imagine a better future.
Title: *Click, Clack, Moo Cows that Type* Author and Illustrator: Doreen Cronin (Author), Betsy Lewin (Illustrator) Grade Level Band: PreK-3	In this simple story of barnyard animals, teachers and children alike can learn how to take steps to advocate for what matters.
Title: *The Teachers March! How Selma's Teachers Changed History* Author and Illustrator: Sandra Neil Wallace & Rich Wallace Awards: *Orbis Pictus Award for Outstanding Nonfiction for Children, Jane Addams Children's Book Award (Short List)* Grade Level Band: 1–4	This nonfiction picture book is based on firsthand interviews and historical documents of the little known Selma Teachers' March in 1965. It tells the story of principal and teacher Reverend Frederick Douglas Reese, Coach Lawrence Higgins, and the 104 Black teachers who risked their safety and jobs to march for voting rights. Additional resources are listed for teachers and students to learn more about the Selma Teachers' March and other important events of the Civil Rights Movement.
Title: *New Kid* Author and Illustrator: Jerry Craft Awards: *Kirkus Prize; John Newberry Medal; Coretta Scott King Book Award* Grade Level Band: 3–7	This middle grades graphic novel tells the story of seventh grader Jordan Banks as he faces not only becoming a new student at a prestigious private school, but one of the only students (or teachers) of color in a predominately White space. Jordan finds himself navigating his neighborhood friends, his own identity, and his desire to fit in at his new school. This book explores issues of identity, belonging, and racism.
Title: *Change Sings: A Children's Anthem* Author and Illustrator: Amanda Gorman (Author) & Loren Long (Illustrator) Awards: *Cybils Awards* Grade Level Band: 1–3	In this picture book, activist and youngest presidential inaugural poet, Amanda Gorman, tells a story of hope and calls for children to create change. Written as a poem about a young girl who leads a group on a musical journey to create change in their community and accompanied by Loren Long's uplifting illustrations, children are invited to use their own power to take action.

Additional Resources

- Learning for Justice Webinar: Equity Literacy
- AFT Share My Lesson Webinar: Affirming Students Through a Language and Literacy Equity Audit
- Visions of Education [Podcast]: Episode 14: Equity Literacy with Paul Gorski
- Equity Literacy Institute: Intro to Equity Literacy

References

Anyon, J. (2014). *Radical possibilities: Public policy, urban education, and a new social movement* (2nd ed.). Routledge. https://doi.org/10.4324/9780203092965.

Au, K. H. (2011). *Literacy achievement and diversity: Keys to success for students, teachers, and schools* (Multicultural Education Series). Teachers College Press.

Baker, E. L., Barton, P. E., Darling-Hammond, L., Haertel, E., Ladd, H. F., Linn, R. L., Ravitch, D., Rothstein, R., Shalveson, R. J., & Shepard, L. A. (2010). *Problems with the use of student test scores to evaluate teachers* (Briefing Paper #278). Economic Policy Institute. www.epi.org/publication/bp278/.

Botzakis, S. G. (2007). Becoming life-long readers: Insights from a comic book reader. In D. E. Alvermann, & K. A. Hinchman (Eds.), *Reconceptualizing the literacies in adolescents' lives* (pp. 29–48). Routledge.

Bower, J., & Thomas, P. L. (2013). *De-testing and de-grading schools: Authentic alternatives to accountability and standardization*. Peter Lang.

Comber, B. (2015). Critical literacy and social justice. *Journal of Adolescent & Adult Literacy*, 58(5), 362–367.

Comber, B., & Nixon, H. (2009). Teachers' work and pedagogy in an era of accountability. *Discourse: Studies in the Cultural Politics of Education*, 30(3), 333–345.

Cramer, E., Little, M. E., & McHatton, P. A. (2018). Equity, equality, and standardization: Expanding the conversations. *Education and Urban Society*, 50 (5), 483–501.

Crocco, M. S., & Costigan, A. T. (2007). The narrowing of curriculum and pedagogy in the age of accountability urban educators speak out. *Urban Education*, 42(6), 512–535.

Darling-Hammond, L. (2004). Standards, accountability, and school reform. *Teachers College Record*, 106(6), 1047–1085.

Darling-Hammond, L. (2007). Race, inequality and educational accountability: The irony of 'No Child Left Behind'. *Race Ethnicity and Education*, 10(3), 245–260.

Dillon, J. J. (2019). No child left behind?. In *Inside today's elementary schools* (pp. 143–164). Palgrave Macmillan.

DuBose, M., & Gorski, P. (2020). *Equity literacy during the COVID19 crisis*. Equity Literacy Institute. www.equityliteracy.org/equity-covid-19.

Dutro, E. (2010). What 'hard times' means: Mandated curricula, class-privileged assumptions, and the lives of poor children. *Research in the Teaching of English*, 255–291.

Eisner, E. W. (1967). Franklin Bobbitt and the "science" of curriculum making. *The School Review*, 75(1), 29–47.

Feierman, J., Levick, M., & Mody, A. (2009). The school-to-prison pipeline… and back: Obstacles and remedies for the re-enrollment of adjudicated youth. *New York Law School Law Review*, 54, 1115–1129.

Fennimore, B. S. (2017). Permission not required: The power of parents to disrupt educational hypocrisy. *Review of Research in Education*, 41(1), 159–181.

Friedman, J., & Tager, J. (2021). Educational gag orders: Legislative restrictions on the freedom to read, learn, and teach. http://arks.princeton.edu/ark:/88435/dsp01f4752k89d.

Gay, G. (1994). *A synthesis of scholarship in multicultural education*. Urban Monograph Series.(Report #142). Office of Educational Research and Improvement.

González, N., Moll, L. C., & Amanti, C. (Eds.). (2006). *Funds of knowledge: Theorizing practices in households, communities, and classrooms*. Routledge.

Gorski, P. (2016). Rethinking the role of "culture" in educational equity: From cultural competence to equity literacy. *Multicultural perspectives*, 18(4), 221–226.

Gorski, P. C., & Swalwell, K. (2015). Equity literacy for all. *Educational leadership*, 72(6), 34–40.

Grant, C.A., & Sleeter, C.E. (2011). *Doing multicultural education for achievement and equity* (2nd ed.). Routledge. https://doi.org/10.4324/9780203831397.

Green, T. L. (2017). From positivism to critical theory: School-community relations toward community equity literacy. *International Journal of Qualitative Studies in Education*, 30(4), 370–387. https://doi.org/10.1080/09518398.2016.1253892.

Green, T. L. (2018). Enriching educational leadership through community equity literacy: A conceptual foundation. *Leadership and Policy in Schools*, 17(4), 487–515.

Haberman, M. (2005). Teacher burnout in black and white. *The New Educator*, 1 (3), 153–175.

Harrison, L., Hurd, E., & Brinegar, K. (2021). But is it really about critical race theory?: The attack on teaching about systemic racism and why we must care. *Middle School Journal*, 52(4), 2–3.

Harry, B., & Anderson, M. G. (1994). The disproportionate placement of African American males in special education programs: A critique of the process. *The Journal of Negro Education*, 63(4), 602–619.

Hawkins, J. N. (2007). The intractable dominant educational paradigm. In M. Mason, P. D. Hershock, & J. N. Hawkins (Eds.), *Changing Education* (pp. 137–162). CERC Studies in Comparative Education, vol 20. Springer.

Heitzeg, N. A. (2009). Education or incarceration: Zero tolerance policies and the school to prison pipeline. In *Forum on public policy online*, 2. Oxford Round Table.

Imig, D. G., & Imig, S. R. (2006). The teacher effectiveness movement: How 80 years of essentialist control have shaped the teacher education profession. *Journal of Teacher Education*, 57(2), 167–180.

Kendall, J. & Marzano, R. (2004). *Content knowledge: A compendium of standards and benchmarks for K-12 education*. 4th edition. Aurora, CO: Mid-continent Research for Education and Learning (McREL).

Klehr, D. G. (2009). Addressing the unintended consequences of No Child Left Behind and zero tolerance: Better strategies for safe schools and successful students. *Georgetown Journal on Poverty Law & Policy*, 16, 585.

Kohn, A. (2000). *The case against standardized testing: Raising the scores, ruining the schools*. Heinemann.

Knoester, M., & Au, W. (2017). Standardized testing and school segregation: like tinder for fire?. *Race Ethnicity and Education*, 20(1), 1–14.

Kumashiro, K. (2012). Reflections on "bad teachers". *Berkeley Review of Education*, 3(1), 5–16.

Lee, C. D. (1998). Culturally responsive pedagogy and performance-based assessment. *The Journal of Negro Education*, 67(3), 268–279.

Love, B. L. (2019). *We want to do more than survive: Abolitionist teaching and the pursuit of educational freedom*. Beacon Press.

Mallett, C. A. (2016). The school-to-prison pipeline: A critical review of the punitive paradigm shift. *Child and Adolescent Social Work Journal*, 33(1), 15–24.

Miller, K., & Weilbacher, G. (2020). Examining the intersection of social justice and state standards with elementary preservice teachers. *Action in Teacher Education*, 42(4), 368–386.

Muhammad, G. (2020). *Cultivating genius: An equity framework for culturally and historically responsive literacy*. Scholastic Incorporated.

Muhammad, G.E. & Mosley, L.T. (2021). Why we need identity and equity learning in literacy practices: Moving research, practice, and policy forward. *Language Arts*, 98(4), 189–196.

National Commission on Excellence in Education. (1983). A nation at risk: The imperative for educational reform. *The Elementary School Journal*, 84(2), 113–130.

National Governors Association. (2011). *Common core state standards initiative: About the standards*.

Nichols, S. L., & Berliner, D. C. (2008). Testing the joy out of learning. *Educational Leadership*, 65(6), 14–18.

Norton, M. I., & Ariely, D. (2011). Building a better America—One wealth quintile at a time. *Perspectives on psychological science*, 6(1), 9–12.

Null, W. (2017). *Curriculum: From theory to practice* (2nd edition). Rowman & Littlefield.

Panos, A. (2021). The devil's armpit and other tales from the rural rustbelt: Interrogating the practice and process of Un/masking in a postcritical ethnography about place. *International Journal of Qualitative Studies in Education*, 34(9), 800–811.

Paris, D., & Alim, H. S. (Eds.). (2017). *Culturally sustaining pedagogies: Teaching and learning for justice in a changing world*. Teachers College Press.

Paris, D., & Winn, M. T. (2014). Preface: To humanize research. In *Humanizing research: Decolonizing qualitative inquiry with youth and communities* (pp. 8–10). Sage Publications.

Parker, L. (2022). Critical moments in education. *Journal of Teaching and Learning*, 16(1), 1–4.

Pollock, M., Rogers, J., Kwako, A., Matschiner, A., Kendall, R., Bingener, C., & Howard, J. (2022). The conflict campaign: Exploring local experiences of the campaign to ban "critical race theory" in Public K–12 education in the U.S., 2020–2021. https://idea.gseis.ucla.edu/publications/the-conflict-campaign/.

Ravitch, D. (Ed.). (2010). *Debating the future of american education: Do we meet national standards and assessments?*Brookings Institution Press.

Sachs, J. (2022, January 24). Steep rise in gag orders, many sloppily drafted. https://pen.org/steep-rise-gag-orders-many-sloppily-drafted/.

Sachs, J, Young, J. C., & Friedman, J. (2022, April 24). For educational gag orders, the vagueness is the point. https://pen.org/for-educational-gag-orders-the-vagueness-is-the-point/.

Smith, M. L. (1991). Put to the test: The effects of external testing on teachers. *Educational Researcher*, 20(5), 8–11.

Smith, J. M., & Kovacs, P. E. (2011). The impact of standards-based reform on teachers: The case of 'No Child Left Behind'. *Teachers and Teaching: Theory and Practice*, 17(2), 201–225.

Smith, P., Lee, J., & Chang, R. (2022). Characterizing competing tensions in Black immigrant literacies: Beyond partial representations of success. *Reading Research Quarterly*, 57(1), 59–90.

Spring, J. (2011). *The politics of American education*. Routledge.

Stedman, L. C. (2010). How well does the standards movement measure up? An analysis of achievement trends, academic course-taking, student learning, NCLB, and changes in school culture and graduation rates. *Critical Education*, 1(10), 1–41.

Stein, S. J. (2004). *The culture of education policy*. Teachers College Press.

Swalwell, K. (2011). Why our students need "equity literacy.". *Teaching Tolerance Blog*. Retrieved from: www.learningforjustice.org/magazine/why-our-students-need-equity-literacy.

U.S. Department of Education. (2001). No Child Left Behind Act. U.S. Department of Education. (n.d.). Overview: Four pillars of NCLB. Retrieved from www.ed.gov/nclb/overview/intro/4pillars.html http://www2.ed.gov/policy/elsec.

U.S. Department of Education. (2010). Race to the Top executive summary. www2.ed.gov/programs/racetothetop/executive-summary.pdf.

van Sluys, K., Lewison, M., & Flint, A. S. (2006). Researching critical literacy: A critical study of analysis of classroom discourse. *Journal of Literacy Research*, 38(2), 197–233.

Vasquez, V. M., Janks, H., & Comber, B. (2019). Critical literacy as a way of being and doing. *Language Arts*, 96(5), 300–311.

Wessel-Powell, C., Panos, A., & Weir, R. (2021). A year of equity literacy: Community actions and invitations. *Literacy*, 55(1), 62–76. https://doi.org/10.1111/lit.12237.

Wun, C. (2014). The anti-black order of No Child Left Behind: Using Lacanian psychoanalysis and critical race theory to examine NCLB. *Educational Philosophy and Theory*, 46(5), 462–474.

Zancanella, D., & Moore, M. (2014). The origins of the Common Core: Untold stories. *Language Arts*, 91(4), 273–279.

Children's Literature Cited

Alexander, K. (2019). *The undefeated*. K. Nelson, Illus. Versify.

Craft, J. (2019). *New Kid*. J. Craft, Illus. Quill Tree Books.

Cronin, D. (2000). *Click, clack, moo: cows that type*. B. Lewin, Illus. Simon & Schuster.

Gorman, A. (2021). *Change sings: A children's anthem*. L. Long, Illus. Viking Books for Young Readers.

Hudson, W. & Hudson, C. W. (Eds.). (2018). *We rise, we resist, we raise our voices*. Crown Books for Young Readers.

Tonatiuh, D. (2014). *Separate is never equal: Sylvia Mendez & her family's fight for desegregation*. D. Tonatiuh, Illus. Abrams Books for Young Readers.

Wallace, S. N. & Wallace, R. (2020). *The teachers march! How Selma's teachers changed history*. Calkins Creek.

5 Censorship

Book Challenges in Classrooms and School Libraries

Kaya van Beynen and Allison N. Symulevich

We all know that encouraging children to read is critically important to teach literacy, foster creativity, and develop critical thinking skills. But whether we should provide access-to or teach difficult or controversial books is in question in our schools, libraries, and society. As Judge Richard Posner stated, "People are unlikely to become well-functioning, independent-minded adults and responsible citizens if they are raised in an intellectual bubble" (*American Amusement Machine Association v. Kendrick*, 2001, at 577). According to the First Amendment of the United States, we have a fundamental right to a freedom of speech and expression. This same amendment also enshrines our right to peacefully petition the government to redress our grievances. Supreme Court rulings since the 1970s have added some nuance to the First Amendment; children have the right to choose what they read, school boards have authority over school curriculum and sponsored activities, parents have the right to parent according to their beliefs, and individuals have the right to challenge public schools as a branch of local government. Thus, this tension across these different First Amendment rights frames the ongoing discourse surrounding book bans.

With this in mind, we posit that teachers be empowered to select and teach and school librarians should select and provide access to a vibrant range of quality and engaging books that reflect the multicultural and literary diversity of young readers. Sadly, teachers and librarians may encounter book challenges in their professional career. Thus, this chapter is geared to practically equip elementary school educators with articulated values on why they should teach controversial books, provide an overview of the legal and educational history of schoolbook challenges, the First Amendment, and outline resources for and best practices to avert, prepare for, and respond to book challenges and ultimately support our students' right to read.

Rationale: Why Teach Challenged Books?

The metaphor of windows, mirrors, and sliding glass doors permeates conversations about children's literature and frames many arguments on

DOI: 10.4324/9781003321941-6

why educators should teach books that could be considered controversial (Bishop, 1990). In essence, sliding glass doors highlight the role of a book's creators; their readers pass through the doors and enter into the imagination of the book's authors and illustrators. Authors have the freedom to create and tell their stories, whether or not these stories are disturbing or challenge traditional hierarchies. These books are the windows that enable children to experience wondrous worlds of thrill, humor, and adventure both real and imaginary. As such, they open up new worlds to young readers, and they expose youth to the lives and experiences of others and provide a way for children to expand their horizons and foster understanding across cultural, social, and historical differences (Bishop, 1990). To complete the metaphor, in some lights, the windows become mirrors that can reflect the experiences of the reader and affirm their lives as part of the larger human conversation.

Children from racial and ethnic minority groups now comprise more than 50% of the children in public schools. Increasingly, publishers are publishing more children's books by minority authors, and many teachers and libraries are conscientiously adding them to their curriculum and library shelves. With more books accessible, students are enabled and empowered to choose what they want to read and to see reflections of their lived experiences. But a disproportionate amount of book challenges target minority characters and portrayals of racial injustices; sex, gender identity, and alternative family structures; and depictions of violence, profanity, and defiance of parent authority (Fletcher-Spear & Tyler, 2014; NTCE, 2018; Town, 2014). Because literature can be a mirror of reality, the content can be controversial. Most parents and adults would easily agree that we should protect children. Childhood is a time of innocence and wonder; toddlers begin to explore their world, and children start to develop their own sense of self and experiences. Preserving this innocence is one mode of parental protection. Many book challenges in elementary schools are geared to prevent children from being exposed to difficult or uncomfortable issues, situations, or deviant behaviors (Town, 2014).

Sherman Alexie explained, "I read books about monsters and monstrous things, often written with monstrous language, because they taught me how to battle the real monsters in my life" (Alexie, 2011). Alexie counters this stance regarding preserving innocence, arguing many children are already "poverty-stricken, sexually and physically abused," and protecting them from books is both ineffectual and too late. It is in these heart-wrenching cases that books matter even more, as children yearn to know they are not alone and can use the stories of their colleagues to learn how to battle their own monsters. The second quote at the beginning of this chapter, by 7th District Judge Richard Posner, highlights that attempts to protect children from exposure to real life can also serve to wrap children in an intellectual bubble, preventing them from learning about the lives of others. While we want to preserve the innocence of youth and protect them from trauma, raising them in a cultural and intellectual bubble is a disservice both to their societal and intellectual growth and ultimately to our democracy at large.

Controversial books can encourage students to read. Comic books and graphic novels are a frequently challenged category of books. Reluctant readers, however, are particularly drawn to comic books with their exciting stories and mix of visual and textual storytelling. Their inclusion in a school library is a common strategy to encourage reading and improve student reading abilities. Connecting students to books that spark their interest is a surefire approach to make students want to read and ultimately improve literacy (Cart, 2008).

Teaching controversial books can also prepare students to become critical thinkers and active members of a democratic society. Teachers can use controversial books to expose their students to new ideas and engage them in big issues, not as a means of indoctrination, but as a way of getting their students to ask questions (NCTE, 2018). Through collective reading and classroom discussion, students can explore their questions and perspectives and hear about the reactions of their colleagues, all under the guidance of a moderating teacher. Within a democracy, we all have opinions but should learn to how to discuss, disagree, come to consensus, and see larger themes beyond the individual.

Why Do Book Challenges Happen?

With the best of motives, a parent might ask their child's teacher or librarian whether a controversial book is available to students in the school. Or else, a political action committee might organize a national campaign directing its members to challenge books that run counter to their cultural or religious values. Recently, some elected officials are waging a public war against children's and young adult books that feature racialized narratives and history or cover LGBTQ+ perspectives and themes (PEN America, 2022a). While their motives might derive from many reasons, book challenges serve to impose a person's own values and beliefs on children, educators, schools, and the educational system. When challenged books are removed from classrooms and school libraries, this limits the choices of students and narrows their exposure to new ideas, perspectives, and the rich fabric of American history and life.

Challenging a book is not necessarily censorship. Some common definitions can help us in this regard. According to the American Library Association (ALA 2010), a book challenge can be:

1. An oral complaint: A verbal objection to a book included or accessible within a classroom or library collection.
2. A written complaint: A written challenge submitted to a library or a school questioning whether a book is appropriate within that school or library.

3. A public attack: A challenge issued in a public, governmental, or media forum questioning whether a book is appropriate for inclusion in a library or school. Public attacks are designed to garner media attention and to harness public opinion in support of book banning or censorship.

The same rights that protect our intellectual freedom also support a person's capacity to challenge a government institution, even public schools. The school board has legal authority to set the curriculum standards, and ultimately, has oversight of what is taught within their jurisdiction. As previously mentioned in the chapter introduction, a core tenant of the First Amendment is students have the freedom to read, and this freedom is based on the notion of choice (NCTE, 2018). Educators facilitate this freedom through classroom and school libraries that provide a range of appropriate materials and a safe space for students to choose what genre, subjects, or authors they want to read. These choices, however, should not be limited by the racial, religious, or social prejudices of non-relatives, community members, or political interest groups (NCTE, 2018). Instead, professional selection criteria is based on variables such as addressing instructional objectives, interest to children, developmental readiness, quality, accuracy, and diversity of perspectives. We describe a more detailed discussion of the principles of selection in the Appendix to this chapter.

Bound by budgets, space, and other variables, schools, teachers, and school libraries cannot offer limitless options to students, thus a critical role of professional educators is to select quality materials that support their instruction and school community. Thus, it can be an entirely legitimate concern that a parent might challenge a book in a library or in a school classroom. A parent always has authority of what their own child reads, but they do not have authority over what other children read.

Due to this inherent conflict over First Amendment rights, schools and school boards need to have a transparent process for review of challenged material. School boards are supposed to follow these procedures detailed within state statutes and school board policies. Challengers can then appeal school board decisions in lawsuits filed within the court system. As these rights may sometimes collide, educators need to know about the legal and educational history of book challenges and censorship because they will confront these issues in their classrooms, libraries, and in their interactions with parents, administrators, and the community.

Book Challenges: The Usual Suspects

A disproportionate amount of book challenges target authors and characters of color (Fletcher-Spear & Tyler, 2014; NTCE, 2018; Town, 2014). By banning books by and about African American, Native American,

Asian American, and Latinx people, this serves to effectively erase their voices and lived experiences from the curriculum and obscure the flaws of our nation's history (Natanson, 2022). Many frequently challenged novels present racialized history and non-White perspectives and experiences that counter the notion of American exceptionalism. For example, elementary age books include *New Kid* by Jerry Craft and *Something Happened in Our Town: A Child's Story about Racial Injustice* by Marianne Celano. Books for middle and high school students illustrate this in *The Hate U Give* by Angie Thomas, *The Bluest Eye* by Toni Morrison, or *Out of Darkness* by Ashley Hope Perez. By this logic, censors argue books depicting these alternate narratives are "unpatriotic" or "uncomfortable" (ALA, 2017). Classroom and school libraries that only include White middle-class stories, however, only present part of the lived experience of America; this lack of literary inclusion is undemocratic.

A fundamental power of children's books is that they both reflect changes to our social and political discourse and help shape the attitudes of the younger generations. Limiting access to controversial books is a means of stopping social, attitudinal, and generational change. As such, books with LGBTQ+ characters or themes, such as *This Day in June* by Gayle Pitman, can serve as catalyst for acceptance and or a challenge for being against "family values," "obscene," or as "grooming children" (Natanson, 2022). As a touchstone of our changing society, picture books that portrayed alternative family units, such as *And Tango Makes Three* by Peter Parnell and Justin Richardson and *Prince & Knight* by Daniel Haack or that chronicle the lives of transgender individuals, such as *I am Jazz* by Jessica Herthel and Jazz Jennings and *George* by Alex Gino, are frequent targets for book banning efforts. Most recently, YA books that focus on the intersectionality between race/ethnicity and sexual orientation, such as *All Boys Aren't Blue* by George Johnson and *Lawn Boy* by Jonathan Evison, quickly moved to the top of the ALA's Top 10 Most Challenged Books List (ALA OIF, 2022).

Finally, children's books with naughty or mischievous characters that defy parental authority or remain unpunished for their deviant behavior are also frequently challenged by concerned parents. For example, the books in the *Captain Underpants* series by Dav Pilkey, the *Harry Potter* series by J. K. Rowling, and *Harriet the Spy* by Louise Fitzhugh regularly appear in the ALA's Frequently challenged books. These books are also fun to read and can be particularly engaging to reluctant readers who might not otherwise be interested in reading.

Historical Perspectives

Legal History

We begin with a brief overview of the legal history of schoolbook challenges in the United States. The most relevant cases presented to the

Supreme Court regarding public schools, student and parental rights, and school board authority are *Board of Education, Island Trees Union Free School District No. 26 vs Pico*, 457 U.S. 853 (1982) and *Hazelwood School District v. Kuhlmeier*, 484 U.S. 260 (1988). As you will see, rulings made of the U.S. Supreme Court have created broad legal guidelines that frame this debate, but undecided or gray areas in U.S. law still exist.

Board of Education, Island Trees Union Free School District No. 26 vs Pico was the first Supreme Court case to consider the First Amendment and the right to receive information in a library setting. In 1975, school board members from the Island Trees Union Free School District of New York received a list of books from a conservative organization deemed "objectionable" and "improper" (*Board of Education v. Pico*, 1982 at 856). The school board initially followed procedures and created a review committee to review the books based on educational suitability, good taste, relevance, and appropriateness to age and grade level. The committee recommended five books be retained, two books be removed, and one book be available with parental consent. With no public explanation, the school board summarily rejected the report and ordered all the books be removed from the curriculum and district school libraries (*Board of Education v. Pico*, 1982). In response, five high school and one middle school students filed a lawsuit arguing that the school board violated their First Amendment rights (*Board of Education v. Pico*, 1982). The case moved its way through the New York District Courts, the U.S. Court of Appeals, and ultimately made its way to the U.S. Supreme Court in 1982. In its decision, the U.S. Supreme Court recognized the students' First Amendment rights to receive a range of information and the right to read books of their own choosing. Additionally, while school boards had significant discretion to determine the content of their school libraries, they could not remove materials based on politics, nationalism, religion, or opinion (*Board of Education v. Pico*, 1982 at 872).

Hazelwood School District v. Kuhlmeier, 484 U.S. 260 (1988), also plays a significant role in book banning. In *Hazelwood*, the principal of a school removed two stories from a student newspaper due to concerns over age-appropriateness of the material. The U.S. Supreme Court held that the student newspaper was not a public forum, and the school did not infringe on the students' First Amendment rights by removing the articles, "so long as their actions are reasonably related to legitimate pedagogical concerns." (*Hazelwood v. Kuhlmeier*, 1988 at 273). Although it dealt with a school newspaper, it has implications for banning materials based on "vulgarity" or "indecency" (Reichman, 2000). Some school boards used this standard to remove books based on explicit sexuality and excessive vulgar language.

It is important to understand these cases to recognize the proper procedures that must be followed by school boards when reviewing materials for both school curriculum and school libraries. Because *Pico* is a plurality opinion and thus not binding, lower courts may not follow this standard regarding removal based on politics, nationalism, religion, or other matters of opinion. Courts might instead follow *Hazelwood's* standard of removal based on vulgarity or indecency.

Educational History

Censorship in schools was infrequent before World War II (Town, 2014). Jongsma (1991) posits censorship increases during times of social and political polarizations. In the 1960s and the start of the racial, gender, and LGBTQ+ civil rights movements and changes in school racial and ethnic demographics, the curriculum and books in school libraries started to include minority characters and coming of age novels filled with themes of social angst, violence, sex, and racial injustice. Legal challenges to books taught in classrooms or present in the school libraries started in 1972; most of these challenges focused on young adult rather than children's literature (Reichman, 2000). In the 1980s, conservative Christian organizations, such as the Moral Majority and the Heritage Foundation, led a political movement to ban books, both young adult and children's literature, considered obscene or disrespectful to America's patriotic heritage (Pincus, 2022; Shopgren & Frantz, 1993). Many conservative parents and community groups responded, and schools and libraries started to experience an influx of challenges to books, particularly those pertaining to race and America's racial history or sexual orientation and same sex families. These public challenges were a critical strategy to rally public opinion around the growing Christian conservatism movement and its increased engagement in federal politics.

In response, libraries, publishers, and intellectual freedom advocates began their own political campaigns. In 1982, the American Library Association (ALA) in collaboration with the Association of American Publishers initiated an annual Banned Books Week celebration to promote reading and raise awareness of threats of censorship. That same year, the People for the American Way (Pfaw), a liberal public interest group, followed later by the ALA in 1990, started to track book challenges in order to get a better understanding of the breadth and magnitude of this issue (ALA, 2000).

Pfaw identified several obvious trends in the 1980s and 1990s. Parents instigated the majority of book challenges, and initially, few challenges resulted in the removal of the item from the school or library (ALA, 2000). However, as the number of book challenges steadily increased into the 1990s, the percentage of book bans (the removal of the books from the classroom or library) also rose. At its peak in 1995, 762 titles were challenged across the United States (a book title could be challenged multiple times), and 50% of these challenges resulted in the removal or restriction of the items in questions (ALA, 2000).

By the twenty-first century, book-banning efforts in the United States declined but did not disappear. The ALA found an average of 510 book titles challenged per year from 2000 to 2009, subsequently falling to an average of 310 books challenged per year from 2010 to 2019 (ALA, 2022). But with the decline of book challenges, various pundits and scholars began to question the value of Banned Books Week. Cultural scholars criticized the capitalistic focus of Banned Books Week, its focus on book sales, and performative support of intellectual freedom (Kuecker, 2018; Lee, 2002). By 2009, Mitchell Muncy, a columnist from the *Wall Street Journal*, argued that some parents may still challenge books; libraries no longer actually removed them from their shelves. Additionally, as parents, not a governmental authority, initiated many of these challenges, they could not be considered an act of censorship but rather a valid removal of inappropriate material (Muncy, 2009).

Pending Challenges

Since 2020, however, book challenges, public attacks, and censorship efforts are gaining momentum. For a nine-month period spanning 2021 and 2022, PEN America, a public interest group devoted to the intersection of literature and intellectual freedom, tracked book bans in school libraries and classrooms in America in order to gain a better understanding of how pervasive this issue had become (PEN America, 2022a). During this short period, they determined that 1,586 books were banned, representing 1,145 unique titles and 874 different authors. These bans came from 86 school districts in 26 states, affecting 2,899 public schools and over 2 million students.

Most disturbingly, PEN America found elected state officials initiated 41% of the book challenges (PEN America, 2022a). Politicians in Texas and Florida proposed statewide banned book lists for local school districts, calling for them to remove these books from their collections (PEN America, 2022a). Several states with conservative governors or legislative majorities introduced legislation to require schools to publish their library collections (EveryLibrary, 2022). By providing public access to library catalogs, book-banning activists are better able to conduct keyword and title searches to identify targeted materials. Based on a journalist's analysis of the challenged titles, this strategy possibly occurred in Texas, when a member of the state House of Representatives created a list of 850 LGBTQ+ books for removal from public school library across the state (PEN America, 2022a). Finally, several states have proposed fining or prosecuting public and school libraries' employees for the distribution of obscene or harmful materials to minors (EveryLibrary, 2022).

These challenges represent blatant acts of censorship through governmental actions to ban books based on a few words, the personal morality of a political group, and attempts to whitewash history. As many of these challenges are pending at the state level, they have not yet become law and have not yet risen to the federal courts.

Conclusion

Removing "controversial" political, racial, gender, or religions books from classrooms and libraries can be damaging to millions of children and young adults. Gay, trans, queer, African American, Asian American, Native American, and Latinx children are less able to access and read books that reflect their experiences and world; sheltered children are kept ignorant about their queer or minority colleagues, and the injustices and traumas of American racial history are erased from the reading curriculum. As we confront increased social isolation, young adults are inhibited from finding a community, a sense of belonging, or reading beyond the immediacy of their own lives and reluctant readers have less options that encourage and engage their attention and imagination.

As the legal and political battles continue, the war against censorship requires a marathon effort, and teachers, librarians, and educators cannot think it will go away. We hope this chapter provides a useful overview of book banning in schools and libraries in the United States. In our Appendix, we discuss best practices to avert or manage book challenges. We hope this too will be of use to educators as they serve their students, schools, and communities.

Reflection Questions

1. How do the historical perspectives of books impact your thinking in how the U.S. Courts supports or declines book challenges? Provide a specific example.
2. How do cultural markers (race, religion, sexuality, class, language, age) impact books that are challenged?
3. How does the Freedom to Read impact your students and their book selections?
4. After reviewing several of the resources, what are ways you can build trust with parents?
5. Read one of the most challenged books from Table 5.1. Identify elements that caused the challenge. Would you use this book in your classroom? Why or why not?

Recommended Children's Literature

Table 5.1 Frequently challenged books for elementary aged classrooms.

Book Information	Summary
Title: *And Tango Makes Three* **Authors:** Justine Richardson and Peter Parnell **Illustrator:** Henry Cole **Awards:** Lambda Literary Award; Storytelling World Resource Award; Henry Bergh Children's Book Award for Environment and Ecology **Ages:** 4–8 yrs	**Summary:** The story of two male penguins, Roy and Silo, who create a family together. **Brief Description of Why Challenged:** LGBTQ+ content
Title: *Something Happened in Our Town: A Child's Story About Racial Injustice* **Author:** Marianne Celano, Marietta Collins, and Ann Hazzard **Illustrator:** Jennifer Zivoin **Awards:** IndieFab Book of the Year Awards (finalist); National Parenting Product Award Winner **Ages:** 4–8 yrs	**Summary:** Follows two families — one White, one Black — as they discuss a police shooting of a Black man in their community. The story aims to answer children's questions about such traumatic events and to help children identify and counter racial injustice in their own lives. **Brief Description of Why Challenged:** divisive language, promotes anti-police views
Title: *This Day in June* **Author:** Gayle Pitman **Illustrator:** Kristyna Litten **Awards:** American Library Association Rainbow List; Global Society Awards; Stonewall Book Award **Ages:** 4–8 yrs	**Summary:** A picture book illustrating a Pride parade. Includes facts about LGBT history and culture and a Note to Parents and Caregivers with information on how to talk to children about sexual orientation and gender identity in age-appropriate ways. **Brief Description of Why Challenged:** LGBTQ+ content and promoting "perversion" and the "gay lifestyle."
Title: *Prince & Knight* **Author:** Daniel Haack **Illustrator:** Stevie Lewis **Awards:** Cybils Awards (Nominee) **Ages:** 4–9 yrs	**Summary:** A modern fairy tale where a noble prince and a brave knight come together to defeat a terrible monster and, in the process, find true love in a most unexpected place. **Brief Description of Why Challenged:** Features gay marriage and LGBTQ+ content; a deliberate attempt to "indoctrinate" young children with the potential to cause confusion, curiosity, and gender dysphoria; and for conflicting with a religious viewpoint.

Book Information	Summary
Title: *I am Jazz* **Author:** Jessica Herthel and Jazz Jennings **Illustrator:** Shelagh McNicholas **Awards:** Australian Family Therapists' Award for Children's Literature; Rainbow Project Book List **Ages:** 5–10 yrs	**Summary:** The story of a transgender child based on the real-life experience of Jazz Jennings, who has become a spokesperson for trans-kids everywhere. **Brief Description of Why Challenged:** LGBTQ+ content, for a transgender character, and for confronting a topic that is "sensitive, controversial, and politically charged"
Title: *Nasreen's Secret School: A True Story from Afghanistan* **Author:** Jeanette Winter **Awards:** Jane Addams Children's Book; Skipping Stones Honor Award; Storytelling World Resource Award **Ages:** 6–9 yrs	**Summary:** The story of a young girl in Afghanistan who attends a secret school for girls. **Brief Description of Why Challenged:** religious viewpoint, unsuited to age group, and violence.
Title: *Stamped (For Kids): Racism, Antiracism, and You* **Authors:** Jason Reynolds and Ibram X. Kendi **Adapter:** Sonja Cherry-Paul **Illustrator:** Rachelle Baker **Awards:** ALA Notable Children's Book; Kirkus Reviews Best Book of the Year; Kirkus Prize, Finalist **Ages:** 6–10 yrs	**Summary:** Adapted from the award-winning Stamped: Racism, Antiracism, and You, this children's edition teaches where racist ideas came from, how it impacts America today, and introduces readers to people who have fought racism with antiracism. **Brief Description of Why Challenged:** Author's public statements, contains divisive topics, foul and vulgar language, gross generalizations about historical racism.
Title: *Captain Underpants (Series)* **Author and Illustrator:** Dav Pilkey **Ages:** 7–12 yrs	**Summary:** The series revolves around two fourth graders, George and Harold, and Captain Underpants, an aptly named superhero from one of the boys' homemade comic books, who accidentally becomes real when the boys hypnotize their cruel, bossy, and ill-tempered principal, Mr. Krupp. **Brief Description of Why Challenged:** Adult authoritative figures depicted as "bad guys," violent imagery, encourages disruptive behavior, main character unpunished for naughty behavior.

Book Information	Summary
Title: New Kid **Author and Illustrator:** Jerry Craft **Awards:** Coretta Scott King Award; Cybils Award; Kirkus Prize; Newbery Medal **Ages:** 8–12 yrs	**Summary:** A graphic novel that tells the story of a 12-year-old black boy, Jordan Banks, who experiences culture shock when he enrolls at a private school. **Brief Description of Why Challenged:** Promotes Critical Race Theory, Marxism, and makes students feel "discomfort, guilt" over systemic depiction of racism within the legal system
Title: George **Author and Illustrator:** Alex Gino **Awards:** California Book Award; Cybils Award; Lambda Literary Award; Stonewall Book Award **Ages:** 8–12 yrs	**Summary:** A story of Melissa, a fourth-grade transgender girl who is struggling to be herself, when the rest of the world sees Melissa as George, a boy. **Brief Description of Why Challenged:** LGBTQ+ content, conflicting with a religious viewpoint, and not reflecting community values.

Resources

- American Library Association (ALA) Office of Intellectual Freedom (OIF). The mission of the ALA Office of Intellectual Freedom is to:

  1. Systematically collected book challenges data through their *Materials Challenge Reporting form* (www.ala.org/tools/challenge support/report),
  2. Track censorship trends through the annual *Top 10 Most Challenged Books List* (www.ala.org/advocacy/bbooks/frequentlycha llengedbooks/top10), and
  3. Supply librarians with tools, resources, and training to defend library resources and effectively respond to book challenges (www.ala.org/advocacy/fight-censorship). Offers confidential consultations to teachers and librarians facing a book challenge.

- EveryLibrary, www.everylibrary.org/. A national organization dedicated to building voter support for libraries. Provides pro-bono consultants to help libraries battle book challenges through petitions, targeted communication to public officials, and social-influencing campaigns.
- Freedom to Read Foundation (FTRF), www.ftrf.org/. A non-profit legal and educational organization dedicated to protecting and defending the First Amendment and supporting the rights of libraries and individuals. FTRF also provides financial and legal assistance to libraries and librarians facing book challenges.

- Kirkus Book Reviews, www.kirkusreviews.com/. One of the largest sites for professional and crowd sourced book reviews. Reviews searchable by genre, age categories, format, and more.
- National Coalition Against Censorship, ncac.org/. Maintains the *Free Expression Educators Handbook* to help teachers, librarians, and school administrators respond to book challenges, created in collaboration with the National Council of Teachers of English. ncac.org/resource/educator-handbook.
- National Council of Teachers of English (NCTE) Intellectual Freedom Center ncte.org/resources/ncte-intellectual-freedom-center/. NCTE offers advice, resources, and a hotline for teachers seeing assistance for a challenge. NCTE manages a book challenge crisis hotline and promises confidentiality response within 24 hours. ncac.org/resource/book-challenge-resource-center. In their *Responding to Book Challenges: A Handbook for Educators*, NCTE provides a *Material Reconsideration Form* template for schools, libraries, and school districts.
- School Library Journal Reviews, www.slj.com/section/reviews. The premiere publication for librarians and information specialists who work with children and teens. A source reviews and evaluations on a broad range of resources, from books and digital content to databases. More than 6000+ reviews published annually.
- Young Adult Library Services Association (YALSA). Hosts an Intellectual Freedom email listserv for young adult librarians to discuss issues pertaining to teens and intellectual freedom in school and public libraries. www.ala.org/yalsa/workingwithyalsa/committees/intellectual

References

Alexie, S. (2011). Why the best kids books are written in blood. *The Wall Street Journal*. www.wsj.com/articles/BL-SEB-65604.

ALA. (2022). Frequently challenged books. www.ala.org/advocacy/bbooks/frequentlychallengedbooks.

ALA. (2017) Hate speech and hate crime. www.ala.org/advocacy/intfreedom/hate.

ALA. (2010). *Intellectual freedom manual*. American Library Association.

ALA OIF. (2022). Top 10 most challenged books lists. www.ala.org/advocacy/bbooks/frequentlychallengedbooks/top10.

Bishop, R. S. (1990). Windows, mirrors, and sliding glass doors. *Perspectives*, 6(3), ix–xi.

Cart, M. (2008). *The value of young adult literature*. Young Adult Library Services Association.

Daly, K. C. (2001). *Balancing act: Teachers' classroom speech and the first amendment*. JL & Educ., 30, 1.

EveryLibrary (2022, April 3). Legislation of concern. www.everylibrary.org/2022_legislative_attacks.

Fletcher-Spear, K. & Tyler, K. (2014). *Intellectual freedom for teens: A practical guide for young adult and school librarians*, American Library Association.

Hartsfield, D. E., & Kimmel, S. C. (2021). Supporting the right to read: Principles for selecting children's books. *The Reading Teacher*, 74(4), 419–427.

Hickson, M. (2022, February 3). What's it like to be the target of a book banning effort? School librarian Martha Hickson tells her story. *School Library Journal.* www.slj.com/story/from-the-breaking-point-to-fighting-anew-school-libraria n-martha-hickson-shares-her-story-of-battling-book-banning-censorship.

Jongsma, K. S. (1991). Concerns about censorship and intellectual freedom. *The Reading Teacher*, 45(2), 152.

Kuecker, E. (2018). *Questioning the dogma of banned books week.* University of Georgia.

Lee, E. (2002). Almost banned books: A brief history. *Counterpoise*, 5(2), 16.

Muncy, M., (2009, September 25). Finding censorship where there is none. *Wall Street Journal.* www.wsj.com/articles/SB10001424052970204518504574420882837440304.

Natanson, H. (2022, April 7). More books are banned than ever before, as congress takes on the issue. *Washington Post.* www.washingtonpost.com/education/2022/04/07/book-bans-congress-student-library/.

NCTE. (2018). The students right to read. https://ncte.org/statement/righttoreadgui deline/.

Pen America. (2022a). Banned in the U.S.A. https://pen.org/banned-in-the-usa/.

Pen America. (2022b). Education gag orders. https://pen.org/report/educational-ga g-orders/.

Pincus, F.L. (2022, March 8). Battles over book bans reflect conflicts from the 1980s. *New Hampshire Bulletin*, https://newhampshirebulletin.com/2022/03/08/ commentary-battles-over-book-bans-reflect-conflicts-from-the-1980s/.

Reichman, H. (2000). Censorship and selection: issues and answers for. https:// ebookcentral.proquest.com/lib/usf/detail.action?docID=3001634.

Shopgren, E. & Frantz D., (1993, September 2). Political, religious right lead school book ban efforts. *Los Angeles Times*, www.latimes.com/archives/la-xpm -1993-09-02-mn-32709-story.html.

Town, C. J. (2014). *"Unsuitable" books: young adult fiction and censorship.* McFarland.

Children's Literature Cited

Celano, M., Collins, M., Hazzard, A., & Zivoin, J. (2018). *Something happened in our town: a child's story about racial injustice.* Magination Press.

Craft, J. (2019). *New kid.* HarperCollins Publishers.

Evison, J. (2018). *Lawn boy: a novel.* Algonquin Books of Chapel Hill.

Fitzhugh, L. (1964). *Harriet, the spy.* Harper & Row.

Gino, A. (2015). *George* (1st edition.). Scholastic Press.

Haack, D. (2018). *Prince & knight.* Little Bee Books.

Herthel, J., Jennings, J., & McNicholas, S. (2014). *I am jazz!*Penguin.

Johnson, G. (2020). *All boys aren't blue: a memoir-manifesto.* Farrar Straus Giroux.

Morrison, T. (2000). *The bluest eye.* Knopf.

Pérez, A.H. (2015). *Out of darkness.* Carolrhoda Lab.

Pilkey, D. (1997). *The adventures of captain underpants: an epic novel.* Scholastic.

Pitman, G.E. (2014). *This day in June.* Magination Press.

Richardson, Parnell, P., & Cole, H. (2005). *And Tango makes three.* Simon & Schuster.

Rowling, J. K., (1998). *Harry potter and the sorcerer's stone.* Scholastic Press.

Thomas, A. (2017). *The hate u give.* HarperCollins Publishers.

Winter, J. (2009). *Nasreen's secret school: a true story from Afghanistan.* Beach Lane Books.

Appendix: Best Practices to Avert or Respond to a Book Challenge

Before a Book Challenge

The extent of free speech rights for teachers in the classroom is legally unclear in the United States (Daly, 2001). Thus, teachers need to carefully balance their own academic freedom, students and parents first amendment rights, and authority of the school board to make decisions regarding the curriculum. One strategy to navigate this rocky path, it to develop and document a book selection process.

Reading is the first place to start. Teachers should read all of the books that they assign or include in their classroom libraries. While word of mouth recommendations, publishers' notices, and book reviews are helpful, teachers need to critically read the materials and carefully weigh their strengths and weaknesses on whether to include them in the curriculum. Hartsfield and Kimmel (2021) created the following Principles of Selection with these questions to guide this consideration:

Table 5A.1. Principles of selection.

Supporting the curriculum	Does the book address instructional objectives?
Appealing to children	Is this topic or treatment interesting to children?
Developmentally appropriate	Does this book address the range of social, emotional, and academic readiness of the students?
Merit	Does this book represent the standards of literary excellence?
Accuracy and authenticity	Does the author's research, knowledge, or experience provide evidence of accuracy and authenticity?
Diverse perspectives	Does this book offer a unique or diverse perspective?

Source: Hartsfield, D. E., & Kimmel, S. C. (2021). Supporting the right to read: Principles for selecting children's books. *The Reading Teacher*, 74(4), 419–427.

With these questions in mind, teachers should consider writing a rationale for any book or novel that they require their students to read. This rationale can help the teachers think through the value of the material, pull together supporting documents such as critical book reviews, whether the book won any awards, and if it appeared on any recommended reading lists. We suggest *Kirkus Reviews* and the *School Library Journal* as two great sites for teachers to find descriptive information about the books, awards and thematic lists, and professional and lay reviews. With this evidence in hand, crafting the book rationale can help the teachers organize their talking points and proactively prepare for any potential book challenge (NCTE, 2018; Town, 2014).

Librarians and school media specialists should develop a Collection Management Policy (Fletcher-Spear & Tyler, 2014). Librarians, because they regularly consider hundreds if not thousands of books each year for inclusion in their school or public libraries, do not have the capacity to read every single book. But librarians have greater leeway than classroom teachers, with their mandate to include a diverse array of books and materials that reflect the interests and demographic of a larger community. This collection management policy should formally define what material should be added to the collection and positively affirm the value of including a range of books and materials to support their targeted audience.

Elements of a collection management policy should include the following:

- A description of your library's and institution's mission, service population, and associated collection development goal statement,
- Name and titles of the people who are responsible for collection management. This could be an individual teacher or librarian, or a school committee,
- The type of materials that should be included in the library, such as genre, reading levels, and format. For example, does the library acquire picture books, chapter books, graphic novels, non-fiction, print and/or ebooks, etc.?
- A description of the library's deselection guidelines. These guidelines are usually based on such variables as material currency, usage, physical condition, and relevancy to school curriculum.

Once complete, the library's Collection Management Policy should be on file with the school administration (NCTE, 2018).

In Response to a Book Challenge

In the advent of a verbal book complaint, calmly listen to the person's concern; remember, all members of the public have a constitutional right to question a public institution (Fletcher-Spear & Tyler, 2014). Share the library's collection management policy with the challenger. Your collection management policy demonstrates that the library has carefully considered the collection content and provides an intellectual framework to explain why various materials are included in a collection and that a library must provide a range of materials that engage all members of its community. Many times, this conversation and respectful listening are sufficient to avert a more formal challenger.

Should this approach not suffice, request that the individual formally submit their challenge. The NCTE Students' Right to Read (NTCE, 2018) provides a helpful "Request for Reconsideration of a Text" form for schools can adopt for their use. The Reconsideration form should ask:

- What book is the person challenging? Collect the title, creator, and format (i.e., picture or chapter book, a graphic novel, etc.) of the material.
- Ask for the name and affiliation of the challenger, for example are they a parent, a teacher, a community member, or are they representing a group?
- What is the reason for the challenge?
- Is the challenge to the whole or part of the book? If it is only to a part, what are the page numbers or sections that the individual considers objectionable?
- What action is the person requesting? For example, do they want the book completely removed from the library, moved to from the elementary library to middle school library, require minors to provide written permission from their parents to access the material, etc.

A library or school's reconsideration process should be outlined in your collection management policy. This reconsideration process should include the following best practices (ALA, 2010; NCTE, 2018):

- Submit the documented challenge immediately to school principal, who then shares the complaint with the School-Based Instructional Materials Reconsideration Committee
- Communicate to the challenger that no decision will be made without due review through the reconsideration committee. During the reconsideration process, the item under review should NOT be removed from the library.
- Membership of the School-Based Instructional Materials Reconsideration Committee should include a teacher or librarian familiar with the material or that may have used the book in their curriculum, at least two English or reading teachers, and the challenger; the committee may also include a student, parents, and/or a member of

the public. Committee membership should be anonymous and comprise an odd number to avoid a tied decision.

- Once formed, the reconsideration committee should review the collection management policy and discuss the principles of intellectual
freedom and the freedom to read as core tenants of our democracy.
- A librarian or teacher on the committee should gather their evidence
and prepare their argument on why the book should be included in
the curriculum or library. For example: did the book win any awards
or is it on any state reading lists? The librarian can find professional
book review, and all the educators can reach out to their colleagues
and professional networks for advice and support.
- The reconsideration committee should be a closed meeting, although
members of the public should be allowed to submit comments to the
library director or school principal.
- The committee review should consider the value of the total book
and not just extracted parts or specific words. Finally, the book
should be objectively evaluated within the context of the library's
collection management policy.
- The committee's decision should be documented and include both
the majority and minority opinions, the recommended action, and be
presented to the school principal.

At this point, the complainant can accept the decision or appeal it to the
district school board. As the district school board is legally responsible for
the adoption of course instructional materials, they have broader discretion
to review, make their own decision, and apply it either to individual schools
or across the county. By law, school boards have more rights to remove
materials from the school's curriculum than from the school library.

In Response to a Public Attack

This is a more difficult issue to confront, mired in the increased polarization
of American society and the increased number and broader scale of recent
book challenges. If the challenge is a public attack through the news or
social media, interest group, or politician, the best strategies differ.

If legal action is threatened, immediately contact your legal counsel.
The Freedom to Read Foundation has lawyers available to provide legal
assistance and support to local counsel. Centrally coordinate your com-
munications to the media. School administrators, teachers, and librarians
should all be aware of the message that the school's spokesperson is
communicating to the media. The spokesperson should stick to facts, not
offer personal opinions, and avoid answering questions without carefully
consideration. Prepare your talking points with a concise focus on high
principles, such as the importance of the First Amendment, a school's
responsibility to educate students to live within a diverse society, and

supporting students' choice and freedom to read as fundamental elements of our demography (Reichman, 2000).

Educators should try to build a coalition of supporters, by reaching out to their colleagues who might have experienced book challenges already and connect with intellectual freedom organizations (suggestions organizations listed in the Recommended Resources section). The Intellectual Freedom Centers for both the American Library Association (ALA) Office of Intellectual Freedom and the National Council of Teachers of English (NCTE) are great places to start. Reach out to your union for support. Educators can also try to rally their school, library, or community advocates to publicly refute censorship attempts. Does your school have any student clubs that might identify with the challenged material? Consider asking these students to speak out against the challenge and testify as to the value of the book.

Personally, teachers and librarians should be sure to practice self-care. Public attacks and challenges are difficult (Hickson, 2022). Sadly, teachers and librarians faced with a public book challenge may receive hate mail, be personally confronted by angry parents, or be branded with the vilest labels of racist, pornographer, or of sexually "grooming" children. As a result, the challenges can be both demoralizing and divisive within a school or library, particularly when some of the students or staff agree with the book challenges against the efforts of the teachers or librarians. Ideally, administrators should support their teachers and have their backs at all stages of this Herculean effort.

Part II

Diverse and Marginalized Groups of People

6 Exploring Social Class and Poverty through Children's Literature

Barbara J. Peterson, Susan V. Bennett, and AnnMarie Alberton Gunn

Rationale

In the United States and across the globe, the rise of income inequality persists (Hartsfield, 2022; Horowitz et al., 2020). In 2020, 11.6 million children (16 %) in the U.S. were living in poverty (Shrider et al., 2021), with 9 % of children living in deep poverty (i.e. 50% below the federal poverty line; Nyugen et al., 2020). Historical, systemic racism and institutional barriers contribute to disproportionately high poverty rates for children of color, with children of color comprising 71% of children living in poverty (Koball et al., 2021). The COVID-19 pandemic has further exacerbated financial hardships for children and families, particularly those living in ethnically diverse, low-income communities, due to long-standing health system and socioeconomic inequities. Today more than ever, it is imperative for educators to be responsive to the needs of children and families experiencing poverty and economic challenges. Although children from low-economic backgrounds comprise a significant portion of U.S. students, socioeconomic class and poverty is a relatively less-explored aspect of diversity explored within culturally responsive, multicultural education.

Educators need to critically examine their own class-based perspectives to develop a class-sensitive pedagogy that draws upon children's assets, while considering the challenges of coping with economic hardships, and navigating literacy curriculum and instructional practices often centered in middle-class ideologies (Jones & Vagle, 2013). Effective educational strategies to support children from low-socioeconomic backgrounds include making the curriculum relevant to students' lives and experiences, teaching about socioeconomic issues and income inequality, and analyzing curriculum materials to avoid reinforcement of negative stereotypes and ideological assumptions about social class and poverty (Gorski, 2013; Hartsfield, 2022; Jones & Vagle, 2013; Peters, 2022).

Teachers can incorporate books about socioeconomic hardships and poverty into language arts instruction to explore these issues with children as they discuss and respond to literature (Labadie, et al., 2013;

DOI: 10.4324/9781003321941-8

McLeod, 2008). Moreover, including children's books about socio-economic hardships and poverty as part of a multicultural curricular framework provides "mirrors" to affirm the lives of children experiencing these challenges and "windows" to promote empathy and understanding amongst children from middle class and more affluent families (Bishop, 1990). However, educators must critically evaluate these children's books to ensure portrayals are authentic, respectful, and reflect the diverse experiences of this cultural group – free from harmful stereotypes or messages (Hartsfield, 2022; Jones & Vagle, 2013; Peters, 2022).

In the following sections, I provide an overview of historical perspectives on socioeconomic class and poverty in U.S. schools and curriculum, how socioeconomic class and poverty has been portrayed in children's literature, as well as strategies for selection and exploration of K-5 children's literature depicting socioeconomic class and poverty situated within a class-sensitive pedagogy. I then offer reflection questions and activities, recommended children's literature, additional resources, and suggestions for sharing diverse books about social class and poverty within the elementary classroom.

Historical Perspectives on Socioeconomic Class and Poverty

The income level in households, since the 1970s, increased, where the median income is now 49% higher (Horowitz et al., 2020). As the income continued to rise, two recessions occurred in the last 22 years, and the rise lessened between 2000 and 2018. Although household incomes grew, from 1971, the middle class became smaller, decreasing from 61% to 51% of the population. Starting in 1980, the top 5% of household incomes rose even faster, especially in the 1990s, resulting in economic inequality. Between 2001 and 2010, all families endured deficits in income, but the families in lower socioeconomic brackets had an even greater loss. The top 5% upper-class continues to rise at much faster rates than the middle- and lower-class household incomes. The gap remains and continues to expand between upper- and lower- classes. This inequality is highly significant as it limits opportunities and chances for upward mobility for these families in lower-economic households.

U.S. Schools

The inequality also impacts children in educational contexts. In 2019, 24% of children in public schools attended high-poverty schools and 20% low-poverty; therefore, 44% of children were enrolled in a school in a low socioeconomic area (National Center for Education Statistics, 2022). The highest percentage of children in high-poverty schools were Blacks (45%), Hispanics (43%), and American Indian/Alaska Native (37%), and the highest in low poverty schools were Asian (40%) and

White (30%). With these high percentages, it is necessary for teachers to have understandings about children who live and attend school in high poverty areas, especially because most teachers are from White, middle-class backgrounds.

Gorski (2008) discussed a significant issue within education and society, Lewis's theory of *culture of poverty*, "that people in poverty share a consistent and observable 'culture'" (p. 1), such as violence, laziness, weak work ethic, or lack of motivation. Researchers debunked this idea; "There is no such thing as the culture of poverty" (p. 2). However, 60 years later, this deficit perspective persists in education. Gorski suggests classism is what is occurring and is a much more harmful deficit theory, where stereotypes are perpetuated, and systematic conditions are ignored. For example, parents from low-income families do not care about their child's education, yet they do care about their child's education. They are just more likely to not attend school events or be involved, possibly because they are working. Another myth or stereotype, the parents are lazy and unmotivated to work, yet 83% of children have one parent or more who are employed.

As the culture of poverty and myths prevail, issues around poverty continue to impact children. Children from low socioeconomic areas have inequitable access and opportunities to high-quality schools (Gorski, 2008). Schools considered low and high poverty are more likely to have less funding, lower teacher salaries, limited technology, less experienced teachers, health hazards, teacher vacancies, and inadequate and outdated materials or facilities.

Portrayals of Poverty in Children's Literature

Children's literature has the potential of "mirrors," where children to see themselves, and "windows," where they develop empathy and understand as they see individuals from different backgrounds than their own (Bennett et al., 2021a, 2021b; Bishop, 1990; Botelho & Rudman, 2009; Gunn et al., 2020, 2022, in press). Hence, children's literature can be not only a powerful tool for teachers to open dialogue about social class and poverty but to affirm children's identity and create a positive space for empowerment (Forest, 2014). However, it is imperative for teachers to carefully select books that are authentic, accurate, respectful, and affirming, while avoiding stereotypes (Hartsfield, 2022).

Classroom libraries might be the first interaction children have with books, yet libraries in higher socioeconomic schools offer a larger selection of books (Crisp, et al., 2016). Although libraries now include more multicultural books, researchers found children's books still encompass primarily White, middle-class characters. Around 1965, scholars began to critically analyze and evaluate how characters were portrayed in children's literature, in particular the work of Larrick, who focused on how

African Americans were represented in children's literature (Forest, 2014). After Larrick's article, other scholars followed and presently continue to examine how children's literature portrays characters from diverse cultural backgrounds, which might include race, ethnicity, religion, sexuality, or disabilities. Yet, one aspect of identity and diversity still neglected and explored less in children's literature is socioeconomic status.

In children's literature, working class and poor characters center around African American and Latino (Jones, 2008). This discrepancy reinforces stereotypes and heightens class privilege in which light skin characters are wealthy and dark skin characters poor. "There is a great void in children's literature, and it is one that attaches itself to working-class and poor families, classism, and structural understandings about money and power" (Jones, 2008, p. 46). In addition, children's literature and society emphasize the idea of "rags to riches" or upward mobility, where someone from a poor, working-class life because wealthy or moves up in status but is an unlikely situation in the real world (Forest, 2014). Therefore, it is imperative that children's literature is examined and evaluated so that it does not perpetuate stereotypes and offers a space to navigate discussions about poverty and social class.

Class-Sensitive Strategies for Selecting and Exploring Children's Literature

As discussed above, as inequity in the United States continues to rise, it becomes increasingly important for schools to embrace curriculum and be responsive to the needs of their students' experiencing these challenges. Books are powerful tools for classroom discussion, but it is important for teachers and students to critically examine texts as they convey ideologies that can affirm or marginalize children's culture and experiences (Hartsfield, 2022).

Hartsfield (2022) discussed themes that educators can apply when making their selection of children's literature for classroom use. Table 6.1 includes selected themes based on multiple research projects presented in Hartsfield's framework for evaluating children's literature about poverty, which illustrates negative stereotypes portrayed in books that feature working class characters. If the themes about lower social class characters are prevalent in a piece of children's literature, the researcher suggests to seek other books that present different points to avoid reinforcing negative stereotypes. Further, Hartsfield notes that educators should use collections of books that offer diverse viewpoints to allow students to gain multiple perspectives on social issues. It should be noted this is not an exhausted list, and educators should critically examine books for other issues that may arise.

Table 6.1 Selected themes for educators to consider while evaluating books representing working class themes.

Themes	Example of How this Theme May Provide a Negative Stereotype about Working Class or Poor People
Caricature	Character(s) is shown as unintelligent.
Charity	Character(s) is shown to need assistance from a more powerful or higher social class person.
Dependency	Character(s) is shown to be dependent on federal, state or local assistance.
Exceptionalism	Character(s) is shown to "make it out" into a higher social class and is now happy.
Fading Blue Collar	Character(s) is shown to not be happy in their job or not working enough
Insignificance	Character(s) is shown to be looked down upon by someone in a higher social or economic status
Irresponsibility	Character(s) is shown to be involved in irresponsible behavior
Shady	Character(s) is shown to be involved in delinquent behavior
Sympathetic	Character(s) is shown to be deserving of pity.

Note: Please see Hartsfield (2022) for more detailed information.

Educators of elementary aged children can engage discussions by using books to critically explore issues of inequity (Bennett, et al., 2017). Together students guided by their teacher can explore and construct knowledge in order to understand the challenges of unequal social relationships presented in books. "Children know when they are treated unfairly, and they question ways things are done in their school and community that result in unequal treatment of individuals or groups" (Bennett et al., 2017, p. 244).

Reflection Questions and Activities

1. In what ways have your personal, cultural and educational experiences contributed to your own perspectives on socioeconomic class and poverty? How do these perspectives compare or contrast with the historical and literature-based perspectives presented in this chapter?
2. What are the benefits of sharing diverse literature reflecting socioeconomic class and poverty with elementary grade children? What challenges might teachers face in selecting and exploring this literature with children as part of a class-sensitive pedagogy?
3. Choose three titles from the children's literature recommended in this chapter to read and analyze. In what ways do the texts and illustrations portray the diverse experiences of children and families

living in poverty? How are these books similar or different in their portrayals of characters and experiences? How might you incorporate these books within your classroom instruction?

4. Explore the resources and references offered in this chapter. How might you utilize these to further your own understanding of children and families from poor or working-class backgrounds and support your own development of a class-sensitive pedagogy?

Recommended Children's Literature

Educators may refer to book awards and book lists to assist them in finding quality literature for children. Awards and book lists that specifically focus on and celebrate high-quality, culturally diverse books include the Coretta Scott King Award, which honors African American authors/illustrators; the Pura Belpré Award and the Tomas Rivera Awards, which honors Latinx authors/illustrators; and Notable Books for a Global Society, which recognizes excellent children's books about cultures across the world. The Jane Addams Book Award recognizes children's books that effectively promote the cause of peace, social justice, world community, and the equality of the sexes and all races. Although socioeconomic diversity is included as a dimension of diversity in children's literature, there currently are no book awards that specifically acknowledge children's literature with respectful and authentic portrayals of characters who are from working-class backgrounds or living in poverty.

Table 6.2 describes some high-quality, contemporary children's literature that may be shared in K-5 classrooms. The books portray characters who are poor or from working-class backgrounds in positive and multi-dimensional ways. Most of these selections are multi-award-winning books, with writing and illustrations that will engage young readers, promote empathy, and spark meaningful conversations surrounding socioeconomic issues. Two titles on this list are nonfiction picture books on the topics of poverty, food insufficiency and homelessness; four are realistic fiction picture books; and two are realistic fiction chapter books. Beyond these titles, there are many excellent historical fiction books with sensitive and authentic portrayals of socioeconomic challenges and poverty that can also be shared in the classroom to broaden children's sense of the past and understandings of socioeconomic struggles within different historical time periods. However, the recommended list focuses on contemporary portrayals in order to foreground socioeconomic issues faced by children and families today, rather than framing these problems as "phenomena of yesteryear" (Hartsfield, 2022, p. 85). This list is by no means exhaustive but is intended as a launching point for a diverse classroom library.

Table 6.2 K-5 multicultural literature with portrayals of poor and working-class characters.

Book Information	Summary
Title: *Last Stop on Market Street* **Author and Illustrator:** Matt de la Peña (Author), Christian Robinson (Illustrator) **Awards:** *Caldecott Award Honoree; Newbery Award; Coretta Scott King Award; Charlotte Zolotow Award; Charlotte Huck Award; ALSC Notable Book; Notable Social Studies Trade Book for Young People; CCBC Choice* **Grade Level Band:** K-2	**Summary:** An African American boy and his grandmother travel by a bus across town to a soup kitchen where they volunteer each week. His grandmother responds to his questions about what they do not have (e.g., a car, an iPod), by engaging him in observations and conversations focused on appreciation of the beauty that can be found in unexpected places, and on the richness of daily routines and relationships within their culturally diverse, urban community.
Title: *A Chair for My Mother* **Author and Illustrator:** Vera B. Williams **Awards:** *Caldecott Award Honoree; American Library Association (ALA) Notable Children's Book; Boston Globe Best Children's Book Illustration Award* **Grade Level Band:** K-3	**Summary:** After losing all of their belongings in a house fire, a girl, her mother, and grandmother save coins in a jar for over a year to finally purchase a big comfortable chair for their home. Events in the story highlight the caring relationships within this family, as well as with their relatives and neighbors who rally to support them in crisis.
Title: *A Different Pond* **Author and Illustrator:** Bao Phi (Author); Thi Bui (Illustrator) **Awards:** *Caldecott Award Honoree; Charlotte Zolotow Award; Asian/Pacific American Award for Literature; Ezra Jack Keats New Writer and New Illustrator Awards; Notable Social Studies Trade Book for Young People* **Grade Level Band:** K-3	**Summary:** A Vietnamese American boy and his father embark on a fishing outing before their work and school day begin. Their catch will provide food for their family, who face economic hardships as new immigrants. Their shared time is filled with quiet moments and conversation about linguistic differences, fellow fishermen, the necessity for parents to work multiple jobs, as well as the father's recollections of fishing with his brother who died in the Vietnam war.
Title: *Those Shoes* **Author and Illustrator:** Marianne Boelts (Author); Norah Z. Jones (illustrator) **Awards:** *Highly Commended Selection, 2008 Charlotte Zolotow Award; Cooperative Children's Book Center Choices 2008* **Grade Level Band:** K-4	**Summary:** Jeremy's grandmother says the new sneakers he *really wants* are too expensive. The almost-new pair of "those shoes" they find at a thrift store are too small for Jeremy. When his grandmother refuses to buy them, Jeremy uses his own money. After hobbling around in too-tight shoes, Jeremy wears his hand-me-down pair. He passes on the too-small shoes to Antonio, a smaller classmate, whose desire and need for "those shoes" are similar to his own.

Book Information	Summary
Title: *I Don't Have Enough: A First Look at Poverty* **Author and Illustrator:** Pat Thomas (Author); Clare Keay (Illustrator) **Awards:** N/A **Grade Level Band:** K-3	**Summary:** This nonfiction picture book focuses directly on the emotions and social problems surrounding poverty, homelessness and food insecurity, told from the perspective of a young child. Simple text and pictures can serve as a launching point for introductory conversations about these topics, and about how sharing what we have with those in need can make an important difference.
Title: *On Our Street: Our First Talk About Poverty* **Author and Illustrator:** Jillian Roberts & Jaime Casap (Authors); Jane Heinrichs (Illustrator) **Awards:** *Notable Social Studies Trade Books for Young People* **Grade Level Band:** 2–5	**Summary:** This nonfiction text uses a question-and-answer format to introduce the realities of people who lack adequate resources and live in poverty conditions in the U.S. and across the world. Through age-appropriate language and photographs, the book addresses issues of homelessness and food insufficiency, as well as the connections between mental illness or refugee status with homelessness and poverty.
Title: *Hold Fast* **Author:** Blue Balliet **Awards:** *Notable Social Studies Trade Books for Young People; CCBC Choices; Notable Children's Book in the Language Arts Award; Junior Library Guild Selection* **Grade Level Band:** 3–7	**Summary:** A young girl, Early, falls into the Chicago homeless shelter system with her family after her father, Dash, mysteriously disappears on the way home from his job at the library. Langston Hughes's poetry fuels Early's determination to "hold fast" to her family's core values, goals and dreams for the future, to discover the truth of her father's disappearance and persevere through a series of life crises to reunite her family.
Title: *The Junction of Sunshine and Lucky* **Author and Illustrator:** Holly Schindler **Awards:** *Numerous state book awards and recognition lists.* **Grade Level Band:** 4–6	**Summary:** "Auggie" Jones lives with Grandpa Gus, a trash hauler, in a poor part of town. Auggie and her friends encounter classist-attitudes at their new school, when the town's beautification committee targets her working-class neighborhood with code violations and fines. A home renovation project with "trash-to-treasure" folk art becomes much more, as Auggie and her grandpa discover new artistic talents, inspire their community to challenge injustice, and help redefine the town's perception of beauty and worth.

Resources

- *National Center for Children Living in Poverty* www.nccp.org/
- *Institute for Children, Poverty & Homelessness* www.icphusa.org/
- *U. S. Hunger* www.ushunger.org
- UNICEF www.unicef.org
- *Global Coalition to End Child Poverty* www.endchildhoodpoverty.org/
- *Children's Defense Fund* www.childrensdefense.org/
- *Save the Children* www.savethechildren.org/
- *End Book Deserts* is an organization whose mission is to increase children and families' access to books, particularly within low-income communities. This website offers many excellent resources, including articles, podcasts, and a literacy advocacy forum related to this aim. www.end bookdeserts.com/
- *The Cooperative Children's Book Center (CCBC), School of Education, University of Wisconsin-Madison* compiles statistics and resources about books by and about people of Color and from the First/Five Nations, as well as other aspects of diversity and representation in children's and young adult literature. Resources include book lists, bibliographies, and a searchable database of recommended titles. https://ccbc.education.wisc.edu/
- *Diverse BookFinder* is a searchable database of thousands of children's picture books featuring Black and Indigenous people and people of Color (BIPOC), published and distributed in the U.S. since 2002. The website also offers powerful tools to analyze picture book collections, and other resources to assist literacy stakeholders in expanding diversity in young children's literature and promoting deeper conversations for change. https://diversebookfinder.org/
- *Social Justice Books*, a Teaching for Change project, offers tools to identify and promote high-quality multicultural and social justice children's books. Resources include articles, curated book lists, book reviews, and Louise Derman-Sparks's *Guide for Selecting Anti-Bias Children's Books.* https://socialjusticebooks.org/
- Adichie, C. N. (2009). *The danger of a single story* [Video]. TED Conferences. www.ted.com/talks/chimamanda_ngozi_adichie_the_dange_ of_a_single_story?language=en
- Tussey, J. T., & Haas, L. (Eds.). (2022). *Poverty impacts on literacy education.* IGI Global.

References

Bennett, S.V., Gunn, A.A., Gayle-Evans, G., Barrera, E.S., & Leung, C. (2017). Culturally responsive literacy practices in an early childhood community. *Early Childhood Education Journal, 46*(2), 241–248. doi:10.1007/s10643-017-0839-9.

Bennett, S. V., Gunn, A. A., & Peterson, B. (2021a) Access to Multicultural Children's Literature During COVID-19. *The Reading Teacher, 74*(6), 785–796.

Bennett, S. V., Gunn, A. A., van Beynen, K., & Morton, M. L. (2021b). Religiously diverse multicultural literature for early childhood. *Early Childhood Education Journal*. https://doi.org/10.1007/s10643-021-01180-7.

Bishop, R. S. (1990). Mirrors, windows, and sliding glass doors. *Perspectives: Choosing and using books for the classroom*, 6(3), ix–xi. https://scenicregional.org/wp-content/uploads/2017/08/Mirrors-Windows-and-Sliding-Glass-Doors.pdf.

Botelho, M. J., & Rudman, M. K. (2009). *Critical multicultural analysis of children's literature: Mirrors, windows, and doors*. Routledge.

Crisp, T., Knezek, S. M., Quinn, M., Bingham, G. E., Girardeau, K., & Starrks, F. (2016). What's on our bookshelves: The diversity of children's literature in early childhood classroom libraries. *Journal of Children's Literature*, 42(2), 29–42.

Forest, D. E. (2014). From rags to "rich as Rockefeller": Potrayals of class mobility in Newbury titles. *Curriculum Inquiry*, 44(5), 591–619. https://doi.org/10.1111/curi.12067.

Gorski, P. (2008). The myth of the "culture of poverty." *Educational Leadership*, 65(7), 32–36.

Gorski, P. (2013). Building a pedagogy of engagement for students in poverty. *Kappan*, 95(1), 48–52. www.edchange.net/publications/PDK-Pedagogy-of-Engagement.pdf.

Gunn, A. A., Bennett, S. V., & Peterson, B. J. (in press). Exploring multicultural picture books with social-emotional themes. *The Reading Teacher*.

Gunn. A.A., Bennett. S. V., & Peterson, B. (2022). "She looks like me:" Putting high-quality multicultural literature in children's hands during COVID-19. *Journal of Research in Childhood Education*, 36(3), 363–380.

Gunn, A. A., & Bennett, S. V., van Beynen, K. (2020). Talking About Religious Diversity: Using multicultural literature as a tool. *Social Studies and the Young Learner*, 33(1), 10–16.

Hartsfield, D. E. (2022). A framework for evaluating children's books about poverty. In J. T. Tussey & L. Haas (Eds.), *Poverty impacts on literacy education* (pp. 77–94). IGI Global.

Horowitz, J. M., Igielnik, R., & Kochhar, R. (2020). *Most Americans say there is too much economic inequality in the U. S., but than half call it a top priority*. Pew Research Center.

Jones, S. (2008). Grass houses: Representations and reinventions of social class through children's literature. *Journal of Language & Literacy Education*, 4(2), 40–58. https://files.eric.ed.gov/fulltext/EJ1068167.pdf.

Jones, S., & Vagle, M. D. (2013). Living contradictions and working for change: Toward a theory of social class sensitive pedagogy. *Educational Researcher*, 42(3), 129–141. https://doi.org10.3102/0013189X13481381.

Koball, H., Moore, A., & Hernandez, J. (2021, April). *Basic facts about low-income children: Children under 18 years, 2019*. National Center for Children in Poverty [NCCP], Bank Street College of Education. www.nccp.org/wp-content/uploads/2021/03/NCCP_FactSheets_All-Kids_FINAL.pdf.

Labadie, M., Pole, K., & Rogers, R. (2013). How kindergarten students connect and critically respond to themes of social class in children's literature. *Literacy Research and Instruction*, 52(4), 387–404. https://doi.org/10.1080/01626620.2019.1710728.

McLeod, C. (2008). Class discussions: Locating social class in novels for children and young adults. *Journal of Language & Literacy Education*, 4(2), 73–79. https://jolle.coe.uga.edu/wp-content/uploads/2013/03/class.pdf.

National Center for Education Statistics. (2022). Concentration of public school students eligible for free or reduced-price lunch. Retrieved from https://nces. ed.gov/programs/coe/pdf/2022/clb_508.pdf.

Nguyen, U. S., Smith, S., & Granja, M. R. (2020). *Young children living in deep poverty: Racial/ethnic disparaties and child well-being compared to other income groups.* National Center for Children Living in Poverty. www.nccp.org/wp-content/uploa ds/2020/10/Deep-Poverty-Report-11.11.20_Final.pdf.

Peters, K. M. (2022). Challenging the poverty narrative through children's literature. In J. T. Tussey & L. Haas (Eds.), *Poverty impacts on literacy education* (pp. 191–212). IGI Global.

Shrider, E. A., Kollar, M., Chen, F., & Semega, J. (2021, Sept. 14). Income and poverty in the United States: 2020. www.census.gov/library/publications/2021/ demo/p60-273.html.

Children's Literature Cited

Balliet, B. (2013). *Hold fast*. Scholastic Press.

Boelts, M. (2009). *Those shoes*. Candlewick Press.

de la Peña, M. (2015). *Last stop on Market Street*. G. Putnam's Sons.

Phi, B. (2017). *A different pond*. Capstone Young Readers.

Roberts, J., & Casap, J. (2018). *On our street: A first talk about poverty*. Orca Book Publishers.

Schindler, H. (2014). *The junction of sunshine and lucky*. Dial Books.

Thomas, P. (2021). *I don't have enough: A first look at poverty*. BES Publishing.

Williams, V. (1982). *A chair for my mother*. Greenwillow Books.

Appendix

The following resources provide foundational tips for planning and implementing effective interactive read-alouds and social-justice oriented discussions of diverse literature, as well as classroom scenarios that may serve as examplars for instruction:

- Birkins, J. M. Strategy guide: Teacher read-aloud that models reading for deep understanding. Read-Write-Think www.readwritethink.org/professional-development/strategy-guides/teacher-read-aloud
- Kesler, T., Mills, M., & Reilly, M. (2020). I hear you: Teaching social justice in interactive read-alouds. Language Arts, 97(4), 207–222.
- Kruger, M. W., Rolander, S., & Stires, S. (Eds.) (2020). Facilitating conversations on difficult topics in the classroom: Teachers' stories of opening spaces using children's literature. *Bank Street Education Occasional Paper Series, 2020*(44). https://educate.bankstreet.edu/occasional-paper-series/vol2020/iss44/14
- Labadie, M., Pole, K., & Rogers, R. (2013). How kindergarten students connect and critically respond to themes of social class in children's literature. *Literacy Research and Instruction, 52*(4), 387–404. https://doi.org/10.1080/01626620.2019.1710728
- McLeod, C. (2008). Class discussions: Locating social class in novels for children and young adults. *Journal of Language & Literacy Education, 4*(2), 73–79. https://jolle.coe.uga.edu/wp-content/uploads/2013/03/class.pdf

7 Reading the African American Family

The Exploration of the Historical-Political and Sociocultural Representation of African American Families in Picture Books

Shanetia P. Clark

Rationale

The familial unit is the cornerstone of the African American community. It reaches beyond the nuclear and immediate members—parents and siblings—and extends into aunts, uncles, cousins, grandparents, and other caregivers who may not have hereditary bonds. The family and caregivers take care of and are responsible for young children and have a direct connection to their development, level of stress, and complex brain function (Lally & Mangione, 2017). Therefore, it is absolutely essential that the relationship between the school setting works in concert and partnership with the families and caregivers. One way in which classroom-family partnership is realized is access to children's literature that authentically reflect their lives. For African American families, these texts needs to present families—in its various configurations—in ways that are both honoring and affirming. In the chapter, I discuss examples of children's literature that present African American families positively.

Historical Perspectives

Family is fundamental to the life of a child; children's physical survival and psychological development are dependent on the adult caregivers who surround them. The familial unit can be composed of parents, siblings, extended relatives, and other caregivers. Thus, educators must be mindful of how families, specifically African American families, are presented in children's literature. Scholar Jonda McNair defines African American children's literature "as books written by and about African Americans that are intended for youth" (McNair, 2013, p. 192). As she states, this distinction of authorship is important because they are able to exhibit and write from "insider perspectives as a result of their lived

DOI: 10.4324/9781003321941-9

experiences" (ibid.). In other words, these authors center African American children as their implied readers more credibly.

African American children's literature provides a metaphorical window, mirror, and sliding glass door for young children (Bishop, 1990). This literature reflects the realities of young African American children in both real and fantastic settings. The urgency of inviting young people to read books that are culturally accurate—"the truthfulness of the represented facts about a culture or cultural group and cultural authenticity refers to the trustworthiness of the represented cultural nuances" (Haghanikar, 2020, p. 12)—should be at the forefront of any preservice teacher education program, as well as in-service professional development sessions. The implied (and actual) readers must be able to trust the author to not force readers to assimilate into the dominant culture but to invite readers into a renewed appreciation and visibility of their home lives. Therefore, the importance of African American authors writing the stories of young African American children's familial units is the guiding principle of this chapter.

In Bishop's pivotal study analyzing children's literature, she divided literature into three categories: social conscience books, melting pot books, and culturally conscious books (Bishop, 2012, pp. 6–7). The selected children's literature within this chapter fits into the third category—culturally conscious—because they are written by African American authors, center on African American characters, and emphasize cultural markers that are immersed in the African American community. These books intentionally "reflect both the distinctiveness of African American cultural experiences and the universality of human experiences" (Bishop, 2012, p. 7).

Likewise, "African American children's literature provides one way to support children of African descent through the process of developing a sense of identity given its authentic perspectives, flavor, and illustrations" (Collier, 2000, p. 235). These books are "reflective of their heritage, historical, and cultural context" (Collier, 2000, p. 236).

It is vital that preservice and in-service teachers provide children with authentic opportunities to unpack and interact with African American children's literature. This access illuminates the viewpoint that African American children are valued, seen, and present in the classroom because their stories are welcomed into fundamentally important spaces. Kruse (2001) notes, "Because educators can do little to change the ethnic composition of the communities in which they teach, multicultural literature represents a way to help learners expand their understanding of parallel cultures" (p. 26); thereby, she does advocate the use of multicultural children's literature as a viable means to broaden students' knowledge base and cultural understandings. Thus, pre-service and in-service teachers must include African American children's literature that depicts various configurations of African American families.

The African American Family

Research about the African American family, its make-up, and its social-economic status has evolved. Scholars Browne and Battle explained:

> Given the interplay of historical, structural, economical, and cultural forces, African American households are among the most diverse family structures. For example, in 2015, 55% of Black children lived with biological parent(s). Of those, 24% lived with their mothers and fathers, 28% lived with only their mothers, and slightly over 3% lived with only their fathers (US Statistical Abstract, 2015). Further, in 2015, 65% of Black single mothers with children under 18 had never been married, while 17% were divorced, 16% were separated, and 3% were widowed. During the same time period, 49% of Black single fathers with children under 18 were never married, while 21% were divorced, 25% were separated, and 5% were widowed (US Statistical Abstract, 2015).
>
> (Browne & Battle, 2018, p. 79)

Likewise, the Pew Research Center reports similar statistics. It includes that "[f]ewer than a quarter (24%) [African Americans] are part of non-family households" (Tamir et al., 2002). These data illustrate the fact that there are many configurations of African American families. Throughout history, particularly since the 1960s, the "[w]idespread changes in living arrangements, along with economic and cultural transformations, placed the traditional nuclear family under greater strain which disproportionately impacted Black families" (Browne & Battle, 2018, p. 78).

Research centering on African American families has moved away from a deficit model. Taylor asserts there was a "shift away from the social pathology perspective to one emphasizing the resilience and adaptiveness of [B]lack families under a variety of social and economic conditions" (Briscoe, 2000, p. 99). Recognizing and celebrating the resourcefulness of expanding families to extended families and friends are vital to understanding and unpacking the African American family. The African American family reaches beyond the nuclear, immediate members. This shift moves in concert with the expansion of children's literature that centers African American children and their families and caregivers.

The union of the trends in research and the expansion of African American children's picture books invites a deep inspection into the ways families are depicted. In the following sections, I give examples of African American children's literature and provide a set of reflection questions that can be used as anchors to guide discussions in the classroom. African American children's literature has the ability to empower young African American children and to make visible the various family and home structures.

Evaluating Children's Literature

Many early childhood and elementary teacher education programs have a course in children's literature for pre-service teachers. This course serves a multitude of overarching purposes:

1. to increase pre-service teachers' exposure and access to children's literature;
2. to expand their knowledge base about the genres and format;
3. to critique and evaluate texts for young readers in order to identify sexism, racism, and other prejudices;
4. to consider ways in which to authentically integrate children's literature into literacy learning; and
5. to build young readers' enthusiasm, access, and experiences with children's literature.

As pre-service teachers consider their future early childhood or elementary students, they learn ways in which children's literature has an additional task: to be a mirror, window, or sliding glass (Bishop, 1990).

To support the ways in which pre-service teachers can evaluate picture books, in particular, with African American families, I outlined a set of reflection questions in Table 7.1. Next, I offer a detailed example reading of *Crown: An Ode to the Fresh Cut* (Barnes, 2017) using the reflection questions.

Crown: An Ode to the Fresh Cut

The beautiful, affirming picture book *Crown: An Ode to the Fresh Cut* (Barnes, 2017) is a celebration of the transformation that happens to a young African American boy after getting a new fresh haircut. This story centers around a young African American boy going to get a haircut in the neighborhood barbershop. In the shop, other patrons are present. The narrator imagines one is a CEO of a tech company; another looks "majestic," while others stare and admire the intricate fades, waves, and

Table 7.1 Reflection questions to analyze African American families in picture books.

Reflection Questions
1. *Who is the author and illustrator of this book? Does their background provide an "insider" connection to the text? If not, then this book is not African American children's literature?*
2. *Within the book, who are the members of African American family unit? How is the family presented? Is it presented positively? If so or if not, explain. Is the African American family centered within the story?*
3. *Does the book disrupt common stereotypes or other misconceptions? If so, in what ways?*

Figure 7.1 Cover of children's book to use with reflection questions provided above.

designs in their hair. The narrator talks of the young boy getting hugs and kisses from his mom once she sees him and the young girls whispering and giggling about how good he looks—"Girlllll ... he's so fine!" (Barnes, 2017, p 7). This important picture book affirms the talents of this young boy. He earns good grades and prize ribbons in school, plays the trumpet, and is well liked by his peers.

Who is the author and illustrator of this book? Does their background provide an "insider" connection to the text? If not, is this African American children's literature?

Derrick Barnes, the author, originally wrote the text as a poem and later partnered with Gordon C. James, the illustrator, to create a picture book that earned the Newbery Honor, Caldecott Honor, Coretta Scott King (author and illustrator), and a host of other awards (2018). Both are African American men raising sons. Barnes noted that going to the barbershop for the fresh cut is "how we develop swagger, and when we begin to care about how we present ourselves to the world. It's also the time when most of us become privy to the conversations of and company of hardworking [B]lack men from all walks of life" (Bird, 2017, para. 4; Barnes, 2018).

The insider language of "we" and "us" signals commonality, a kinship, with both the text and the implied readers.

Within the book, who are the members of the African American family unit? How is the family presented? Is it presented positively? If so or if not, explain. Is the African American family centered within the story?

Crown: An Ode to the Fresh Cut displays a representation of a family. The narrator, who may be the father or a father figure, depicts the ritual of going to "the shop." One may posit that the narrator is Barnes because of his personal background of being the father to four sons, and he explained:

> I wrote this book for our sons, nephews, grandsons, and godsons. [It] is for the African American boys that reside in suburban cul-de-sacs, urban landscapes, and every place in between that this great country has to offer. We love them all. Unfortunately, because of the negative stereotypical images from pop culture, the nightly news, and films that have been burned into the psyche of America—especially for those who have little to no interaction with our boys—we have no control over the way they are perceived outside of our communities, our circles, our families. I just wanted the world to know that we love and cherish them immensely. I wrote this book for African American boys. Point blank.
>
> (Barnes, 2018, p. 136)

The positive relationship and the bonding between a father and son during the ritual of visiting the barbershop are essential in the African American community. The barbershop is a space wherein clients and community members, in particular African American boys and men, fellowship and discuss various aspects of life.

In *Crown: An Ode to the Fresh Cut*, readers learn who comprises the family unit. The narrator, one who can be read as the father and the mother. Readers will recognize the positive relationship between the mother and young son. As seen in the illustration, the mother leans in and kisses him on the cheek, and he smiles while playing the trumpet. She calls him beautiful; "Being viewed in your mother's eyes as someone that matters—now that's beautiful. And you'll take it. You don't mind at all" (Barnes, 2017, np).

The family serves an important role in affirming the young boy's self-esteem. The life at home appears to be caring and loving. It is a positive space. As stated before, the mother shows affection to the young boy. The father (figure) spends time with the young boy by shepherding him through the ritualistic experience of going to the barbershop; it's a rite of passage. The young boy earns good grades, and he's able to develop his artistic talents. The affection and joy he has at home transfers to school. This young boy is well liked and admired by his peers. The development and shaping of whom he will become starts in the home.

Does the book disrupt common stereotypes or other misconceptions? If so, in what ways?

Barnes and James positively portray the family and those around the young boy. He is celebrated, honored, cherished, and loved. A variety of skin shades are presented in the book, and the young boy and his family are darker-skinned. The protagonist as a deep chocolate brown skin impacts young readers who are this shade; they will view themselves as the hero, the one who is smart. The deliberate choice to present this young African American boy as darker-skinned, as the hero, disrupts colorism and its potential harm. There is significant research on which colorism negatively affects darker-skinned children in schools (Hunter, 2016; Keith & Monroe, 2016). "The skin-tone hierarchy in the United States is largely a legacy of White supremacy and racial mixing that resulted from European colonization, transcontinental trade, and subjugation" (Keith & Monroe, 2016, p. 6). It is important to note that African American children, especially boys, of all skin shades personally connect to this book.

Does the book disrupt common stereotypes or other misconceptions? If so, in what ways?

Children who are raised in caring environments enable them to have positive brain development:

> [O]ne of the clearest findings is that early brain development is directly influenced by babies' day-to-day interactions with their caregivers. Even before birth, babies have a built-in expectation that adults will be available and care for their needs.
>
> (Lally & Mangione, 2017, p. 17)

It is evident that the young boy in *Crown: An Ode of the Fresh Cut* is cared for, feels loved, and is having his needs met; therefore, his brain development is progressing positively. By going to get his haircut, he exhibits good hygiene, and it improves his self-esteem and self-concept.

Discussion

As illustrated in the example, unpacking African American children's literature by examining the ways in which African American families are presented goes beyond the surface. While pre-service and in-service teachers become immersed in children's literature and consider ways to share them with their (future) students, being mindful of the families presented is vital. Because African American children spend a significant amount of their time in a classroom, feeling a sense of community and belonging are especially important. A way to do this is to make visible different types of families through classroom literature.

Table 7.2 lists a small collection of African American children's literature. Teachers can use this evaluation to question if African American children's families are presented in ways that support African American children. Thus far, there is a glaring absence of picture books with African American LBGT+ families written by African American authors; publishing lacks this category of picture books. The book *I Am Perfectly Designed* (2019) is written by Karamo Brown, a gay man, and his son Jason "Rachel," who identifies as pansexual. While reviewing this list, it is clear see what types of families are underrepresented.

Table 7.2 Recommended African American children's literature showcasing African American families.

Book Information	Summary
Title: *My Cold Plum Lemon Pie Bluesy Mood* **Author and Illustrator:** Tameka Fryer Brown (Author) and Shane W. Evans (Illustrator) **Awards:** *N/A* **Grade Level Band:** K-5	**Summary:** Jaime is in a mood. This narrative concept color book describes his various moods. For example, when Jaime is in a purple mood, he is feeling good like when he bites into a juicy plum. His mood turns gray when he's kicked out of the family room by his brothers or gentle green when he draws his sister a dragon. This book showcases his mood when he is around different members of his family.
Title: *Knock Knock: My Dad's Dream for Me* **Author and Illustrator:** Daniel Beaty (Author), Bryan Collier (Illustrator) **Awards: Coretta Scott King Award (Illustrator);** Marion Vannett Ridgway Award (Honor), Boston Globe-Horn Book Awards (Honor), Notable Social Studies Trade Books for Young People, Junior Library Guild Selections; ALSC Notable Children's Books; Notable Children's Books in the Language Arts Award; Center for the Study of Multicultural Children's Literature Best Books **Grade Level Band:** 3rd grade and up	**Summary:** Pretending to be asleep, a little boy plays a game of "Knock Knock" with his father each day. One day, the knock doesn't come. The son waits each day for his father to knock on his door again. The little boy grows up to be a man with a family and business. Later, he is reunited with his father. This story is inspired by a poem written by Beaty and performed on "Def Poetry Jam."
Title: *Granddaddy's Turn: A Journey to the Ballot Box* **Author and Illustrator:** Michael S. Randy and Eric Stein (Authors) and James E. Ransome (Illustrator) **Awards:** Notable Social Studies Trade Books for Young People; CCBC Choices **Grade Level Band:** 2nd grade and up	**Summary:** In the rural south, a grandson goes with his grandfather to vote for the first time. His grandfather gets dressed up for the "happiest day of his life"—voting day. When they arrived at the voting booth, the boy's grandfather was denied because he could not read a thick book. The grandfather never got the chance to vote before he died, so years later his grandson votes and holds a picture of grandfather.
Title: *Aunt Flossie's Hats and (Crab Cakes Later)* **Author and Illustrator:** Elizabeth Fitzgerald Howard (Author) and James Ransome (Illustrator) **Awards:** CCBC Choices **Grade Level Band:** 1st grade and up	**Summary:** Two sisters, Sarah and Susan, go to visit their Great-great Aunt Flossie. At her house, they go to drink tea, eat snacks, and try on hats! As the girls pull out hats from Aunt Flossie's collection, Aunt Flossie reminiscences and tells the stories of the hats' histories such the fire in Baltimore and the African American troops in the 92nd Division returning from the Great War.

Book Information	Summary
Title: *These Hands* **Author and Illustrator:** Margaret H Mason (Author); Floyd Cooper (Illustrator) **Awards:** Charlotte Zolotow Award (Commended); ALSC Notable Children's Books, (Commended); CCBC Choices; Notable Books for a Global Society, Golden Kite Awards; Notable Children's Books in the Language Arts Award; **Grade Level Band:** K-5	**Summary:** A grandfather and his grandson Joseph enjoy spending time together. His grandfather's hands tied shoes, played the piano, did fancy card tricks, and swung a baseball bat. His grandfather, however, could not use his hands to bake bread at the Wonder Factory due to White people not eating the bread that Black hands touched. His grandfather mobilized, gathered others to sign petitions, and protested, which resulted in the Wonder Factory abandoning the discriminatory practices.
Title: *Just Like a Mama* **Author and Illustrator:** Alice Faye **Duncan (Author);** Charnelle Pinkney Barlow (illustrator) **Awards:** Charlotte Zolotow Highly Recommended; Kansas NEA Reading Circle List PrimaryTitle **Grade Level Band:** K-5	**Summary:** Young Carol Olivia Clementine is being raised by Mama Rose. Her parents are away, so Mama Rose steps in. Mama rose teaches Clementine how to ride a bike, clean her room, and tell time. Mama Rose is Clemetine's caregiver and her "home," even though she is not an immediate relative. This book shares the relationship between a caregiver and a young girl and how important it is to make her feel safe, protected, and valued.
Title: *Me and Mama* **Author and Illustrator:** Cozbi A. Cabrera **Awards:** Coretta Scott King Award (Illustrator); Caldecott Honor; CCBC Choices; ALSC Notable Children's Books (Commended); El día de los niños / El día de los libros **Grade Level Band:** K-5	**Summary:** A little Black girl loves her mother so very much. Mama's "love is brighter than the sun, even on the rainiest of days." The two spend the rainy day together. A beautiful book sharing the relationship between a mother and daughter.
Title: *Soul Food Sunday* **Author and Illustrator:** Winsome Bingham (Author) and C.G. Esperanza (Illustrator) **Awards:** Coretta Scott King Book Awards (Illustrator Honor); ALSC Notable Children's Books (Commended); CCBC Choices; Charlotte Zolotow Award (Commended); Golden Kite Awards (Picture Book Text Honor) **Grade Level Band:** PreK and higher	**Summary:** On Sundays, the entire family gathers for "Soul Food Sunday." The ritual of the preparation of the food and the tradition of coming together for fellowship, family, and food are the heart of the story. The young Black boy narrates the story.

Book Information	Summary
Title: *Carrimebac: The Town that Walked* **Author and Illustrator:** David Barclay Moore (Author) and John Holyfield (Illustrator) **Awards:** N/A **Grade Band:** 6 and up	**Summary:** After the Civil War and the end of slavery, Rootilla Redgums and her grandson Julius Jefferson walked to Walkerton. There, the former enslaved people were in dire straits because the White neighbors refused to buy their goods. Rootilla and Julius taught the people to special skills. The White neighbors accused them of using magic; in "white hoods," they terrorized and threatened to burn Walkertown down. Rootilla and Julius used their magic to protect the town.
Title: *Girl Dad* **Author and Illustrator:** Sean Williams (Author) and Jay Davis (Illustrator) **Awards:** N/A **Grade Band:** PreK and up	This book celebrates the relationship between two dads and their daughters; it shows each dad having a positive and lovely relationship with their own daughters. Filled illustrations of, for example, dads dancing ballet, doing their daughter's hair, caring for and tending to boo-boos, and being the best cheerleader.
Title: *I Am Perfectly Designed* **Author and Illustrator:** Karamo Brown and Jason "Rachel" Brown (Authors), Anoosha Syed (Illustrator) **Awards:** N/A **Grade Band:** PreK and up	The Browns, a real-life father and son team, write a semi-autobiographical story about their relationship. The story begins, "First there was you, Dad. Then there was me. And now there is us." As the two walk around the city, the son asks his father recall memories of fun times together or moments when he was sad or confused, and his father supported and hugged him. This story speaks to the unique bond of a father and son.

References

Barnes, D. (2018). Why our boys deserve a crown: The social responsibility of the Black artist to create affirming images for Black children. *Language Arts*, 96(2), 135–138.

Bird, B., (2017). Review of the day: Crown by Derrick Barnes, ill. Gordon C. James. *School Library Journal*. Retrieved from https://afuse8production.slj.com/2017/09/29/review-of-the-day-crown-by-derrick-barnes-ill-gordon-c-james/.

Bishop, R. S. (1990). Mirrors, windows, and sliding glass doors. *Perspectives: Choosing and Using Books for the Classroom*, 6(3). Retrieved from https://scenicregional.org/wp-content/uploads/2017/08/Mirrors-Windows-and-Sliding-Glass-Doors.pdf.

Bishop, R. S. (2012). Reflections on the development of African American children's literature. *Journal of Children's Literature*, 38(2), 5–13.

Briscoe, D. L., (2000). Distinctive features of the African-American family: Debunking the Myth of the deficit model. *Ethnic Studies Review*, 23(1), 97–122.

Browne, A. P., & Battle, J. (2018). Black family structure and educational outcomes: The role of household structure and intersectionality. *Journal of African American Studies*, 22(1), 77–93.

Collier, M. D. (2000). Through the looking glass: Harnessing the power of African American children's literature. *The Journal of Negro Education*, 69(3), 235–242.

Fox, M. (2022). A read-aloud lesson. Retrieved from https://memfox.com/for-tea chers/for-anyone-interested-a-read-aloud-lesson/.

Haghanikar, T. M. (2020). The ethnicity of the implied author and the implied reader in multicultural children's literature. *Children's Literature and English Language Education*, 8(1), 10–30.

Hunter, M. (2016) Colorism in the classroom: How skin tone stratifies African American and Latina/o students. *Theory Into Practice*, 55(1), 54–61, doi:10.1080/00405841.2016.1119019.

Keith, V. M., & Monroe, C. R. (2016). Histories of colorism and implications for education. *Theory Into Practice*, 55(1), 4–10, doi:10.1080/00405841.2016.1116847.

Kruse, M. (2001). Escaping ethnic encapsulation: The role of multicultural children's literature. *The Delta Kappa Gamma Bulletin*, 67(4), 26–32.

Lally, J. R., & Mangione, P. L. (2017). Caring relationships: The heart of early brain development. *YC: Young Children*, 72(2), 17–24.

McNair, J. (2013). "I never knew there were so many books about us": Parents and children reading and responding to African American children's literature together. *Children's Literature in Education*, 44, 191–207. doi:10.1007/s10583-012-9191-2.

Tamir, C., Budiman, A., Noe-Bustamante, L., & Mora, L. (2021). Black population. Retrieved from www.pewresearch.org/social-trends/fact-sheet/facts-about-the-us-black-population/.

Children's Literature Cited

Bandy, M. S. (2015). *Granddaddy's turn: A journey to the ballot box*. Candlewick Press.

Barnes, D. (2017). *Crown: An ode to the fresh cut*. Bolden.

Beaty, D. (2013). *Knock knock: My dad's dream for me*. Little, Brown and Company.

Bingham, W. (2021). *Soul food Sunday*. Abrams Books for Young Readers.

Brown, K., & Brown, J. (2019). *I am perfectly designed*. Henry Holt and Company.

Brown, T. F. (2013). *My cold plum lemon pie bluesy mood*. Viking.

Cabrera, C. A. (2020). *Me & Mama*. Simon and Schuster.

Duncan, A. F. (2020). *Just like mama*. Simon and Schuster.

Howard, E. F. (1991). *Aunt Flossie's hats (and crab cakes later)*. Clarion Books.

Mason, M. H. (2010). *These hands*. Houghton Mifflin Harcourt.

Moore, D. B. (2022). *Carrimebac: The town that walked*. Candlewick Press.

Williams, S. (2022). *Girl dad*. Harper.

Appendix: Foundational Teaching Tips

1. The recommended picture books within this chapter are ones that will engage young readers. Each book is inspired by and center special moments between a young person and his/her/their family member or caregiver. After reading, invite young readers to think of a special memory with a family member or caregiver. Once they have a moment in mind, ask them to share, either in writing or orally, what makes it special. What happened in this moment? Describe it by including bits of conversation, the setting, other people involved, and why it stands out in their memory. These questions can spart the initial inquiry into a memoir paper.

2. Each of the highlighted books is a strong read-aloud. Let the students enjoy the cadence, rhythm, and energy of the stories. Invite students to be engaged with the illustrations while listening to the read-aloud. To learn ways to improve the act of reading aloud, visit author Mem Fox's "A Read-Aloud Lesson" (2022). In this lesson, Fox discusses ways to improve the experience of the read-aloud by, for example, emphasizing the beginning of the stories and paying extra attention to the words and the intention of the text. After reading, encourage children to discuss how families are represented and what parts of the stories stand out.

3. Invite the children to create a portrait or an artistic rendering of a family member or caregiver. The children should give their artistic creation a title and write paragraphs describing the art piece—including the materials used—and its inspiration. Finally, have a gallery walk showcasing and celebrating the artistic creations.

8 Southeast Asian Refugee Children's Literature

A Pedagogical Tool to Critically Juxtapose War and Migration

Sohyun An

Rationale

"The United States is not at war. The United States is war" (Han, quoted in Smith, 2016, p. 69). Born out of war against the British empire, the United States has been at war with or invaded other countries in all but eleven years of its existence (Torreon & Plagakis, 2018; Vine, 2020). These wars are often remembered in the U.S. collective memory as grim but inevitable and necessary to bring freedom, democracy, and safety in the world (Zinn, 2011). In reality, U.S. wars have engendered more violence and suffering and served the economic and political interests of elites, while leaving tens of millions at home and abroad dead, devastated, and displaced with trauma and pain (Vine, 2020). In the United States' post-9/11 wars alone, nearly 15,000 U.S. military personnel lost their lives, and 1.7 million U.S. veterans returned from their deployments with physical and mental damage (Vine et al., 2021). In the countries where the U.S. post-9/11 wars were fought, 4 million combatants and civilians lost their lives, and 10 million became refugees abroad or internally displaced (Vine et al., 2021).

To prevent future wars and suffering, U.S. wars need to be taught in an honest and critical way beyond simply glorifying them as noble and moral missions in defense of freedom and democracy (Gibbs, 2020; Vine, 2020; Zinn, 2011). Research has shown that war-related attitudes begin to develop in early childhood (Bat-Ami, 1994) and that children can explore the difficult knowledge of war when supported by teachers (An, 2021a, 2021b, 2022a; Burns, 2009). Without critical learning about war at school, children may be left with inaccurate messages from the larger society. In the U.S. rituals, such as Memorial Day and Independence Day, U.S. wars become, to children, honorable events that are unfortunate but necessary for national security, progress, or world peace (Nguyen, 2017). In popular movies and video games, U.S. wars even become an amusement to children, in which fighting is glamorized, the enemy is dehumanized, and the United States is always right and just (Nguyen, 2017). These messages will not help children make informed

DOI: 10.4324/9781003321941-10

future decisions about whether, why, and how the United States should go to war, nor will they ultimately prevent future wars and violence (Gibbs, 2020; Noddings, 2012).

In teaching about U.S. wars, what is often missing is the role of U.S. wars in inducing and exacerbating refugee crises and displacement (Espiritu, 2014). Regarding Asian migration to the United States, for example, Roland Coloma (2017) poignantly stated, "we are here because you were there" (p. 94). That is, many Asians have entered the United States as refugees, orphans, adoptees, military spouses, laborers, or immigrants partly because the United States has gone to Asia for its military and imperialist gains, instigating the conditions for displacement (Lee, 2016). School textbooks, however, tend to decouple U.S. wars in Asia and Asian migration to the United States as if they were separate events (An, 2016). U.S. wars in Asia are typically presented in textbooks as rescue and liberation missions, while Asian migration to the United States is generally explained as Asians fleeing from poverty and oppression in their home countries and finding freedom and prosperity in the United States (An, 2022c; Suh et al., 2015). In these accounts, the U.S. implications for Asian displacements and diasporas through war and military intervention are largely absent (An, 2022c).

Such decoupling is not just inaccurate but also dangerous because it reinforces the national myth of U.S. wars as always noble and necessary (Espiritu, 2014; Palumbo-Liu, 1999). This myth, as history shows, has allowed, justified, and promoted the status quo of endless U.S. military interventions around the world (Vine, 2020; Zinn, 2011). Moreover, the decoupling promotes an ahistorical understanding of Asian migration to the United States, which has contributed to abundant anti-Asian violence and discrimination, ranging from verbal attacks such as "Go back to your country!" to hate crimes and physical violence throughout U.S. history (Lee, 2016). To stop anti-Asian violence and prevent future wars, Asian migration to the United States and U.S. wars in Asia should be critically juxtaposed and taught together.

This chapter focuses on the Southeast Asian migration and the Vietnam War and proposes teaching these two events in critical juxtaposition through Southeast Asian refugee children's literature. Unlike textbooks, children's books about Southeast Asian refugees naturally bring together the war and the refugee displacement by telling a story of the Vietnam War through Southeast Asian experiences of war and displacement (An, 2022a, 2022b). In the following sections, I first present the historical perspectives on the Vietnam War and Southeast Asian migration. Next, I discuss the pedagogical values of Southeast Asian refugee children's literature along with reflection questions for the critical use of the literature. Last, I offer recommendations of books and instructional approaches and resources.

Figure 8.1 Vietnam War map.

Before proceeding, it is important to note that Southeast Asian populations in the United States are diverse, including not only Vietnamese, Cambodian, Lao, and Hmong but also Bruneian, Burmese, Indonesian, and Malaysian people, to name a few (Kula & Paik, 2016). Yet, this chapter concentrates on people from Vietnam, Laos, and Cambodia because they constitute the largest Southeast Asian populations in the United States and their lives were profoundly affected by the Vietnam War.

Historical Perspectives

Before the War

Present-day Vietnam, Laos, and Cambodia were once colonized by France (Lawrence, 2008). During World War II, Japan drove the French out and occupied the region. In 1945, hours after Japan's surrender in World War II, Vietnam declared its independence. Yet France ignored the declaration and sought to recolonize it (Young, 1991). This led to the First Indochina War (1946–1954), in which the United States sided with France, preferring French imperial rule to an independent, communist-led government in Vietnam as well as in Laos and Cambodia (Young, 1991). After eight years of fighting, the war ended with a French defeat, resulting in the temporary division of Vietnam into North and South Vietnam while providing Laos and Cambodia independence (Lawrence, 2008).

Vietnam War

In this context, the United States began to intervene more deeply in the region to contain communism (Lawrence, 2008). In South Vietnam, the United States supported a series of anti-communist regimes to quell the communist forces who sought to reunite Vietnam under an independent communist government (Nguyen, 2012). By the 1960s, the United States became involved in a full-blown war against North Vietnamese forces and their allies in South Vietnam. The war ended with a U.S. defeat in 1975, killing about 58,000 Americans and 3 million Vietnamese. Further, 12 million Vietnamese became refugees, and most infrastructure in Vietnam was destroyed (Lawrence, 2008).

Even worse, the war spread to Cambodia and Laos as North Vietnamese forces moved into the region. The U.S. bombings over Cambodia killed tens of thousands of Cambodians and motivated Cambodian civilians to support the Khmer Rouge, a communist force in Cambodia that initiated a brutal genocide of many Cambodians upon taking power in 1975 (Schlund-Vials, 2012). Laos was also heavily bombed. Two million tons of U.S. bombs were dropped over Laos from 1964 to 1973, which was equivalent to a planeload of bombs every eight minutes, twenty-four hours a day for nine years (Chan, 1994). This bombing was intended to support the U.S.-backed Royal Lao government in its fight against Lao communist forces as well as destroy the pathway that North Vietnamese forces used to attack South Vietnam (Kurlantzick, 2017). To shield such military actions from U.S. public scrutiny and minimize American casualties, the United States recruited the Hmong, an ethnic minority living in Laos, to fight in its "secret war" (Kurlantzick, 2017).

Refugee Crisis

When the United States left the region in 1975, communist governments came to power in Vietnam, Laos, and Cambodia (Lawrence, 2008). Those who had supported the U.S. military actions during the war or who suffered from the new regimes began to flee. Thousands of people packed airports and boats or fled on foot (Lee, 2016). These refugees were routed to makeshift camps in Thailand, the Philippines, Guam, and other Asian Pacific islands, then moved to receiving countries (Espiritu, 2014). From 1975 to 1978, the first wave of 140,000 Southeast Asian refugees arrived in the United States (Lee, 2016).

Beginning in 1979, the second wave of Southeast Asian refugees started to enter the United States. Fleeing from deteriorating economic conditions and political persecution, hundreds of thousands of people in Vietnam, Laos, and Cambodia undertook a perilous journey to seek refuge (Lee, 2016). Many died from drowning, shipwreck, starvation, thirst, or violent pirate attacks during their journey (Vo, 2006). Those who survived still had to endure poor conditions in refugee camps in the first asylum countries while waiting uncertainly and sometimes indefinitely to be reviewed for resettlement in refugee-receiving countries (Robinson, 1998).

Resettlement

The American response to the Southeast Asian refugee crisis was mixed. According to a poll taken in 1979, 62% of Americans disapproved of admitting the refugees for fear they would become economic or cultural threats (DeSilver, 2015). Although some were received warmly, many others experienced hostility and discrimination from American neighbors (Lee, 2016). For instance, the 1989 Cleveland Elementary School shooting revealed American hostility in its extreme. A White gunman, who reportedly hated Asian immigrants, entered an elementary school in Stockton, California and killed five children of Southeast Asian refugee families (Escalante, 2019).

Often resettled in poverty-stricken neighborhoods plagued by gang violence, racial tension, and failing schools while recuperating from the trauma of war and forced displacement, many Southeast Asian refugees struggled to rebuild their lives (Lee & Ramakrishnan, 2021). Over 18% of Cambodian families and 27% of Hmong families lived below the poverty line, compared with 11% of U.S. families overall (U.S. Census Bureau, 2010). Over 34% of Cambodian, Lao, and Hmong Americans did not complete high school, compared with 13% of the general population (U.S. Census Bureau, 2010). Southeast Asian Americans are also three times more likely to be deported based on an old criminal conviction, compared to other immigrants (Southeast Asian Resource Action Center, n.d.).

In sum, Southeast Asian Americans represent the largest refugee community ever to be resettled in the United States, after being forcefully displaced by the U.S. wars and their aftermath in Vietnam, Laos, and Cambodia (Lee, 2016). Their stories of war, displacement, and resettlement reveal the complex legacies of the Vietnam War (Espiritu, 2014).

Teaching about Southeast Asian Migration

The U.S. collective memory and school curricula are largely silent on the interwoven histories of the Vietnam War and Southeast Asian migration (An, 2022c; Espiritu, 2014; Marciano, 2011). The Vietnam Veterans Memorial, for example, lists and honors the names of the 58,000 Americans who were killed during the war, yet the names of Southeast Asians who fought with American soldiers and were killed are nowhere to be found in the memorial (Espiritu, 2014). Popular movies, novels, and textbooks also center American experiences of the war, ignoring the effects of the war on Southeast Asians (Leahey, 2010; Nguyen, 2017; Wood, 2016).

Meanwhile, popular memories and textbook accounts of Southeast Asian migration tend to present the United States as a safe refuge for desperate Southeast Asians fleeing from communism, while neglecting the United States' role in inducing the refugee exodus in the first place through war (An, 2022c). Southeast Asian refugees' struggles with racism, poverty, and discrimination when resettling to the United States are also largely erased in the popular discourse and school lessons on immigration, which often tell a single story of European immigrants entering Ellis Island and achieving the American Dream (Nguyen, 2017; Rich & An, 2022).

This chapter proposes Southeast Asian refugee children's literature as a pedagogical tool to disrupt the dominant narratives about the Vietnam War and the Southeast Asian migration. Telling a story of the Vietnam War through Southeast Asian refugees' experiences, this literature naturally strings together war, forced displacement, and migration (An, 2022b). Extant research has noted this value. That is, the Southeast Asian refugee children's literature moves Southeast Asian experiences from the periphery to the center of the Vietnam War narrative and disrupts the decoupling of war and migration (An, 2022b; Levy, 2000). However, previous research has also found limitations to children's literature. Most, but not all, Southeast Asian refugee children's books tend to avoid difficult topics, such as the United States' role as a violent war aggressor that spurred the deaths and displacements of Southeast Asians; instead, the United States does not appear in these books or appears only as a benevolent rescuer or a safe and welcoming refuge for the refugees (An, 2022b). Extant research, therefore, suggests the critical selection and use of Southeast Asian refugee children's literature.

Recommended Children's Literature and Teaching Suggestions

There are many Southeast Asian refugee children's books. In Table 8.1 I recommend two books each about Vietnamese, Cambodian, Hmong, and Lao refugees with brief story lines and instructional suggestions. These

Table 8.1 Recommended children's literature.

Books about Vietnamese Refugees

Title: *Inside Out and Back Again*
Author and Illustrator: Thanhha Lai
Awards: *Newbery Honor; National Book Award for Young People's Literature*
Grade Level Band: 3–5

Summary: Ten-year-old Hà, the protagonist and narrator of the book, describes her life in South Vietnam prior to the Fall of Saigon, the difficult journey at sea fleeing Vietnam, and the effort to rebuild life in the United States.

Instructional Suggestions: This semi-autobiographical novel naturally strings together the war, refugee displacement, and resettlement. The author does not shy away from the racism and poverty that the refugee family faced in the United States. It also shows Vietnamese refugees may have diverse and divergent feelings and thoughts about the war, forced displacement, and resettlement. Therefore, the book can be a great tool to engage children in learning about the war and the migration from the Vietnamese refugee perspectives. Given the length of the novel, teachers may assign the book for independent reading prior to a book discussion. To facilitate independent reading, teachers may need to provide students with a reading guide with question prompts, such as those in the previous section.

Title: *A Different Pond*
Author and Illustrator: Bao Phi (Author) Thi Bui (Illustrator)
Awards: *Caldecott Honor Book; Ezra Jack Keats New Writer Honor and New Illustrator Honor; Charlotte Zolotow Award*
Grade Level Band: 3–5

Summary: Bao, a young Vietnamese American boy, wakes up early in the morning to accompany his father who goes fishing for the family dinner. His parents need to work even on weekends to support the family. While his parents are at work, Bao takes care of his little siblings. At school, Bao often hears his classmates make fun of his father's "broken" English. Despite these challenges, Bao's family finds joy in being together.

Instructional Suggestions: This semi-autobiographical picture book has great value in highlighting the struggle and resilience of Vietnamese refugee families. Yet, the story line lacks details on the Vietnam War as a main driver of Vietnamese displacement. Teachers, therefore, would need to ask students why Bao's family came to the United States. Teachers could also have students closely read the author's note and find some historical background of the war and its impact on the refugee crisis.

Books about Cambodian refugees

Title: *Half Spoon of Rice*
Author and Illustrator: Icy Smith (Author), Sopaul Nhem (Illustrator)

Summary: Nine-year-old Nat and his family are among the thousands of Cambodians who were sent to the forced labor camps by the Khmer Rouge. There, Nat and other children are separated from their parents and endure harsh labors. Eventually, Nat escapes to Thailand where he is reunited with his family. After many months in a Thai refugee camp, Nat's family gets permission to resettle in the U.S.

Awards:
National Association for Multicultural Education Multicultural Children's Publication Award; Society of School Librarians International Honor Award
Grade Level Band: 3–5

Instructional Suggestions: The author in this historical fiction picture book vividly describes how the Vietnam War profoundly changed the lives of the Cambodian people. The story line is complemented by the information pages at the end of the book, which explain how the U.S. secret war in Cambodia exacerbated the Cambodian refugee crisis. Thus, teachers could have students read Nat's story first and then closely read the information pages to put the story line into a larger historical context.

Title: *A Path of Stars*
Author and Illustrator: Anne Sibley O'Brien
Awards: *Asian/Pacific American Award for Literature for Picture Book Honor*
Grade Level Band: 3–5

Summary: Dara, a young Cambodian American girl, listens to her grandmother talk about her family's journey to the United States. Grandmother's story begins with a peaceful life in Cambodia, which was suddenly disrupted by war. Grandmother lost many family members and had to take a perilous journey to find refuge. After many years waiting in a Thai refugee camp, her grandmother gets to resettle and rebuild life in the United States.

Instructional Suggestions: The great value of this book is in highlighting the struggles and resilience of Cambodian refugees. Yet, the book is silent on the role of the United States in the Cambodian refugee crisis other than as a good refuge for displaced Cambodians. To address this limitation, teachers could pair this book with *Half Spoon of Rice*, so students could have a more complete understanding of Cambodian refugee experiences of the war, displacement, and resettlement.

Books about Hmong Refugees

Title: *Dia's Story Cloth*
Author and Illustrator: Dia Cha
Awards: *Children's Books of Distinction Award from Hungry Mind Review*
Grade Level Band: 3–5

Summary: Dia, the author and narrator of the book, uses a Hmong story cloth to illustrate her family history. Her father was one of many Hmong men who were recruited by the United States to fight the communist forces during the Vietnam War. When the war ended with a communist victory, Dia's family joined many Hmong people who fled to Thailand to escape political persecution. After four years of struggling in a Thai refugee camp, Dia's family finally received permission from the U.S. government to resettle in America. Although Dia struggled with adjusting to American life, she persisted and eventually became an anthropologist.

Instructional Suggestions: Dia's story strings together the U.S. secret war in Laos, Hmong displacement, and resettlement. Information pages at the end of the book provide more details on Hmong history and culture. Thus, teachers could have children read Dia's story first and then go deeper into learning more about Hmong refugees through the information pages.

Title: *Grandfather's Story Cloth*
Author and Illustrator: Linda Gerdner and Sarah Langford (Author), Stuart Loughridge (Illustrator)
Awards: *Most Outstanding Health and Safety Children's Book; Gold Medal Winner*
Grade Level Band: 3–5

Summary: Chersheng, a Hmong American boy, lives with his grandfather who is losing his memory because of Alzheimer's. His grandfather has a story cloth that tells his family history. Using the story cloth, Chersheng asks the grandfather to talk about his journey to America. Because the story cloth does not include his grandfather's life after arriving in the United States, Chersheng decides to make a new story cloth for him that includes the missing piece.
Instructional Suggestions: The great value of this historical fiction picture book is in highlighting the struggles and resilience of Hmong refugees. However, this book is silent on the whys of the war and the complex roles that the U.S. played in Hmong lives. The United States only appears as a good refuge that allowed the grandfather to resettle. Thus, teachers can pair this book with *Dia's Story Cloth* and guide students to fill the gap in this book.

Lao Refugees

Title: *Mali Under the Night Sky*
Author and Illustrator: Youme Landowne
Awards: *Skipping Stones Honor Award*
Grade Level Band: K-5

Summary: Mali, a little girl in Laos, enjoys her happy childhood, which is suddenly disrupted by war. Like other families, Mali's family also decide to undertake the treacherous journey to escape war. Unfortunately, Mali's family gets caught by soldiers. While locked up in jail, Mali does not lose hope. She dreams of being free and safe someday.
Instructional Suggestions: This picture book brings to light how the Vietnam War profoundly changed the lives of the Lao people. Although the story line does not include much historical context of the war, the end pages offer some information about the U.S. secret war in Laos and its implications for the Lao refugee crisis. Thus, teachers can have students read Mali's story first and then move on to the end page to fill the gap in the story line.

Title: *When Everything Was Everything*
Author and Illustrator: Saymoukda Duangphouxay Vongsay (Author), Cory Nakamura Lin (Illustrator)
Awards:
Grade Level Band: 3–5

Summary: A young Lao refugee girl tells a story about her daily life in the United States. She is raised on food stamps, continuously shuttled from one public housing address to the next, forced into ESL classes, and ridiculed by her classmates. Yet, the girl finds resilience and joy amid challenges.
Instructional Suggestions: This semi-autobiographical picture book shows both the struggles and resilience of Lao refugees in rebuilding life in the United States. Yet, the author does not talk about why and how the girl and her family came to the United States. Thus, teachers can pair this book with *Mali Under the Night Sky*, so students can connect the dots between the U.S. secret war in Laos and the Lao displacement and migration to the United States.

books are chosen based on accessibility as well as the opportunity to present a more authentic portrayal of the war and forced migration.

Teachers can use a single text or a group of texts to take advantage of the benefits of the literature (that is, critically juxtaposing war and migration), while being mindful of its limitations (that is, silence on the complex roles that the United States played in the war and forced migration). When engaging children in critical reading and discussion of the books, teachers can use guiding questions such as the following:

- Characters and setting:
    - Who are the main characters?
    - Which Southeast Asian group is this story about?
    - When and where is the story taking place?

- War:
    - What were the causes of the war?
    - Who was involved in the war?
    - What roles did the United States play in the war?
    - How did the war affect the main characters and their communities?
    - Who was responsible for the war atrocities?
    - How did the main characters respond to the war?
    - What did the main characters feel and think about the war?

- Displacement:
    - What happened in the aftermath of the war?
    - Why did the main characters decide to escape their country?
    - What challenges did the main characters face during their escape?
    - What challenges did the main characters face in the refugee camps?
    - How did the main characters navigate these challenges?
    - What did the main characters feel and think about the displacement?

- Resettlement:
    - When and where did the main characters resettle in the United States?
    - How did Americans treat the main characters?
    - What challenges did the main characters face in rebuilding life in the United States?
    - How did the main characters navigate the challenges?
    - What did the main characters feel and think about resettlement?

- Connecting the dots:
  - How were the Vietnam War and Southeast Asian migration interconnected?
  - Whose experiences and perspectives are included and whose are not in the book?
  - What new understanding and questions do you have about the Vietnam War and Southeast Asian migration?

Critically reading and discussing the books with these guiding questions would help children develop a more critical and nuanced understanding of the Vietnam War and Southeast Asian migration. Specifically, students would see the Vietnam War through the eyes of Southeast Asian refugees, inquire into the complex roles that the United States played in the war and in forced migration, and recognize the struggles and resilience of Southeast Asian refugees.

Resources

In conclusion, the critical selection and use of Southeast Asian refugee children's literature can support students to critically juxtapose the Vietnam War and the Southeast Asian migration to build a more nuanced and critical understanding of Southeast Asian communities in the United States. Below are suggested resources for teachers to learn more about the intertwined history of the Vietnam War and Southeast Asian migration. I hope many teachers find this chapter helpful for reimaging their teaching about Southeast Asian Americans.

- *Southeast Asian Refugee Stories* from University of Minnesota Immigration History Research Center [oral history interview clips] https://cla.umn.edu/ihrc/immigrant-stories/story-collections/southeast-asian-refugee-stories
- *After-lives of the Vietnam War: The Art of Southeast Asian Refugees* [virtual exhibit] https://calisphere.org/exhibitions/88/after-lives-vietnam-war/
- *The Vietnam War* by Ken Burns & Lynn Novick [film] www.pbs.org/kenburns/the-vietnam-war/
- Southeast Asian Deportation from Southeast Asian Resource Action Center [website] www.searac.org/programming/national-state-policy-advocacy/immigration/
- *Body counts: The Vietnam War and militarized refuge(es)* by Yến Lê Espiritu [book]
- *Nothing ever dies: Vietnam and the memory of war* by Viet Thanh. Nguyen [book]
- *War, genocide, and justice: Cambodian American memory work* by Cathy Schlund-Vials [book]

Reflection Questions for Teacher Education Classrooms

1. How did the U.S. wars in Vietnam, Laos, and Cambodia affect Southeast Asian lives?
2. Why is it important to critically juxtapose the Vietnam War and Southeast Asian migration?
3. What are benefits and limitations of Southeast Asian refugee children's books in teaching about the Vietnam War and Southeast Asian migration?
4. How can we use Southeast Asian refugee children's literature to teach the Vietnam War and Southeast Asian migration in a critical way?

References

An, S. (2016). Asian Americans in American history: An AsianCrit perspective on Asian American representation in U.S. history curriculum standards. *Theory and Research in Social Education*, 44(2), 244–276.

An, S. (2021a). Fifth-grade inquiry into a convergence of U.S. imperialism, racism, and war: A World War II lesson. *Social Studies Teaching and Learning*, 2 (3), 147–161.

An, S. (2021b). Teaching difficult knowledge of the Korean War through international children's literature. *Social Studies and Young Learner*, 33(3), 24–32.

An, S. (2022a). Teaching about the Vietnam War: Centering Southeast Asian refugee voices through children's literature. *Social Studies and Young Learner*, 34(4), 24–32.

An, S. (2022b). Critical juxtaposing of war and migration: A critical content analysis of Southeast Asian refugee children's literature. *The Social Studies*, 113(5), 249–263. https://doi.org/10.1080/00377996.2022.2046996.

An, S. (2022c). Re/presentation of Asian Americans in 50 states U.S. history standards. *The Social Studies*. https://doi.org/10.1080/00377996.2021.2023083.

Bat-Ami, M. (1994). War and peace in the early elementary classroom. *Children's Literature in Education*, 25(2), 83–99.

Burns, T. J. (2009). Searching for peace: Exploring issues of war with young children. *Language Arts*, 86(6), 421–430.

Chan, S. (1994). *Hmong means free: Life in Laos and America*. Temple University Press.

Coloma, R. (2017). "We are here because you were there": On curriculum, empire, and global migration. *Curriculum Inquiry*, 47(1), 92–102.

DeSilver, D. (2015). *U.S. Public seldom has welcomed refugees into country*. Pew Research Center. www.pewresearch.org/fact-tank/2015/11/19/u-s-public-seldom -has-welcomed-refugees-into-country/.

Escalante, E. (2019, January 17). Need to know: The 1989 Cleveland School Shooting. *ABC10*. www.abc10.com/article/news/local/stockton/need-to-know-the-1989-cleveland-school-shooting/103-bf6463b2-ce78-4ba1-9216-fc2c79907f82.

Espiritu, Y. L. (2006). The 'we-win-even-when-we-lose' syndrome: U.S. press coverage of the twenty-fifth anniversary of the 'Fall of Saigon.'" *American Quarterly*, 58(2), 329–352.

Espiritu, Y. L. (2014). *Body counts: The Vietnam War and militarized refuge(es)*. University of California Press.

Gibbs, B. (2020). The foot and the flag: Patriotism, place, and the teaching of war in a military town. *Democracy and Education, 28*(2), 1–14.

Kula, S., & Paik, S. (2016). A historical analysis of Southeast Asian refugee communities: Post-war acculturation and education in the U.S. *Journal of Southeast Asian American Education and Advancement, 11*(1), 1–23.

Kurlantzick, J. (2017). *A great place to have a war: America in Laos and the birth of a military CIA*. Simon & Schuster.

Lawrence, M. (2008). *The Vietnam War: A concise international history*. Oxford University Press.

Leahey, C. (2010). *Whitewashing war: Historical myth, corporate textbooks, and possibilities for democratic education*. Teachers College Press.

Lee, E. (2016). *The making of Asian America*. Basic Books.

Lee, J., & Ramakrishnan, K. (2021). From narrative scarcity to research plentitude for Asian Americans. *Journal of the Social Sciences, 7*(2), 1–20.

Levy, M. (2000). *Portrayal of Southeast Asian refugees in recent American children's books*. Edwin Mellen Press.

Marciano, J. (2011). Civic illiteracy and American history textbooks: The U.S.–Vietnam War. In J. L. DeVitis (Ed.), *Critical civic literacy: A reader* (pp. 319–342). Peter Lang Publishing.

Marshall, G. N., Schell, T. L., Elliott, M. N., Berthold, S. M., & Chun, C. (2005). Mental health of Cambodian refugees two decades after resettlement in the United States. *Journal of the American Medical Association, 294*(5), 571–579.

Nguyen, L.T. (2012). *Hanoi's War*. University of North Carolina Press.

Nguyen, V.T. (2017). *Nothing ever dies: Vietnam and the memory of war*. Harvard University Press.

Noddings, N. (2012). *Peace education: How we come to love and hate war*. Cambridge University Press.

Palumbo-Liu, D. (1999). *Asian/American: Historical crossings of a racial frontier*. Stanford University Press.

Rich, T., & An, S. (2022). Teaching difficult histories of immigration at the elementary level. In L. Harris, M. Sheppard & S. Levy (Eds.), *Teaching difficult histories in difficult times: Stories of practice* (pp. 167–178). Teachers College Press.

Robinson, C. (1998). *Terms of refuge: The Indochinese exodus and the international response*. Zed Books.

Schlund-Vials, C. (2012). *War, genocide, and justice: Cambodian American memory work*. University of Minnesota Press.

Smith, A. (2016). Heteropatriarchy and the three pillars of white supremacy: Rethinking women of Color organizing. In INCITE (Eds.), *Color of violence* (pp. 66–73). Cambridge, MA: South End Press.

Southeast Asian Resource Action Center. (n.d.). Southeast Asian Americans and school to prison to deportation pipeline. www.searac.org/immigration/southeast-asian-americans-and-the-school-to-prison-to-deportation-pipeline/.

Suh, Y., An, S., & Forest, D. (2015). Immigration, imagined communities, and collective memories of Asian American experiences. *Journal of Social Studies Research, 39*(1), 39–51.

Tang, E. (2013). *Unsettled: Cambodian refugees in the New York City hyperghetto*. Temple University Press.

Torreon, B. & Plagakis, S. (2018). *Instances of use of United States Armed Forces abroad, 1798–2018*. Washington, DC: Congressional Research Service.

U.S. Census Bureau. (2010). 2010 American community survey. www.census.gov/newsroom/releases/archives/american_community_survey_acs/cb11-158.html.

Vine, D. (2020). *The United States of war: A global history of America's endless conflicts from Columbus to the Islamic states.* University of California Press.

Vine, D., Coffman, C., Khoury, K., Lovaxz, M., Bush, H., Leduc, R., & Walkup, J. (2021). Creating refugees? Displacement caused by the United States' post-9/11 wars. https://watson.brown.edu/costsofwar/papers.

Vo, N. M. (2006). *The Vietnamese boat people, 1954 and 1975–1992.* McFarland & Company.

Wood, J. (2016). *Vietnam narratives and the collective memory of the Vietnam War.* Ohio University Press.

Young, M. (1991). *The Vietnam Wars, 1945–1990.* Harper Perennial.

Zinn, H. (2011). *Howard Zinn on war.* Seven Stories Press.

Children's Literature Cited

Cha, D. (1994). *Dia's story cloth.* Lee & Low Books.

Gerdner, L., & Langford, S. (2009). *Grandfather's story cloth.* Shen's Books.

Lai, T. (2013). *Inside out & back again.* HarperCollins.

Landowne, Y. (2010). *Mali under the night sky.* Cinco Puntos Press.

O'Brien, A. (2012). *A path of stars.* Charlesbridge.

Phi, B. (2017). *A different pond.* Capstone Publishing.

Smith, I. (2010). *Half spoon of rice.* East West Discovery Press.

Vongsay, S. D. (2018). *When everything was everything.* Full Circle Publishing.

Appendix

As noted in the chapter, Southeast Asian refugee children's literature has both benefits and drawbacks. Therefore, a critical selection and use of the children's literature is needed. The recommended books and teaching suggestions are offered in the chapter to assist preservice and inservice teachers to use the children's literature critically. For more detailed analysis and discussion of pedagogical values and limitations of Southeast Asian refugee children's literature, I recommend these articles:

- An, S. (2022). Teaching about the Vietnam War: Centering Southeast Asian refugee voices through children's literature. *Social Studies and Young Learner, 34*(4), 24–32.
- An, S. (2022). Critical juxtaposing of war and migration: A critical content analysis of Southeast Asian refugee children's literature. *The Social Studies.* 113(5), 249–263. https://doi.org/10.1080/00377996.2022.2046996

9 Celebrating Latinx Children's Literature

Lynn Atkinson Smolen

Rationale

Rudine Sims Bishop (1990) describes books as offering both a mirror and window into a people's way of life. Books provide a mirror for children to see themselves and their experiences when they read stories with characters that look and act as they do. In this situation, reading becomes "a means of self-affirmation, of reaffirming" (Bishop, 1990, p. 3) their place in the world. When they do not find themselves in books, "or when they see themselves presented only as laughable stereotypes, they learn a powerful lesson about how much they are undervalued in the society in which they are part" (Bishop, 1990, p. 7). It is equally important to understand that books can serve as windows. Students from dominant cultures need to know others who are different from themselves through books. "If they see only reflections of themselves, they will grow up with an exaggerated view of their importance and value in the world—a dangerous ethnocentrism" (Bishop, 1990, p. 7).

The purpose of this chapter is to invite teachers into the world of Latinx books so that they come to appreciate these treasures created by talented Latinx writers and illustrators. The historical background of Latinxs in the U.S., the description of exemplary books, the literature resources, and the suggestions for using these books in the classroom are included so that teachers will have the knowledge and resources to provide young readers with a mirror and a window into Latinx children's literature.

Historical Perspectives of Latinxs in the United States

Latinxs in the U.S. are diverse; some have arrived recently, while others trace their ancestors back 300 years. The largest group of Latinxs is Mexican Americans, who represent 61% of the total Latinxs in the U.S. The rest of the Latinxs are from Puerto Rico, a U.S. territory, Cuba, El Salvador, Dominican Republic, Central America, and South America.

DOI: 10.4324/9781003321941-11

Origins of Latinxs

The three groups of Latinxs discussed in this chapter became part of the U.S. through different circumstances. Mexicans became residents of the U.S. through territorial conquest; Cubans settled in the U.S. as political refugees escaping Fidel Castro's regime in Cuba; and Puerto Ricans became residents of the U.S. after Spain ceded Puerto Rico to the U.S. at the end of the Spanish American War (Bennett, 2003).

History of Spanish Colonization

The history of Spanish colonization of the North American continent (National Geographic, 2022) began in 1493 with the second voyage of Columbus. Spain colonized Puerto Rico in the same year. Cuba quickly followed in 1511 with the arrival of Diego Velázquez de Cuéllar and the founding of Baracoa. In 1519, Hernán Cortés began the conquest of Mexico, and in 1565 Pedro Menéndez de Avilés founded St. Augustine, Florida (National Park Service, 2022).

Mexican Americans

Mexican Americans have a complex history in the U.S. Some Mexican Americans trace generations of their families to the 1600s when Spaniards settled in the area that is now Santa Fe, New Mexico (Britannica, 2022). These Mexican Americans were annexed to the U.S. after the Mexican American War in 1848. After the war, Mexico and the U.S signed the Treaty of Guadalupe Hidalgo, in which Mexico ceded parts of present-day Arizona, California, New Mexico, Texas, Colorado, Nevada, and Utah to the U.S In 1854, Mexico and the U.S ratified the Gadsden Purchase (National Archives, 2022a), making tens of thousands of previous Mexican citizens living in parts of Arizona and New Mexico residents of the U.S.

With the Treaty of Guadalupe Hidalgo, the U.S. promised to respect the land and rights of the Mexican nationals who lived on the ceded lands (National Archives, 2022b). However, the promises were hollow because the federal government lacked the power to enforce the treaty's promises. Anglo-Americans facing no federal enforcement used unscrupulous methods from "lynching, to armed theft, to quasi-legal and legal means such as forcing expensive litigation in American courts to prove land titles to strip the Mexicans of their land" (Bennett, 2003, p. 147).

Mexican immigration occupies a complex position in the U.S. legal system and U.S. public opinion. Immigration law has swung back and forth throughout the twentieth century, at times welcoming Mexican immigrants and at other times slamming the door shut on them. The public reception of this immigrant group has also been unpredictable;

Mexican immigrants have been able to make a place for themselves in communities across the U.S. but frequently have had to endure hostile elements in those same communities to survive (Library of Congress, 2022a). As Feagin and Feagin (1993, as cited in Bennett, 2003, p. 148) point out, "there still remains considerable prejudice and discrimination directed against Mexican Americans, the great bulk of whom are in the working class and lower-class groups."

Puerto Ricans

After the War of 1898 with Spain, The U.S acquired the Island of Puerto Rico. Puerto Ricans, a people of Taino Indian, African, and Spanish heritage, became citizens of the U.S. when President Wilson signed the Jones-Shafroth Act in 1917 (Library of Congress, 2022b). U.S. citizenship facilitated Puerto Ricans' migration to the U.S; however, the change of legal status in 1917 did not immediately produce a wave of migration from Puerto Rico to the U.S. "The large migration of Puerto Ricans to the U.S took place after 1945 due to economic changes having to do with the transformation of the Island's economy from a monocultural plantation economy into a platform for export-production in factories" (Lehman College, 2022). In 1950, the exodus from Puerto Rico exploded to a rate of 43,000 persons a year, so in 1955, 700,000 Puerto Ricans had resettled and increased to one million by the mid-1960s (Library of Congress, 2022c).

Cuban Americans

From the latter part of the nineteenth century and the early part of the twentieth century, Cuba and the U.S. enjoyed peaceful coexistence. As many as 100,000 Cubans moved between Florida and Cuba each year. However, everything changed with the rise of Fidel Castro's regime in 1959. Fear of the Communist government caused an era of mass emigration out of Cuba to the U.S. The first wave of Cubans emigrating to the U.S. was the wealthiest. They came to be known as the "golden exiles" (Library of Congress, 2022d). In 1965, flights between Cuba and the U.S. resumed, and an additional 300,000 Cubans were added to the original 200,000. The second wave of Cubans was also warmly welcomed. However, those who arrived in 1980 as part of the Mariel boatlift found a hostile encounter from those outside the Cuban community. These Marielitos were much less affluent and accompanied by a few thousand who were taken from the jails in Cuba, thus stigmatizing this group. Today, few Cuban emigrants reach the U.S.

Despite the major differences in their history and culture, Puerto Ricans, Cuban Americans, and Mexican Americans share a common language, heritage, and worldview that stems from the cultural fusion of

Spanish and Native American values. They also share a history of cultural conflicts related to the pressures of Americanization and problematic race relations (Bennett, 2003, p. 146).

Latinx Experiences in U.S. Schools

Due to the long history of discrimination and marginalization (Ada, 2016), Latinx children and adolescents have faced many challenges in U.S. schools. They often find their language and culture not valued and not represented adequately in the school curriculum. Additionally, schools and the community often pressure them to conform to mainstream White values. Many Latinx students speak English well, and many of them are fluent in both Spanish and English. However, those who do not speak English well and are identified as English learners (ELs) often find themselves in schools without adequate support. Furthermore, they are often placed in classrooms where the content teacher has little training to support their acquisition of English and learning the subject matter in English.

Despite English learners' (ELs') need for instructional support, few content teachers in U.S. schools know how to scaffold their learning effectively. The lack of preparedness of these teachers to support ELs is primarily due to teacher preparation programs not prioritizing training for this important task (Villegas, 2018). There is a serious need for content teachers to develop research-based instructional strategies to support ELs' learning, particularly because these students spend most of the instructional day with them.

As Villegas (2018) points out, the limited preparation of content teachers to effectively instruct ELs has profound implications for these students' academic outcomes and future opportunities. When teachers lack the pedagogical knowledge and skills this task demands, ELs are placed at a severe disadvantage.

The inadequate preparation of content teachers to teach ELs has significant negative consequences on these students' lives. Often when these teachers have limited confidence to teach ELs, they place this responsibility on the shoulders of ESL and bilingual teachers because they view them as having the expertise to teach them. This often results in content teachers making little effort to scaffold learning for these students to succeed academically (Villegas 2018).

Another serious consequence of content teachers' lack of preparedness to teach linguistically diverse students is their tendency to maintain deficit views of these students. They form negative views of ELs' ability to achieve and ultimately stifle their learning. This negative attitude towards linguistic minorities could result in low academic achievement and future problems with employment (Villegas 2018).

A Brief History of Latinx Children's Literature

According to the Cooperative Children's Book Center (2022), only 6.3% of children's books published in the U.S were about Latinxs in 2019. Latinx children deserve to have many opportunities to see themselves represented in books, and children from other ethnic backgrounds should have the opportunity to read stories from this rich heritage. Fortunately, new writers, editors, and agents are striving to expand the presence of Latinxs in children's literature (NPR, 2020).

The early Spanish speakers who arrived on the Americas' shores brought traditional oral tales: myths, legends, folktales, and adivinanzas (riddles), which are still shared orally amongst Latinxs today. Ada (2016) and Campoy and Ada (2011, as cited in López-Robertson, 2021a) state that the origins of Latinx children's literature can be traced to *La edad de oro* (The Golden Age), a literary magazine. José Martí, a famous Cuban poet, wrote four issues of this magazine for Spanish-speaking children in the Americas, which according to Ada and Campoy (2011, as cited in López-Robertson, 2021a, p. 35), marked the "beginning of Latinx children's literature."

"After Martí's death, the book became widely known (Ada, 2016). In the book, Martí spoke against discrimination and condemned oppression with the hope that "young people will embrace the concept of equality among all human beings and espouse justice as the means for living in a world at peace" (Campoy & Ada, 2011, as cited in López-Robertson, 2021a, p. 36).

Latinx children's literature as we know it today began to emerge in the 1970s at the same time as the Civil Rights Movement. Latinx authors started to become more actively involved and began to write about their experiences growing up as Latinxs in the U.S. (González, 2009, as cited in López-Robertson, 2021a). During this time, authentic literature by Latinx authors started to emerge. Nicolasa Mohr wrote novels and short stories for adolescents about young girls' experiences and oppression growing up in a Puerto Rican community in New York City. Her novels include *Nilda* (1973), and her collections of short stories include *El Bronx Remembered* (1993), an award-winning book. Also, during this period, Rudolfo Anaya, a Mexican American, who became known as the father of *Chicano* literature, wrote books such as *Bless Me Ultima* (1972), which was later adapted into a movie. (Chicano refers to someone who is a native of or descends from Mexico and lives in the U.S, Britannica, 2022).

In the 1990s, Latinx children's literature became more visible partly due to the establishment of three important book awards celebrating Latinx literature and its authors and illustrators. Those awards are the Américas Award for Children's and Young Adult Literature, established in 1993 to "encourage and commend authors, illustrators, and publishers who produce quality children's and young adult books that portray Latin

America, the Caribbean, or Latinx cultures in the United States" (Consortium of Latin American Studies Programs, 2022); the Pura Belpré Award, established in 1996, "is presented annually to a Latinx writer and illustrator whose work best portrays, affirms, and celebrates the Latinx cultural experience in an outstanding work of literature for children and youth" (Association for Library Service to Children, 2022); and the Tomás Rivera Award, established in 1995, which "honors authors and illustrators who create literature depicting the Mexican American experience" (Texas State University, 2022).

Latinx literature for children and young adults came of age in 1990 when new gifted Latinx authors and talented illustrators began writing and illustrating books for children and adolescents. Alma Flor Ada, a Cuban author, has written books for children in different genres, including nonfiction, fiction, folklore, and poetry. Among her numerous books, she wrote *The gold coin* (1994), a fable about a thief who finally learns a lesson, and *Gathering the Sun: An Alphabet Book in Spanish and English* (1997), a beautifully illustrated book that features Mexican American farmers in the Southwest. Gary Soto, a Chicano author, has written picture books for young children, including *Too Many Tamales/¡Qué montón de tamales!* (1993) portrays the traditional festivities that most Latinxs engage in during Christmas. He has also written collections of short stories portraying the everyday life of Chicano adolescents in the *barrio* (the neighborhood where Chicanos live), including the popular *Baseball in April and Other Stories* (2000). Pat Mora's children's poetry collections include *Confetti* (1999), a book of poems that evokes the natural beauty of the Southwest with references to the desert, rivers, and animals. *Listen to the Desert/Oye al desierto* (2001), another book of poems by Mora, uses onomatopoeia words in Spanish and English with a repetitive rhythm to evoke the sounds of desert animals.

Recently, more Latinx authors have contributed to the increasing body of Latinx children's and adolescent literature. Margarita Engle, a Cuban American author, has written many verse novels, memoirs, and children's picture books. In *A Song of Frutas* (2021), a little girl visits her grandfather, a singing fruit seller in Cuba, and enjoys helping him sell mangos, lemons, oranges, and other fruits by singing out their names. Monica Brown, a Peruvian-American author, has written two children's chapter book series and many picture books, including *Waiting for the biblioburro/ Esperando el biblioburro* (2011), a bilingual picture book about a librarian with two burros laden with books visiting the home of a little girl in a remote village.

Even though Latinx children's and adolescent literature "continues to be underrepresented in proportion to the number of books published annually in the United States" (Ada, 2016, p. xvii), there is no doubt that this literature has come of age (Ada, 2016; Naidoo, 2011).

Selection Criteria for Latinx Literature

When choosing Latinx literature for your classroom, selecting books that are authentic and appealing to children at the grade level you teach is important. You must also select books representing a specific place and cultural group rather than a generic Latinx group. Keep in mind that there is no such thing as one Latinx culture.

Bishop (1993) explains that a good way to determine which books are authentic multicultural literature is to read literary works written by insiders of the culture. She elaborates:

> Reading the literature of insiders will help teachers learn to recognize recurring themes, topics, values, attitudes, language features, social mores—those elements that characterize the body of literature the group claims as its own. It will also acquaint them with the variety and diversity within the culture.
>
> (Bishop, 1993, pp. 46–47)

Another way to develop insight into authenticity in Latinx children's literature is by reading books that have won the Pura Belpré Award, the Américas Award, or the Tomás Rivera Award. The judges for these awards use cultural and linguistic authenticity criteria, as well as literary and artistic criteria when selecting exemplary literature. After reading many award-winning books, use a checklist, such as López-Robertson's (2021b) "How to Choose Latinx Literature for Your Classroom," to analyze one of the books you have read. You could do this on your own or with a colleague and then discuss the book's qualities.

Table 9.1 highlights award-winning Latinx children's literature representing three groups who live in the U.S.: Mexican Americans, Puerto Ricans, and Cubans. These books have been written and illustrated by talented Latinxs who have an inside view of their culture and represent it authentically. It is noteworthy that many bilingual books can be used in the classroom to promote biliteracy and provide a mirror for Latinx students to see themselves and their culture represented in literature. Also, many of these literary works have social justice themes that provide Latinx students with insight into the struggles they face. For example, *Separate is Never Equal: Sylvia Mendez & Her Family's Fight for Desegregation* by Tonatiuh (2014) portrays a Latinx family who fought against discrimination in a California school.

Reflection Questions and Activities

1. Select a book that received the author's award for the Pura Belpré Award. Using a checklist for selecting a quality Latino children's book, analyze the book to determine if it authentically represents the Latinx experience.

Table 9.1 Recommended pieces: Multicultural literature for elementary-aged classrooms.

Book Information	Summary
Title: Planting Stories: *The Life of Librarian and Storyteller Pura Belpré* **Spanish edition:** *Sembrando historias: Pura Belpré: bibliotecaria y narradora de cuentos* **Author and Illustrator:** Anika Aldamuy Denise (Author), Paola Escobar (Illustrator) **Ethnic Group:** Puerto Rican **Awards:** Pura Belpré Awards, Américas Award, Orbis Pictus, Notable Books for a Global Society **Grade Level Band:** PK-2nd	**Summary:** In this exquisitely illustrated, award-winning picture book based on the inspirational life of Pura Belpré, readers learn about New York City's first Puerto Rican librarian. In 1921, Pura Belpré came to New York City to visit a relative and stayed to take a job as a bilingual assistant in a library. In this position, she began to tell Puerto Rican folktales to children and community members. Enthusiastic about sharing her stories, she visited library branches and classrooms throughout New York City. Pura Belpré's stories became the first author of Latinx storybooks to be published in the U.S.
Title: *The Golden Flower: A Taino Myth from Puerto Rico* **Author and Illustrator:** Nina Jaffe (Author), Enrique O. Sanchez (Illustrator) **Ethnic Group:** Tainos from Puerto Rico **Awards:** Pura Belpré Awards, Américas Award **Grade Level Band:** 1st-5th	**Summary:** In this myth, illustrated with sumptuous colors, Jaffe retells the creation story of how Puerto Rico and the sea that surrounds it came to be. In a primal land with no water or vegetation, a young boy plants seeds that sprout into a large pumpkin. Two men fight over the pumpkin, causing it to roll down the mountainside. The pumpkin splits open, bringing forth the sea with all its creatures, including crabs, whales, dolphins, and sunfish. This myth is reminiscent of other creation stories in the Caribbean and Latin America.
Title: *The Storyteller's Candle* **Spanish edition:** *La velita de los cuentos* **Author and Illustrator:** Lucia Gonzalez (Author), Lulu Delacre (Illustrator) **Awards:** Pura Belpré Illustrator Honor Award & Author Honor Award, Américas Award, International Latinx Book Awards **Ethnic Group:** Puerto Rican **Grade Level Band:** K-4th	**Summary:** It is wintertime in New York City during the Great Depression (1929–1935). Cousins Hildamar and Santiago rush home from school to warm their hands on the iron stove. They are homesick for Puerto Rico, where they would be warm at this time of year. Soon they discover that there is a Puerto Rican librarian who speaks Spanish at the neighborhood library. They start visiting the library to listen to the traditional folktales this endearing storyteller tells. This book provides insight into the magical effect that Pura Belpré had on the Puerto Rican community when she invited them to celebrate their stories.

Book Information	Summary
Title: *Separate is Never Equal: Sylvia Mendez & Her Family's Fight for Desegregation* **Spanish edition:** *Separados no somos iguales: Sylvia Mendez y la lucha de su familia por la intergración* **Author and Illustrator:** Duncan Tonatiuh **Ethnic Group:** Mexican American **Awards:** Pura Belpré Awards, Robert F. Sibert Informational Book Medal, Carter G. Woodson Book Award, Américas Award, Tomás Rivera Book Award **Grade Level Band:** 2nd-5th	**Summary:** This nonfiction picture book tells the story of the Mendez family, who fought for their children's right to attend their local school. On the first day of school in 1944, the children's aunt drove the three Mendez children and their cousins to school in Westminster. The aunts' two children, who had fair skin, were allowed to attend the school, but the three Mendez children were told they had to attend the Mexican school, which was far inferior. The Mendez family filed a lawsuit which they won after three years of fighting for their rights. As a result of the legal outcome, California schools became desegregated.
Title: *Dreamers* **Spanish edition:** *Soñadores* **Author and Illustrator:** Yuyi Morales **Ethnic Group:** Mexican American **Awards:** Pura Belpré Award, Tomás Rivera Book Award, Notable Books for a Global Society, Notable Social Studies Trade Books for Young People **Grade Level Band:** PK-2nd	**Summary:** In this resplendent picture book, the multi-talented author tells her story of leaving her home in Xalapa, Mexico, to immigrate with her young son, Kelly, to the U.S. At first, they are excited to explore a new country; however, they soon feel lonely, unable to communicate in the new language, and do not know anyone. Then they discover a library where they are welcomed and invited to explore beautiful picture books. Morales includes a two-page biography at the back of the book that provides more details about her life and a list of books that have inspired her.
Title: *Harvesting Hope: The Story of Cesar Chavez* **Author and Illustrator:** Kathleen Krull (Author), Yuyi Morales (Illustrator) **Ethnic Group:** Mexican American **Awards:** Pura Belpré Award, Américas Award, Jane Addams Children's Book Award **Grade Level Band:** 2nd-5th	**Summary:** This biographical picture book tells the life of Cesar Chavez, a brave and determined Mexican American who fought for the human rights of his fellow farm workers. He believed strongly in "la causa" and tirelessly worked to improve living conditions for those he believed deserved a better life. The National Farm Workers Association won the first contract for grape growers through Chavez's leadership. Morales's beautiful illustrations with rounded forms and rich colors powerfully support the text.

Book Information	Summary
Title: My Name is Celia Cruz/ Me llamo Celia: The Life of Celia Cruz/ la vida de Celia Cruz **Author & Illustrator:** Monica Brown (Author), Rafael López (Illustrator) **Ethnic Group:** Cuban **Awards:** Pura Belpré Awards, Américas Award **Grade Level Band:** 2nd-4th	**Summary:** This bilingual book introduces readers to the famous Cuban singer Celia Cruz. As a young woman, she moved to the U. S. due to the revolution in Cuba. In her new home, she became known as the Queen of Salsa as she introduced the rhythm of this music to audiences. The story is told in verse with some lines expressing the sound of the music, as in "Boom boom boom! beat the congas. / Clap clap clap! go the hands." The vibrant colors in the illustrations give a sense of the excitement and enthusiasm that Celia conveyed in her songs.
Title: Drum Dream Girl: How One Girl's Courage Changed Music **Author and Illustrator:** Margarita Engle (Author), Rafael López (Illustrator) **Ethnic Group:** Cuban **Awards:** Pura Belpré, Américas Award, Notable Books for a Global Society **Grade Level Band:** PK-3rd	**Summary:** This stunningly illustrated picture book features a poem that tells the story of Millo Castro Zaldarriaga, a mixed-race girl who longed to become a drummer. Millo dreamed of becoming a drummer, but the rule on the island was that girls could not be drummers. So, she had to drum in her head and on the furniture. One night, an audience recognized her musical talent when she played her bongo drums at a café overlooking a garden. The eloquently composed poem uses rhythmic free verse and alliteration to echo the repetitive beats of drums.
Title: Marti's Song for Freedom/ Martí y sus versos por la Libertad (bilingual book) **Author & Illustrator:** Emma Otheguy (Author), Beatriz Vidal (Illustrator) **Ethnic Group:** Cuban **Awards:** Américas Award, CCBC Choices, Junior Library Guild Selections **Grade Level Band:** 2nd-6th	**Summary:** This bilingual picture book tells the story of Cuba's famous poet and political revolutionary, José Martí. Throughout his life, Martí wrote articles and speeches advocating for Cuba's independence from Spain and the abolition of slavery. He was imprisoned and later exiled from Cuba for his political writings and speeches. Later in life, he returned to Cuba to fight in a war against Spain. The story is written in English and Spanish verse, with stanzas from the poet's *Versos sensillos* interwoven into the text.

2. Describe some benefits of including culturally and linguistically authentic books in your classroom. Discuss two books that you think authentically represent a particular Latinx culture, such as Mexican Americans, Puerto Ricans, or Cuban Americans. State your rationale for why you consider them authentic.

3. Choose a bilingual picture book to read and analyze. What format does the author use to include both Spanish and English (example:

both Spanish and English text throughout the book, separate editions – one for English and one for Spanish, Spanish words sprinkled throughout an English text)? How would you include this book in your curriculum? How would you build a bridge from one language to the other to support students' development of biliteracy?

4. Browse through the list of resources for Latinx literature in this chapter. Choose two of these resources to explore. What did you learn about Latinx children's literature from these resources?

5. Choose two books from the Américas Award with similar topics (example, immigration). Describe what is similar or what is different about these two books in terms of their perspective on the topic. How would you use these two books in your curriculum?

Bilingual Books Promote Latinx Multiculturalism and Biliteracy

Many of the books listed in Table 9.1 are written in English and Spanish. This is an example of a recent trend in Latinx children's literature published in the U.S. Latinx bilingual books have increased in number in the U.S. (Ernst Slavitt & Mulhearn, 2003, as cited in Hadaway & Young, 2010). Published in different formats, these books are found with the Spanish and English text on the same page, for example, Pérez's (2009) *My Diary from Here to There/Mi diario de aquí hasta allá* and Gonzalez's (2008) *The Storyteller's Candle/La velita de los cuentos*; the Spanish edition and the English edition published in separate books, for example, Denise's (2019) *Planting Stories: The Life of Librarian and Storyteller Pura Belpré* (English edition) and *Sembrando historias: Pura Belpré: bibliotecaria y narradora de cuentos* (Spanish edition); and Spanish words and phrases strategically placed throughout the English text, such as Mora's (1996) *Confetti: Poems for Children*, using different devices, such as context clues, the Spanish translation next to the English word or words, and picture clues added so that non-Spanish speakers can understand the meaning.

Translating from one language to another requires a high level of proficiency in both languages and great literary language skills. In the text, both languages need to sound natural, authentic, and flow the way the regional dialect of Spanish or English normally flows. This means the translator must also be knowledgeable of regional dialects in English and Spanish and accurately represent the version of English and Spanish in the narration and dialect. Spanish varies from country to country, mostly in vocabulary and pronunciation. For example, the Spanish spoken in Puerto Rico is different from the Spanish spoken in Mexico, so Latinxs who are immigrants, migrants, or descendants from these places are likely to speak the dialect of those origins. An example of a difference in vocabulary is the word kite. In Puerto Rico, a kite is called *chiringa;* in Mexico, it is called *papalote*. The same is true for English. British English uses the word lorry for a large vehicle that transports materials, whereas American English uses the word truck.

Additionally, the translator and editor need to be careful to avoid presenting one language as superior to the other by where it is placed on the page or by the use of a different font for one language versus another (Hadaway & Young, 2010), and to carefully check for problems with "incorrect lexical constructions, unclear phrases, awkward expression and grammatical, spelling, and/or typographical errors" (Schon, 2004 as cited in Hadaway & Young, 2010, p. 120).

Language is an important part of a person's cultural identity (Hadaway & Young, 2010), so reading bilingual books in Spanish and English is likely to support emerging bilingual Latinx students' pride in their culture and invite them to make connections to the story.

Furthermore, bilingual books support Latinx students' literacy development in both English and Spanish. To promote biliteracy, teachers can ask Latinx students to read the version of the story written in their stronger language first, discuss it with a partner or a group of their peers, then write about it, and finally read the story in the other language and respond to questions in that language. This way, the first reading in their stronger language scaffolds their reading comprehension of the story written in their weaker language. They can also closely read the story in each language, searching for cognates (English and Spanish words with similar sounds, spelling, and meanings such as important and *importante*). They can also search for word parts similar in morphology in both languages, for example, the suffixes in the words information and *información*. Thus, all students benefit from reading bilingual books by using one language as a bridge to the other language.

Resources

Websites

- Association for Library Service to Children. (2022). Pura Belpré award. www.ala.org/alsc/awardsgrants/bookmedia/belpre.
- Consortium of Latin American Studies Programs. (2022). Américas award. www.claspprograms.org/americasaward.
- Texas State University. (2022). Tomás Rivera book award. www.education.txstate.edu/ci/riverabookaward/.
- ¡Colorin colorado!. (2022). A bilingual site for educators and families of English language learners. www.colorincolorado.org/ [See Hispanic Heritage Booklists & Meet the Author Videos]
- Social Justice Books. (2022). Puerto Rican children's literature for social justice: A bibliography for social justice. https://socialjustice-books.org/puerto-rican-childrens-literature-social-justice-bibliography/.
- Book Connections. (2022). Homepage. www.bookconnections.org/.

- Lee and Low Books. (2022). Multicultural children's books. www. leeandlow.com/.
- Latinxs in Kid Lit https://latinosinkidlit.com/.
- López-Robertson, J. (2021b). How to Choose Latinx Children's Literature for Your Classroom. www.scholastic.com/teachers/teaching-tools/articles/professional-development/latinx-childrens-literature-classroom. html.

Books

- Ada, A. F. (2002). A magical encounter: Latino children's literature in the classroom (2nd ed.)
- López-Robertson, J. (2021a). Celebrating our cuentos: Choosing and using Latinx literature in elementary classrooms. Scholastic.
- Naidoo, J. C. (2011). Celebrating cuentos: Promoting Latino children's literature and literacy in classrooms and libraries. Libraries Unlimited.
- Smolen, L. A. & Oswald, R. A. (2011). Multicultural literature and response: Affirming diverse voices. Libraries Unlimited.
- Smolen, L. A. & Ortiz-Castro, V. (2004). Exploring Latino culture through folk tales. In Terrell A. Young (Ed.), Happily ever after: Sharing folk literature with elementary and middle school students (pp. 193–218). International Reading Association.

References

Ada, A. F. (2016). Forward: Literature in the lives of Latino children. In E. Rojas Clark, B. Bustos Flores, H. L. Smith, & D. A. González (Eds.), *Multicultural literature for Latino bilingual children: Their words, their worlds.* (pp. ix–xviii). Rowman & Littlefield.

Association for Library Service to Children. (2022). Pura Belpré award. www.ala. org/alsc/awardsgrants/bookmedia/belpre.

Bennett, C.I. (2003). *Comprehensive multicultural education: Theory and practice*, 5th Ed. Pearson Education.

Bishop, R. S. (1990, March). Windows and mirrors: Children's books and parallel cultures. In *California State University: San Bernardino reading conference: 14th annual conference proceedings* (pp 3–12). In Files.Eric.Ed.gov/fulltext/ED337744.pdf.

Bishop, R. S. (1993). Multicultural literature for children: Making informed choices. In V. J. Harris (Ed.), *Teaching multicultural literature in grades K-8.* (pp. 46–47). Christopher-Gordon.

Britannica. (2022). Chicano. www.britannica.com/topic/Chicano.

Consortium of Latin American Studies Programs. (2022). Américas award. www. claspprograms.org/americasaward.

Cooperative Children's Book Center. (2022). Books by and/or about Black, Indigenous and People of Color. https://ccbc.education.wisc.edu/literature-resources/ccbc-diversity-statistics/books-by-and-or-about-poc-2018/.

Hadaway, N. L., & Young, T. A. (2010). *Matching books & readers: Helping English learners in grades K-6.* Guilford.

Jones, N., Marks, R., Ramirez, R., Ríos-Vargas, M. (2021). 2020 Census illuminates racial and ethnic composition of the country. www.census.gov/library/stories/2021/08/improved-race-ethnicity-measures-reveal-united-states-population-much-more-multiracial.html.

Kiger, P. J. (2020). How St. Augustine became the first European settlement in America St. Augustine, Florida was founded by Spanish explorers long before Jamestown and the Plymouth Colony. www.history.com/news/st-augustine-first-american-settlement.

Lehman College. (2022). Puerto Rican emigration: Why the 1950s?https://lcw.lehman.edu/lehman/depts/latinampuertorican/latinoweb/PuertoRico/1950s.htm.

Library of Congress. (2022a). Immigration and relocation in U.S. History: Mexican. www.loc.gov/classroom-materials/immigration/mexican/.

Library of Congress. (2022b). Jones Act. www.loc.gov/rr/hispanic/1898/jonesact.html.

Library of Congress. (2022c). Migrating to a new land. www.loc.gov/classroom-materials/immigration/puerto-rican-cuban/migrating-to-a-new-land/.

Library of Congress. (2022d). Crossing the straits. www.loc.gov/classroom-materials/immigration/puerto-rican-cuban/crossing-the-straits/.

López-Roberston, J. (2021a). *Celebrating our cuentos: Choosing and using Latinx literature in elementary classrooms.* Scholastic.

López-Roberston, J. (2021b). How to choose Latinx children's literature for your classroom. www.scholastic.com/teachers/teaching-tools/articles/professional-development/latinx-childrens-literature-classroom.html.

Naidoo, J. C. (2011). Introduction: Latino children's literature in today's classrooms and libraries. Celebrating cuentos. In J. C. Naidoo (Ed.), *Promoting Latino children's literature and literacy in classrooms and libraries.* (pp. xiii–xx). Libraries Unlimited.

National Archives. (2022a). Gadsden purchase treaty. www.archives.gov/legislative/features/nm-az-statehood/gadsden.html.

National Archives. (2022b). Treaty of Guadalupe Hidalgo (1848). www.archives.gov/milestone-documents/treaty-of-guadalupe-hidalgo.

National Geographic. (2022). North America: Physical geography. https://education.nationalgeographic.org/resource/north-america-physical-geography.

National Park Service. (2022). Unit 1: Spain in the New World to 1600. www.nps.gov/fora/learn/education/unit-1-spain-in-the-new-world-to-1600.htm.

NPR. (2020). New groups aim to get more Latinx stories to young readers. www.npr.org/2020/09/28/916980190/new-groups-aim-to-get-more-latinx-stories-to-young-readers.

Riojas Clark, E., Bustos Flores, B., Smith, H. L., & González, D. A. (2016). *Multicultural literature for Latino bilingual children: Their words, their worlds.* Rowman & Littlefield.

Texas State University. (2022). Tomás Rivera book award. www.education.txstate.edu/ci/riverabookaward/.

University of South Florida. (2002). Ponce de León: Florida's first Spanish explorer. https://fcit.usf.edu/florida/lessons/de_leon/de_leon1.htm.

Villegas, A. M. (2018). Introduction to preparation and development of mainstream teachers for today's linguistically diverse classrooms. *The Educational Forum, 82,* 131–137. doi:10.1080/00131725.2018.1420848.

Children's Literature Cited

Ada, A. F. (1994) *The gold coin*. N. Waldman (Ills.). Editorial Everest.

Ada, A. F. (1997), *Gathering the sun: An alphabet book in Spanish and English*. S. Silva (Ills.). HarperCollins Español, Bilingual Edition.

Ada, A. F., & Campoy, F. I. (2006). *Tales our abuelitas told: A Hispanic folktale collection*. F. Davalos (Ills.), S. Guevara (Ills.), L. Torres (Ills.), & V. Escriva (Ills.). Atheneum Books for Young Readers.

Aldamuy Denise, A. (2019). *Planting stories: The life of librarian and storyteller Pura Belpré*. P. Escobar (Illus.). Harper.

Anaya, R. (1972) *Bless me Ultima*. Grand Central.

Brown, M. (2004). *My name is Celia: The life of Celia Cruz/Me llamo Celia: La vida de Celia Cruz*. R. López, (Ills.). Luna Rising.

Brown, M. (2011) *Waiting for the biblioburro/ Esperando el biblioburro*. J. Parra (Ills.). Tricycle Press.

Engle, M. (2015). *Drum dream girl: How one girl's courage changed music*. R. López (Ills.). Houghton Mifflin Harcourt.

Engle, M. (2021) *Song of frutas*. S. Palacios. (Ills.). Atheneum Books for Young Readers.

Gonzalez, L. (2008). *The storyteller's candle/La velita de los cuentos* (L. Delacre, Ills.). Children's Book Press.

Jaffe, N. (1996). *The golden flower: A Taino myth from Puerto Rico*. E. O. Sánchez. (Ills.). Simon & Schuster Books for Young Readers.

Krull, K. (2003), *Harvesting hope: The story of Cesar Chavez*. Y. Morales (Ills.). Harcourt Books.

Martí, J. (2020/1905) *La edad de oro*. Independently published.

McDermott, G. (1997) *Musicians of the sun*. G. McDermott (Illus.). Simon & Schuster Children's Publishing.

Mohr, N. (1973). *Nilda*. Arte Público Press.

Mohr, N. (1993). *El Bronx Remembered*. Harper Teen.

Mora, P. (1999) *Confetti: Poems for children*. E. O. Sanchez (Ills.). Lee & Low Books.

Mora, P. (2001) *Listen to the desert/Oye al desierto*. Francisco X. Mora (Ills.). Clarion Books.

Morales, Y. (2018). *Dreamers*. Y. Morales (Ills.). Neal Porter Books.

Otheguy, E. (2017). *Marti's song for freedom/Marti y sus versos por la libertad*. B. Vidal (Ill.). Children's Book Press.

Pérez, A. I. (2009). *My diary from here to there/Mi diario de aquí hasta allá*. M. C. Gonzalez (Ills.). Children's Book Press.

Soto, G. (2000). *Baseball in April*. Clarion Books.

Soto, G. (1993). *Too many tamales/¡Qué montón de tamales!*G. P. Putnam's Sons.

Soto, G. (2003). *Pacific crossing*. Clarion Books.

Soto, G. (2003). *Taking sides*. Hmh Books for Young Readers.

Soto, G. (2003). *Local news: Stories*. Clarion Books.

Tonatiuh, D. (2014). *Separate is never equal: Sylvia Mendez & her family's fight for Desegregation*. D. Tonatiuh (Ills.). Abrams.

Appendix: Foundational Teaching Tips

The following activities are recommended for use with Latinx literature in pre-K to 8th grade.

Interactive Read-Alouds

Teachers can successfully use interactive read-alouds with younger and older students. The teacher reads a story or poem aloud to the class, pausing to involve the students. For young children, the teacher might pause to let the students say a rhyming word out loud in a poem or make the sound of an animal in a story. For older students, the teacher might pause the reading of the story aloud to ask students to discuss a question with their partner about the story. Short poems by Ada or Mora would work well for read-alouds with young students. Short stories by Soto or excerpts from novels by Pam Muñoz Ryan would be effective for read-alouds with adolescents.

Drama

Drama is an excellent way for students to express their response to a story. Younger students can make masks for different characters and act out the story. Young children would enjoy dramatizing Latinx folk tales, like those in *Tales our abuelitas told: A Hispanic folktale collection by Ada & Campoy (2006)*. Older students could engage in frozen statues. In this activity, the teacher asks two or three students to pose as characters in the story at a memorable or dramatic point. The students freeze in a position that portrays the event in the story. The other students try to guess what event the frozen statues represent. Students then take turns dramatizing different events in the story with frozen statues. With this activity, students would enjoy acting out scenes from Esperanza Rising by Pam Muñoz Ryan (2012).

Creating Books Using Mentor Texts

An excellent way to promote students' writing development is to have students create books using mentor texts. The teacher begins the lesson by reading a mentor text (a text chosen to model a particular aspect of writing) to the class, then teaches a mini-lesson on a literary device or writing strategy featured in the mentor text, such as effective dialogue or sensory details. The teacher then explains how students can incorporate the writing feature into their writing. Then, the teacher guides the students as they attempt to use the writing element in their own stories. Pat Mora's (2001) poem, *Listen to the Desert/Oye al desierto*, would be a good choice for a mentor text for teaching students how to use onomatopoeia in a poem.

Reader's Theater

Reader's theater, a type of performance reading that requires students to read from scripts in front of an audience, is effective for improving oral reading. The students do not have to memorize lines; however, this activity requires practice and feedback from the teacher. There is no need to use scenery, props, costumes, or movements; thus, this activity is easy to plan. Students enjoy reader's theater and improve their fluency with this activity (Rasinski, 2010). It is also beneficial for building students' confidence when reading aloud and increasing their enthusiasm for literature. Teachers can write scripts using Latinx literature for their students to perform. They can also teach older students how to write scripts based on their favorite Latinx poems, nonfiction, or narrative writing. Visit Aaron Shepard's Reader's Theater page at www.aaronshep.com/rt/RTE.html to find examples of scripts based on children's literature and tips for using reader's theater in the classroom. Latinx folk tales are excellent choices for scripts. For more information on using readers' theater with folk tales, refer to Smolen and Ortiz-Castro's (2004) discussion of Latinx folk tales written for children and adolescents and their example of a reader's theater script based on McDermott's (1997) *Musicians of the Sun*.

10 Resilience, Courage, Relocation

Deepening Understanding about Immigrants and Refugees with Children's Literature

Grace Enriquez

Introduction

> Someday we will become something we haven't even yet imagined. But right now ... We are stories. We are two languages. We are lucha. We are resilience. We are hope. We are dreamers, soñadores of the world. We are Love Amor Love.
>
> (Morales, 2018)

These lines, spread poetically in two languages across lush, full-page illustrations, all by acclaimed children's author and illustrator, Yuyi Morales, underline the humanity and hope that immigrants and refugees harbor as they attempt to find a home in a new land. Although the experiences of immigrants and refugees are not new content in children's literature, global events over the last decade have thrust it into the media spotlight and increased the number of students in our classrooms who have traversed borders in search of a new home. Political and environmental crises in Syria, Afghanistan, Ukraine, Latin America, and even within the U.S. have forced multitudes of people to leave their homes in recent years with no assurances of returning. In the last two decades, the number of immigrants living in the U.S. grew from roughly 30 million to 45 million, with children 18 years old and younger comprising 25.8% (17.8 million) of the U.S. immigrant population in 2019 (Migration Policy Institute, 2022). Additionally, the United Nations High Commissioner for Refugees (UNHCR) estimated that 84 million people have been displaced globally as of mid-2021, approximately 42% (35 million) of whom are children under the age of 18 (UNHCR, 2022). These statistics have also climbed exponentially in the last decade, prompting the UNHCR to declare "a children's refugee crisis." Indeed, children make up a significant portion of the populations who have left the home they knew, sometimes with little more than hope of a better life elsewhere.

Certainly, such relocation across national borders can be either voluntary or involuntary. However, a common thread is a sense of liminality—

DOI: 10.4324/9781003321941-12

or what Edward Said (2000) articulates as "a fundamentally discontinuous sense of being" (p. 177)—and therefore, the precariousness of identities and daily lived experiences of those who have been displaced and separated from their roots. Geographical and physical uprooting often goes hand in hand with cultural dislocation, thereby precipitating additional kinds of unsettlement—emotional, linguistic, social, professional, etc.—that can accompany the transnational experience. Furthermore, xenophobic government policies and social attitudes only exacerbate the crisis and trauma of those who have been forced to leave their homes. And for undocumented immigrants, resettlement increases a sense of economic and emotional instability and distress (Dreby, 2012).

Before continuing, it's critical to clarify the various terms associated with this discussion and that children may encounter when reading. Although both immigrants and refugees left the home they know to resettle in a different land with different cultural and linguistic practices, they are not the same. What distinguishes them is their reason for **migrating**, or moving from one region to another. Mass migration can lead to **diaspora**, or the scattering of people from their original homeland. **Immigrants** leave their home voluntarily, often for reasons related to work, school, or family; **refugees** must leave home because of persecution, war, and other human rights violations, and therefore, flee from home to seek asylum (Strekalova-Hughes, 2019). **Displacement,** in which people are forced to leave their homes, can also be due to natural disaster; as the repercussions of climate change increase the frequency of wildfires, drought, rising sea levels, flash floods, and extreme weather storms, entire communities have been forced to seek shelter elsewhere. The conflation of these two populations ignores the reasons for leaving home in the first place, giving rise to questionable assumptions about what they are seeking from the U.S. The highly partisan and xenophobic rhetoric around immigrants and refugees exposes a reactionary fear of perceived differences and motivations for leaving home. And yet, immigrants and refugees have always been at the core of our nation's existence.

As Nel (2018) bemoans, educators and children's literature scholars do not have much sway in redressing government policies toward immigrants and refugees, but we "can guide readers to books that harness the imagination's power to nourish empathy, and we can steer them away from those that reinforce bigotry" (p. 359). While educational research about such populations is replete with deficit representations (Karam et al., 2019), children's literature can offer portraits of immigrant and refugee students through an asset-oriented lens. Such texts highlight the resilience, strength, and capabilities of children and families who are working to rebuild their lives and establish a sense of home in a land that is so different from where they came. Additionally, teachers can cultivate students' critical literacy skills to help them interrogate representations of immigrants and refugees for stereotypes and inauthentic representations.

This chapter, then, focuses on children's literature about children and families who have resettled in another land as immigrants or refugees. Although migration is and always has been a global phenomenon, I acknowledge a bias in this chapter that skews toward stories written primarily in English about transnational settlement in Western nations. This bias is partly due to my positionality as a U.S. scholar of children's literature, but also because of my own family's story of immigration to the U.S. from the Philippines in the 1960s and 1970s. Thus, I begin this chapter with a historical background of immigration movements and refugee experiences in the U.S., tracing the corresponding responses of the field of children's literature publishing. Next, I explain why attending to the identities and lived experiences of immigrants and refugees matters, using examples of high-quality children's literature to illustrate how such books can support those goals. In the final section, I offer reflection questions and other professional resources to support pre- and in-service educators in becoming critical consumers and teachers of children's literature about immigrants and refugees.

History of Immigration and Refugee Experiences in the U.S.

Human migration is an undeniable fact of history and as old as humans themselves. People have been moving and resettling across the globe for hundreds of thousands of years, as documented by studies in genetics, anthropology, and cultural storytelling. The earliest fossil evidence traces the roots of modern humans to Africa, and almost universal consensus among researchers supports that people traveled northward from there to the Middle East and then east and west across the globe (Delson, 2019). The official history of the United States traces its founding to the migration of European settlers, though most acknowledge the first inhabitants of North America most likely came across the Bering Strait thousands of years ago, long before those European settlers, between the Pacific and Arctic Oceans from Asia. The story of the English Pilgrims who established the Plymouth Colony in Massachusetts, however, resonates with the notions of opportunity, freedom, and displacement that characterizes much of the attention on immigrants and refugees who move to the U.S. today.

In our current times, the heavy focus by media outlets and the partisan rhetoric on immigrants and displaced peoples may generate a sense that the sheer number of those hoping to resettle and rebuild their lives in the U.S. is a new phenomenon. However, most historians cite four major waves of migration to the U.S. since its founding: (1) the arrival of settlers from England, France, and Spain that marked the colonial development of the U.S., (2) the arrival of people from other Western European countries, especially Ireland, during the first half of the 19th century, (3) the arrival of immigrants from southern and eastern Europe in the late

19th century and into the early 20th century, and (4) the growing number of people from Latin American, Asian, Middle Eastern, and African countries in the second half of the 20th century to current times (Ewing, 2012; U.S. Census Bureau, 2014). These periods do not include the simultaneous enslavement of Africans and African Americans who were forced to leave their homes as merchandise and chattel rather than as human beings. Furthermore, refugees have been a part of these waves from the beginning, seeking safety and solace in the nation whose iconic statue declares, "Give me your tired, your poor, / Your huddled masses yearning to breathe free" (Lazarus, 2002, p. 233). Indeed, continuing this legacy of immigration, the number of people living in the U.S. who resettled from another country has exponentially risen throughout our history (Budiman, 2020).

Children's literature has attempted to address these shifts. With the burgeoning of children's book publishing in the late twentieth century, books about immigrants and refugees began appearing that chronicled the experiences of children from colonial times to present day. However, the majority of these books echoed a narrative of "successful migration stories where children move from unfortunate circumstances in their home countries to happier lives in the host countries" (Orgad et al., 2021, p. 566). In reality, not all stories are "successful" ones. Moreover, what counts as "success" can vary, depending on the challenges immigrants and refugees face during the journey to another land and the challenges experienced once they arrive.

In the last two decades, as the call for social justice and diverse representation in children's literature grew louder, the publishing industry began publishing stories that reveal more nuanced immigrant and refugee experiences. For example, while ending on a hopeful note, *Marwan's Journey* (de Arias, 2018) ends once the child protagonist reaches the border, leaving readers to wonder whether he will "successfully" cross it. Books like *Hear My Voice/Escucha mi voz* (Binford, 2021) and *Between Us and Abuela: A Family Story from the Border* (Perkins, 2019) chronicle the heartrending devastation experienced by children who have been separated from their families at the U.S.–Mexico border. The critically acclaimed novel *Land of Forgotten Girls* (Entrada Kelly, 2016) delivers a heartrending account of two sisters who must deal with the loss of their parents after they immigrate to the U.S. and find a way to sustain hope amidst cruel circumstances. Such books aim to depict a more realistic understanding of the complexities children and families continue to face, even when they are able to cross the border in search of a new home.

Still, many children's books about immigrants and refugees aim to tell about hopeful transitions across borders, but without glossing over the complexities and difficulties that are actually involved. The stunning wordless picture book, *Here I Am* (Kim, 2014), conveys the fear and courage children experience in moving to a place where the language, food, games, and habits are unfamiliar. *Other Words for Home* (Warga, 2021), a Newbery Honor Book, details how determining what is home in a new land also involves grappling with new understandings about one's own identity. *Lubna and Pebble* (Meddour, 2019) is a stirring picture book about a young refugee girl living in the World of Tents who learns to overcome her loneliness to help another child adjust to their new situation. The gorgeous Caldecott Honor picture book, *A Different Pond* (Phi, 2017), poignantly balances the tender moment of a father telling his son about his childhood in Vietnam and the stark reality of the family's poverty in the U.S.

These titles and more show the growing sensibility and responsiveness of children's literature to the nuances and realities of immigrants and refugees. More and more, children's literature is beginning to reflect current issues around immigration and the children's refugee crisis, addressing a variety of reasons for leaving home, assumptions about immigrants and refugees, and the question of what counts as "success" when the journey to establish a new home does not end once national borders are crossed.

Using Children's Literature about Immigrants and Refugees in the Classroom

Why do stories about immigrants and refugees matter? What is the point of sharing them in the classroom? In this section, I address these questions through three lenses: a lens of storytelling; a lens of culturally relevant, responsive, and sustaining teaching; and a lens of critical literacies. Each highlights the power and challenges of using children's literature about immigrants and refugees in classroom pedagogy.

A Lens of Storytelling

Storytelling is a practice as old as the social existence of humans. In tracing the first examples of narrative tradition, Yılmaz and Ciğerci (2019) point out that "human understanding is largely related to storytelling—especially in relation to the concept of 'relocation', which means being able to refer to events belonging to a different time and place than ongoing communication" (p. 2). Indeed, though the forms, modalities, and functions of storytelling have varied and evolved throughout history, stories offer pathways for greater insight about ourselves and empathy for one another (Cunningham, 2015; Parsons, 2014).

With her powerful metaphor, renowned children's literature scholar Rudine Sims Bishop (1990) reminds us that as vehicles for such storytelling purposes, children's literature provides a mirror of a young reader's identities and lived experiences, a window into lives that are different from a reader's own experiences, and a sliding glass door to step through in imagination to become part of the world portrayed. In this sense, sharing stories about immigrants and refugees can provide students multiple entry points for deepening understanding and expanding knowledge.

For example, apart from the immigrant and refugee children in our own classrooms, some elementary students may have heard about the U.S. Deferred Action for Childhood Arrivals (DACA) policy, but many may have a shallow understanding of it. A book like *Ariel is a Dreamer: A True Story* (Morales, 2021) provides a firsthand account via an accessible and engaging picture book format of a young girl who applies for DACA with the same hopes and dreams of a bright future of other children in the U.S. The powerful novel, *The Turtle of Oman* (Shihab Nye, 2014), delves into the last week of an Omani boy before he moves with his parents who will attend graduate school in Michigan, telling the story of immigration from the angle of someone who doesn't want to leave. Its sequel, *The Turtle of Michigan* (Shihab Nye, 2022), continues the story once the family arrives in the U.S. Additionally, children's authors and editors have compiled anthologies of autobiographical stories from immigrant and refugee children, such as the Sibert Honor winning graphic novel, *The Unwanted: Stories of Syrian Refugees* (Brown, 2021), offering more opportunities to use storytelling for developing insight into their experiences of living in the liminal space between nations. Such books exemplify the power of storytelling to humanize those who have come from other lands to make a home alongside us.

Parsons (2014) also lists four distinct functions of storytelling: (1) for courage and inspiration, (2) to heal and as testimonio, (3) to maintain or forge connections, and (4) to entertain. In particular, stories that aim to bear witness for oppressed communities and honor the agency and humanity of collective people, or *testimonios*, can provide connection, deepen understanding, and rally communities to work for a better world for all (Forcinito, 2016; Webb, 2019). Sharing stories about immigrants and refugees can work toward unpacking the discourse and rhetoric around these populations, especially through first-hand accounts that paint a broader picture than what partisan media outlets and government officials depict. But, they can also offer models of courage and inspiration for youth, support connections among communities, and entertain readers of all ages.

A Lens of Culturally Relevant, Responsive, and Sustaining Teaching

Children's literature about immigrants and refugees promotes pedagogies that affirm, support, and sustain students' diverse cultural identities and ways of knowing, being, and learning. Culturally relevant teaching aims to "empower students intellectually, socially, emotionally, and politically by using cultural referents to impart knowledge, skills, and attitudes" (Ladson-Billings, 1994, p. 18), while culturally responsive teaching centers diverse students' cultural knowledge and lived experiences as building blocks for effective teaching (Gay, 2018), and culturally sustaining teaching aims to preserve and celebrate students' unique cultural sense of being (Alim & Paris, 2017). All three approaches build upon decades of educational research that shows the benefits of building instruction upon students' cultural assets rather than any perceived deficit of the dominant culture they may have.

Children's literature about immigrants and refugees, particularly those that depict the experiences of people moving from Latin American, Asian, Middle Eastern, and African countries, support culturally relevant, responsive, and sustaining teaching. Despite the exponential increase in the number of books published for children in recent decades, these populations continue to be underrepresented and missing from the books used in K-12 classrooms. Moreover, if such books are included in classroom libraries and curricula, too often they are relegated to single units or small group and independent reading rather than centered throughout all of teaching and learning (Enriquez, 2019, 2021b). Positioning books about immigrants and refugees as constituent components of curriculum and instruction across the year not only affirms the identities and lived experiences of the diverse students in our classrooms and their families, but it acknowledges them to be valuable assets and foundations for learning.

A Lens of Critical Literacy

Sharing children's literature about immigrants and refugees in classrooms can also take students' literacy learning beyond merely functional skill development, elevating literacy education to learning "'the language of possibility,' enabling learners to recognize and understand their voices within a multitude of discourses in which they must deal" (Freire & Macedo, 1987, p. 54). In this way, sharing these stories, like those about any marginalized people, can work toward developing students' critical literacy skills and supporting goals of equity, diversity, inclusion, and justice.

Critical literacy recognizes that all texts are socially and ideologically constructed, and supports teachers and students to question, evaluate, and act to reassess and reconstruct what constitutes truth and reality (Shor, 1999). In other words, critical literacy aims to investigate and spotlight the relationship between language and power (Janks, 2000). However, critical literacy is not simply a pedagogical approach or skill set; it is "an ongoing stance toward a richer understanding of the world and the efforts to build a more just society" (Enriquez, 2021a, p. 254). Toward this goal, critical literacy often involves integrating diverse texts to gain insight and build empathy around multiple perspectives, deconstructing texts to investigate issues of power and representation, reconstructing narratives to give voice to marginalized perspectives, and engaging in social action to fully realize the potential of one's literacy abilities (Jones, 2006; Leland, Lewison, & Harste, 2017). Using children's literature about immigrants and refugees in the classroom supports critical literacy development in these ways.

Integrating Diverse Texts to Gain Insight and Build Empathy around Multiple Perspectives

This principle aims to help students realize the complexity and connections of the world, social relationships, and human existence. For example, the novel *Refugee* (Gratz, 2017) demonstrates the interdependence we share, despite our different circumstances, by recounting the stories of Josef, a Jewish boy in 1930s Nazi Germany, Isabel, a Cuban girl in 1994, and Mahmoud, a Syrian boy in 2015. The author explained, "I want to show young readers we keep making the same mistakes over and over again, and if we want tomorrow, if we want *mañana* to be any different, we have to make changes here and now today." The picture book *Wishes* (Thi Van, 2021) strips down the narrative to an unnamed child leaving behind an unknown homeland to seek safety in an undisclosed destination, but employs a remarkable combination of brief sentences, figurative language, and full double-page illustrations to evoke an array of emotions about the plight of refugees from various, creative perspectives. *Efren Divided* (Cisneros, 2021), winner of the Pura Belpré Award, highlights, for students who have only ever known one country as their home, the feeling of being pulled between two worlds that many immigrant children feel. Still other books, especially nonfiction texts like the well-researched and engaging informational chapter book *Finding Home: The Journey of Immigrants and Refugees* (Sookfong Lee, 2021), provide a comprehensive account of the issues these populations face. Sharing books like these deepens understanding and encourages students to approach the situations of immigrants and refugees with broader awareness.

Deconstructing Texts to Investigate Issues of Power and Representation

This tenet aims to surface tacit assumptions, values, and worldviews within texts. Deconstructing texts doesn't just mean critiquing them, but also working to understand how a text positions the reader within the broader world. Deconstructing a text can also highlight stereotypes about certain populations, engaging readers in dialogue about where those stereotypes come from, why they exist, and why the author may have included them in the text.

Specifically, research on representations of immigrants indicates they are often depicted through a lens of deficit and victimization that positions characters as "other" and encourage a "sympathetic response for readers through feelings of pity for immigrants and a sense of superiority for their own way of life" (Sung, Fahrenbruck, & López-Robertson, 2017, p. 56). Although such portrayals may stem from good intentions, aiming to shed light on the challenges that immigrants face upon entering a new country and attempting to build a home there, they may also inadvertently strip immigrants of their dignity and humanity, propping them up as "others." For example, *One Green Apple* (Bunting, 2006) is a heartwarming picture book about Farah, a lonely Muslim girl who finally begins to connect with her classmates on a fieldtrip to an apple orchard. But it can also be critiqued for equating Farah's sense of belonging with her attempting to speak English rather than her classmates attempting to learn Arabic to communicate. Readers may also debate whether an author can accurately or authentically write about characters or events that do not reflect their own cultural identity and lived experiences, no matter how renowned the author may be. Strekalova-Hughes (2019) found a preponderance of flight narratives in the children's stories about refugees, thereby revealing a myopic representation of the hurdles they face. Using an eye toward power and representation helps students to critically examine the assumptions behind the portrayal of immigrants and refugees in children's literature.

Reconstructing Narratives to Give Voice to Marginalized Populations

Working in tandem with the tenet of text deconstruction for issues of power and representation is the principle of reconstructing—or retelling— commonly assumed stories in ways that are more equitable, inclusive, and just. The novel *Boy, Everywhere* (Dassu, 2021) challenges perceptions of refugees that separate them as "other", victimize them as "destitute" or "underprivileged," or villainize them as "greedy" or "criminals." Indeed, author A. M. Dassu writes in her author's note for this novel:

> Due to media coverage at the time [of conducting research for *Boy, Everywhere*], many people assumed refugees were poor, uneducated, and wanted to come to Europe because they'd have a better life. But the more Syrian people I met and the more research I did, the more I realized that if it weren't for the war, most Syrians would never have left. It became clear their lives were very similar to ours in the West, and a civil war could easily bring the same fate upon any of us.
>
> (Dassu, 2021, pp. 387–388)

The picture book *A Map into the World* (Yang, 2021) cleverly diverts any sense of pity from the young Hmong immigrant child to her elderly White non-immigrant neighbor. As the seasons change, so does all of their lives, and it's the child who brings hope and healing to those around her. The Charlotte Huck Award winning picture book, *Room on Our Rock* (Temple & Temple, 2019), literally flips the narrative about refugees; after reading a conventional xenophobic and nationalistic response to a group of seals who need shelter, readers can read the sentences in reverse order to discover a more compassionate and uplifting response. The Pura Belpré award winning picture book, *Dreamers* (Morales, 2018), from which the quotation that opens this chapter is drawn, also approaches the immigrant and refugee narrative from an asset-based orientation. Such books emphasize the agency, strengths, and resources that immigrants and refugees already bring with them when they cross borders.

Engaging in Social Action to Realize the Potential of One's Literacy Abilities

For some, since the purpose of critical literacy is to work toward a more just and equitable world, action must accompany such learning in order to realize that goal. Children's literature also reflects his belief, providing stories that exemplify how youth can take action to make the journey of immigrants and refugees less distressing. In the picture book *Mama's Nightingale: A Tale of Immigration and Separation* (Danticat, 2015), the power of writing provides the child protagonist with a sense of hope that her family can be reunited again after her mother is sent to an immigration detention center. And in the compelling picture book *Hear My Voice/ Escucha mi voz: The Testimonies of Children Detained at the Southern Border of the United States* (Binford, 2021), 61 immigrant and refugee children from Central America tell their stories about life in a detention center. Students can flip the book over to read about their experiences in their own Spanish words, and learn more about ways to help with the book' sections on additional information, questions, and action points. Such titles provide examples and guidance for engaging in action–particularly via the potential of reading, writing, speaking, and listening–to build more understanding, empathy, and justice for immigrants and refugees.

Reflection Questions for Pre-service and In-service Teachers

When considering selecting children's literature to teach about immigrants and refugees, we need to be purposeful and thoughtful about that process. Cappiello and Thulin Dawes (2010) identify three layers of consideration for selecting children's literature for use in classrooms: (1) literary/artistic quality, (2) utility as a teaching tool, and (3) text complexity, or appropriateness for students. The questions below build upon these layers, but also add the lenses of (4) storytelling; (5) culturally relevant, responsive, and sustaining teaching; and (6) critical literacy to provide further reflection points to help support meaningful teaching and learning with these books. Invite your colleagues and pre-service/in-service students to work in small groups to answer the questions below with some of books mentioned in this chapter or in Table 10.1. As a model for them, select one of the books and answer one question from each of the sections below.

1. Literary/artistic/storytelling quality:

   - What kinds of professional praise (awards, starred reviews, etc.) did the title receive?
   - Does the text use rich, interesting language and sentences?
   - Does the text include language and vocabulary that authentically and vividly describe the experiences of the immigrant and/or refugee population involved?
   - How do the visuals engage readers with the experience of immigrants and/or refugees?
   - How does the text meet the established criteria for genre and structure?

2. Teaching utility:

   - What is your pedagogical rationale for using this text?
   - How does this text align with your curriculum or standards requirements for teaching about immigration and displacement?
   - How much background knowledge do your students need to fully engage with the content of this text?
   - What support may students need to access the language and vocabulary of the text?
   - How does the book enhance and expand students' current knowledge about immigrants and refugees?
   - What possibilities does this book offer for teaching in multimodal ways?

3. Text complexity:

   - How complex is the book's content in terms of the issues that immigrants and/or refugees face?
   - How complex is the book's text structure, language, and visual support for students to access?

4. Storytelling:

   - How does this book provide a window and/or mirror into the lives of immigrants and/or refugees for my students?
   - How might I use this book as a sliding glass door to support my students' understanding of immigrants and refugees?
   - In what ways might this book be used to model courage and inspiration, heal and provide testimonio, maintain or forge

connections among diverse people, and engage students to enjoy the story?

5. Culturally relevant, responsive, and sustaining teaching:

    •   How does this book align with my students' cultural identities and ways of knowing, being, and living?
    •   How does this book affirm my students' experiences
    •   How does this book position students' cultural identities, knowledge, and experiences as resources for learning?

6. Critical literacy:

    •   What perspectives and voices are included in this text? What perspectives and voices are neglected?
    •   What assumptions and stereotypes are perpetuated in this text?
    •   How might this book help reframe the conventional narrative about immigrants and refugees?
    •   How might this book inspire action toward equity, diversity, inclusion, and justice?

Recommendations for Multicultural Children's Literature to Facilitate Discussion and Cultural Diversity

The following table lists some recommended titles for teaching about immigrants and refugees in elementary aged classrooms. Considering the growing number of high-quality books about this population that are published each year, this list is by no means exhaustive or definitive of the multiple reasons people leave their home to resettle in another, the experiences they undergo during their journey or after they relocate, or the demographics of people who leave home in search of a better life elsewhere. As previously mentioned, the titles I included lean towards those primarily written in English that detail experiences of resettlement in Western nations. Additionally, although a number of high-quality nonfiction and poetry books about immigrants and refugees are available, most of the listed titles are fiction picture books or chapter books due to space limitations. I also only provided titles that have won awards from major children's literature and literacy organizations or have received multiple starred reviews from nationally reputable children's literature publications. Finally, the books in this list are limited to those published within the last five years in order to underscore the relevance and urgency of immigrant and refugee issues and experiences today.

Table 10.1. Recommended pieces multicultural literature for elementary aged classrooms.

Book Information	Publisher's Summary
Title: *Dreamers* **Author and Illustrator:** Yuyi Morales **Genre:** Picture book memoir **Awards:** Pura Belpré Illustrator Award; *New York Times* / New York Public Library Best Illustrated Book; Flora Stieglitz Strauss Award; *Boston Globe-Horn Book* Honor; Bulletin of the Center for Children's Books Blue Ribbon title; Junior Library Guild selection; Children's Literature Assembly (CLA) Notable Children's Book in Language Arts; Bank Street College of Education Best Children's Books of the Year; Kirkus Reviews Best Books; Publishers Weekly Best Books, School Library Journal Best Books **Grade Level Band:** K-3	**Publisher's Summary:** *Dreamers* is a celebration of making your home with the things you always carry: your resilience, your dreams, your hopes and history. It's the story of finding your way in a new place, of navigating an unfamiliar world and finding the best parts of it. In dark times, it's a promise that you can make better tomorrows....It's a story about family. And it's a story to remind us that we are all dreamers, bringing our own strengths wherever we roam.
Title: *A Different Pond* **Author and Illustrator:** Bao Phi; Thi Bui **Genre:** Fiction Picture book **Awards:** Caldecott Honor; Charlotte Zolotow Award; Asian/Pacific American Award for Literature Winner; Ezra Jack Keats New Writer Honor; Ezra Jack Keats New Illustrator Honor; *Boston Globe-Horn Book* Honor Book; Notable Social Studies Trade Books for Young People; Cooperative Children's Book Center (CCBC) Choices; Bank Street College of Education Best Children's Books of the Year; *Huffington Post* Best Picture Books of the Year; *Washington Post* Best Children's Books of the Year; *Boston Globe* Best Children's and YA Books of the Year; Publishers Weekly Best Books of the Year; Kirkus Reviews Best Picture Books of the Year; *School Library Journal* Best Books of the Year; New York Public Library Best Books for Kids **Grade Level Band:** K-4	**Publisher's Summary:** As a young boy, Bao and his father awoke early, hours before his father's long workday began, to fish on the shores of a small pond in Minneapolis. Unlike many other anglers, Bao and his father fished for food, not recreation. A successful catch meant a fed family. Between hope-filled casts, Bao's father told him about a different pond in their homeland of Vietnam.
Title: *Wishes* **Author and Illustrator:** Muon Thi Van; Victo Ngai **Genre:** Fiction Picture book **Awards:** Association for Library Service to Children (ALSC) Notable Children's Book **Grade Level Band:** K-3	**Publisher's Summary:** *Wishes* tells the powerful, honest story about one Vietnamese family's search for a new home on the other side of the world, and the long-lasting and powerful impact that makes on the littlest member of the family. Inspired by actual events in the author's life, this is a narrative that is both timely and timeless.

Book Information	Publisher's Summary
Title: *Mama's Nightingale: A Story of Immigration and Separation* **Author and Illustrator:** Edwidge Danticat; Leslie Staub **Genre:** Fiction Picture book **Awards:** Kirkus Reviews Best Picture Books of the Year **Grade Level Band:** K-3	**Publisher's Summary:** After Saya's mother is sent to an immigration detention center, Saya finds comfort in listening to her mother's warm greeting on their answering machine. To ease the distance between them while she's in jail, Mama begins sending Saya bedtime stories inspired by Haitian folklore on cassette tape. Moved by her mother's tales and her father's attempts to reunite their family, Saya writes a story of her own—one that just might bring her mother home for good.
Title: *Room on Our Rock* **Author and Illustrator:** Kate Temple and Jol Temple; Terri Rose Baynton **Genre:** Fiction Picture book **Awards:** National Council of Teachers of English (NCTE) Charlotte Huck Award **Grade Level Band:** K-3	**Publisher's Summary:** Three seals are perched on a rock. When others need shelter, do they share it? When read from front to back, the group of seals firmly believe there is no room on their rock for the parent and child seal who are seeking a place to rest. Readers are then encouraged to read the story again, from back to front, revealing a welcoming message where the seals make room for others and share their rock.
Title: *Marwan's Journey* **Author and Illustrator:** Patricia de Arias; Laura Borràs **Genre:** Fiction Picture book **Awards:** Notable Social Studies Trade Books for Young People; United States Board on Books for Young People (USBBY) Outstanding International Trade Book; Kirkus Reviews Best Picture Books of the Year; Bank Street College of Education Best Children's Books of the Year **Grade Level Band:** K-3	**Publisher's Summary:** Marwan is a young boy on a journey he never intended to take, bound for a place he doesn't know. On his journey, he relies on courage and memories of his faraway homeland to buoy him. With him are hundreds and thousands of other human beings, crossing the deserts and the seas, fleeing war and hunger in search of safety. He must take one step after another—bringing whatever he can carry, holding on to dreams.

Book Information	Publisher's Summary
Title: *Boy, Everywhere* **Author:** A. M. Dassu **Genre:** Fiction Novel **Awards:** Kirkus Reviews Best Books; Bank Street College of Education Best Children's Books of the Year; American Library Association (ALA) Notable Children's Book **Grade Level Band:** 3–8	**Publisher's Summary:** Forced to sell all their belongings and leave their friends and beloved grandmother behind, Sami and his family travel across the Middle East [and] cross the treacherous waters of the Mediterranean and manage to fly to England, only to be separated and detained in an immigration prison for the "crime" of seeking asylum. Yet the transition from refugee to immigrant in a new life will be the greatest challenge Sami has ever faced.
Title: *Refugee* **Author:** Alan Gratz **Genre:** Fiction novel **Awards:** Notable Social Studies Trade Books for Young People; YALSA Quick Picks for Reluctant Young Readers; YALSA Best Fiction for Young Adults **Grade Level Band:** 6–9	**Publisher's Summary:** This timely and powerful novel tells the story of three different children seeking refuge... , All three kids go on harrowing journeys in search of refuge. All will face unimaginable dangers - from drownings to bombings to betrayals. But there is always the hope of tomorrow. And although Josef, Isabel, and Mahmoud are separated by continents and decades, shocking connections will tie their stories together in the end.
Title: *Efrén Divided* **Author:** Ernesto Cisneros **Genre:** Fiction novel **Awards:** Pura Belpré Award Winner; Bank Street College of Education Best Children's Book of the Year; Chicago Public Library Best of the Best; New York Public Library's Best Books for Kids; School Library Journal (SLJ) Best Book **Grade Level Band:** 3–8	**Publisher's Summary:** Efrén Nava's Amá is his Superwoman—or Soperwoman, named after the delicious Mexican sopes his mother often prepares. Both Amá and Apá work hard all day to provide for the family, making sure Efrén and his younger siblings Max and Mía feel safe and loved. But Efrén worries about his parents; although he's American-born, his parents are undocumented. His worst nightmare comes true one day when Amá doesn't return from work and is deported across the border to Tijuana, México.

Book Information	Publisher's Summary
Title: Hear My Voice/Escucha mi voz **Author and Illustrator:** Warren Binford; 17 Latinx illustrators **Genre:** Nonfiction Informational Book **Grade Level Band:** 2 and up	**Publisher's Summary:** Every day, children in migration are detained at the U.S.–Mexico border. They are scared, alone, and their lives are in limbo. Hear My Voice/Escucha mi voz shares the stories of 61 children, from Honduras, Guatemala, El Salvador, Ecuador, and Mexico, ranging in age from five to seventeen—in their own words from actual sworn testimonies. Befitting the spirit of the project, the book is in English on one side; then flip it over, and there's a complete Spanish version.
Title: Finding Home: The Journey of Immigrants and Refugees **Author and Illustrator:** Jen Sookfong Lee; Drew Shannon **Genre:** Nonfiction Informational Book **Awards:** Notable Social Studies Trade Books for Young People **Grade Level Band:** 4–8	**Publisher's Summary:** What drives people to search for new homes? From war zones to politics, there are many reasons why people have always searched for a place to call home. In Finding Home: The Journey of Immigrants and Refugees, we discover how human migration has shaped our world. We explore its origins and the current issues facing immigrants and refugees today, and we hear the first-hand stories of people who have moved across the globe looking for safety, security and happiness.

Resources for Further Education and Materials for Classrooms

The following list provides professional books, informational websites, and digital databases that can support educators' learning about immigrants and refugees, as well as children's literature that addresses their experiences.

Professional Books

- Bajaj, M., Walsh, D., Bartlett, L., & Martinez, G. (2022). Humanizing education for immigrant and refugee youth: 20 strategies for the classroom and beyond. Teachers College Press.
- Campano, G. (2006). Immigrant students and literacy: Reading, writing, and remembering. Teachers College Press.

- Campano, G., Ghiso, M. P., & Welch, B. J. (2016). *Partnering with immigrant communities: Action through literacy.* Teachers College Press.
- Manning, M., Orozco Sahi, I., Juelke, L., & Monterrey, S. (2022). *Creating a sense of belonging for immigrant and refugee students: Strategies for K-12 educators.* Routledge.

Informational Websites

- Migration Policy Institute:
- www.migrationpolicy.org
- United Nations High Commissioner on Refugees:
- www.unhcr.org/refugee-statistics/

Digital Databases

- Colorín Colorado:
- www.colorincolorado.org/article/using-books-about-immigration-classroom;
- www.colorincolorado.org/booklist/guides-supporting-refugee-students
- Libros for Language:
- https://librosforlanguage.org/
- Social Justice Books: A Teaching for Change Project:
- https://socialjusticebooks.org/booklists/immigration/
- TeachingBooks: www.teachingbooks.net/tb.cgi?lid=9295;
- www.teachingbooks.net/tb.cgi?lid=6501

References

Alim, H. S., & Paris, D. (Eds.). (2017). *Culturally sustaining pedagogies: Teaching and learning for justice in a changing world.* Teachers College Press.

Bishop, R. S. (1990). Mirrors, windows, and sliding glass doors. *Perspectives: Choosing and Using Books for the Classroom, 1*(3), ix–xi.

Budiman, A. (2020.) Key findings about U.S. immigrants. Pew Research Center. www.pewresearch.org/fact-tank/2020/08/20/key-findings-about-u-s-immigrants/.

Cappiello, M. A., & Thulin Dawes, E. (2010). *Teaching with text sets.* Teacher Created Materials.

Cunningham, K. E. (2015). *Story: Still the heart of literacy learning.* Stenhouse Publishers.

Delson, E. (2019, July 10). An early dispersal of modern humans from Africa to Greece. *Nature, 571,* 487–488. https://doi.org/10.1038/d41586-019-02075-9.

Dreby, J. (2012). The burden of deportation on children in Mexican immigrant families. *Journal of Marriage and Family, 74*(4), 829–845.

Enriquez, G. (2019). Rethinking read-alouds: Toward meaningful integration of diverse books in our classrooms. *Primer Calendar, 48*(1), 30, 40.

Enriquez, G. (2021a). Critical approaches to text. In S. Parsons & M. Vaughn (Eds.), *Principles of effective literacy instruction, grades K-5.* (pp. 251–257). New York: Guilford Press.

Enriquez, G. (2021b). Foggy mirrors, tiny windows, and heavy doors: Beyond diverse books toward meaningful literacy instruction. *The Reading Teacher*, 75(1), 103–106. http://doi.org/10.1002/trtr.2030.

Ewing, W. A. (2012). Opportunity and exclusion: A brief history of U.S. immigration policy. www.americanimmigrationcouncil.org/research/opportunity-and-exclusion-brief-history-us-immigration-policy.

Forcinito, A. (2016). Testimonio: The witness, the truth, and the inaudible. In Martínez-San Miguel, Y., Sifuentes-Jáuregui, B., & Belausteguigoitia, M. (Eds). *Critical terms in Caribbean and Latin American thought: New directions in Latino American cultures*. Palgrave Macmillan. https://doi.org/10.1057/9781137547903_22.

Freire, P., & Macedo, D. (1987). *Literacy: Reading the word and the world*. New York: Bergin & Harvey.

Gay, G. (2018). *Culturally responsive teaching: Theory, research, and practice* (3rd edition). Teachers College Press.

Janks, H. (2000). Domination, access, diversity and design: A synthesis for critical literacy education. *Educational Review*, 52(2), 175–186.

Jones, S. (2006). *Girls, social class, and literacy: What teachers can do to make a difference*. Portsmouth, NH: Heinemann.

Karam, F. J., Kersten-Parrish, S., Warren, A. N., & Kibler, A. (2019). Representations of Sudanese/South Sudanese children resettled as refugees in children's literature for the middle grades. *Journal of Children's Literature*, 45(2), 32–42.

Ladson-Billings, G. (1994). *The dreamkeepers: Successful teaching for African American children*. San Francisco, CA: Jossey-Bass.

Lazarus, E. (2002). The new Colossus. In G. Eiselein (Ed.), *Emma Lazarus: Selected poems and other writings*. Broadview Press.

Leland, C., Lewison, M., & Harste, J. (2017). *Teaching children's literature: It's critical!* (2nd ed.) New York: Routledge.

Migration Policy Institute. (2022). Children in U.S. immigrant families (By Age Group and State, 1990 versus 2019). www.migrationpolicy.org/programs/datahub/us-immigration-trends#children.

Nel, P. (2018). Migration, refugees, and diaspora in children's literature. *Children's Literature Association Quarterly*, 357–362.

Orgad, S., Lemish, D., Rahali, M., & Floegel, D. (2021) Representations of migration in U.K. and U.S. children's picture books in the Trump and Brexit era. *Journal of Children and Media*, 15(4), 549–567.

Parsons, L. T. (2014). Storytelling in global children's literature: Its role in the lives of displaced child characters. *Journal of Children's Literature*, 42(2), 2016.

Said, E. W. (2000). *Reflections on exile and other essays*. Harvard University Press.

Shor, I. (1999). What is critical literacy? In I. Shor & C. Pari (Eds.), *Critical literacy in action: Writing words, changing worlds* (pp. 1–30). Portsmouth, NH: Boynton/Cook-Heinemann.

Sookfong Lee, J. (2021). *Finding home: The journey of immigrants and refugees*. Orca Book Publishers.

Sung, Y. K, Fahrenbruck, M. L., & López-Robertson, J. (2017). Using intertextuality to unpack representations of immigration in children's literature. In H. Johnson, J. Mathis, & K. G. Short (Eds.), *Critical content analysis of children's and young adult literature* (pp. 44–60). New York: Routledge.

Strekalova-Hughes, E. (2019). Unpacking refugee flight: Critical content analysis of picture books featuring refugee protagonists. *International Journal of Multicultural Education, 21*(2), 23–44.

UNHCR. (2022). Refugee data finder. www.unhcr.org/refugee-statistics/.

U.S. Census Bureau. (2014). The "second great wave" of immigration: Growth of the foreign-born population since 1970. www.census.gov/library/visualizations/2014/demo/the-second-great-wave-of-immigration-growth-of-the-foreign-born-population-since-1970.html.

Webb, L. (2019). Testimonio, the assumption of hybridity and the issue of genre. *Studies in Testimony, 2*(1), 3–23.

Yılmaz, R., & Ciğerci, F. M. (2019). A brief history of storytelling: From primitive dance to digital narration. In *Handbook of research on transmedia storytelling and narrative strategies* (pp. 1–14). IGI Global.

Children's Literature Cited

Binford, W. (2021). *Hear my voice/Escucha mi voz.* Workman Publishing Co.

Brown, D. (2021). *The unwanted: Stories of Syrian refugees.* Clarion Books.

Bunting, E. (2006). *One green apple.* Clarion Books.

Cisneros, E. (2021). *Efrén divided.* Quill Tree Books.

Danticat, E. (2015). *Mama's nightingale: A tale of immigration and separation.* Dial Books.

Dassu, A. M. (2021). *Boy, everywhere.* Lee & Low Books.

de Arias, P. (2018). *Marwan's journey.* mineditionUS.

Entrada Kelly, E. (2016). *The land of forgotten girls.* Greenwillow Books.

Gratz, A. (2017). *Refugee.* Scholastic Books.

Kim, P. (2014). *Here I am.* Picture Window Books.

Meddour, W. (2019). *Lubna and Pebble.* Oxford University Press.

Morales, A. (2021). *Ariel is a dreamer: A true story.* Random House Studio.

Morales, Y. (2018). *Dreamers.* Neal Porter Books.

Perkins, M. (2019). *Between us and Abuela: A family story from the border.* Farrar, Straus and Giroux.

Phi, B. (2017). *A different pond.* Capstone Young Readers.

Shihab Nye, N. (2014). *The turtle of Oman.* Greenwillow Books.

Shihab Nye, N. (2022). *The turtle of Michigan.* Greenwillow Books.

Temple, K., & Temple, J. (2019). *Room on our rock.* Kane Miller Books.

Thi Van, M. (2021). *Wishes.* Orchard Books.

Warga, J. (2021). *Other words for home.* Balzer + Bray.

Yang, K. K. (2021). *A map into the world.* Lerner Digital.

Appendix: Foundational Tips for Teaching with Children's Literature

It can be easy to assume that using children's literature is like teaching with any other instructional text. However, to teach with children's literature in thoughtful and purposeful ways, especially around a topic like immigrants and refugees, here are some foundational tips to keep in mind:

1. **Choose high-quality children's literature.** Use questions 1–3 listed in this chapter as a guide to ensure you are selecting books that are not only well written and well illustrated, but also appropriate in terms of the complexity of material and potential for instructional effectiveness.

2. **Remember that no text is ever politically neutral. Neither is your approach to using that text.** Just by virtue of choosing a book about a particular topic, you are communicating a stance on that topic. More importantly, though, is how you help your students navigate the political messages—both explicit and implicit—within that book. Use questions 4–6 in this chapter to help you consider your approach to the book in ways that honor and respect the lived experiences, identities, and humanity of immigrants and refugees in the books, in your classroom, and in your community.

3. **Offer multimodal and multilingual opportunities for responding to children's literature.** On their own, readers respond to what they read in a variety of ways, not just through writing and speaking in English. Providing students with opportunities to respond through diverse modalities (e.g., visual art, digital composition, performance, creative writing, etc.), as well as their home languages, recognizes the numerous ways we make meaning of text and the diverse technological, natural, global, linguistic, and artistic resources we can draw upon to do so. Moreover, doing so takes on an asset-based instructional approach that allows students to showcase and build upon their strengths as learners.

11 A Critical Multicultural Call to Action

Culturally Responsive Teaching for Indigenous Populations

Donna Sabis-Burns (Mohawk)

The movements, such as #WeNeedDiverseBooks, have elevated the bar by offering a deeper focus and expanded landscape for celebrating the intricacies that storytelling brings to the classroom. This is especially true for literature written or illustrated by and/or about Indigenous people. In recent times, not only are we seeing an increase in the publication of more books about Indigenous people, but we are also seeing an increase in the number of Indigenous authors and illustrators. Much too often, books featuring Indigenous people are only pulled off the shelf in October (Columbus) and November (Thanksgiving/Native Heritage Month) (Rampey et al., 2021). With more Indigenous literature resources available to families and educators and more award-winning authors and illustrators being honored, the word is spreading that literature by and about Indigenous people is paving a new way towards diversity, equality, and inclusivity in the classroom.

In the eloquent words from the Indigenous author Joseph Bruchac (Abenaki):

> When I speak of the memory of stories, I mean the way stories themselves remember the things that individuals (and nations) find it so easy to forget. Those lessons of moral conduct, of humility and of courage, of survival itself are held firm in the story's grasp. The old stories, those takes that have truly become tradition, are not just interesting for people to hear—they are as necessary as breath itself, the sacred breath that carries the words of life.
>
> (Bruchac, 1998, p. vii)

We are obligated to educate our youth with a truthful account of history and to teach the richness of realistic, authentic, and contemporary literature for children and young adults. We need to promote books where Indigenous characters are up front and visible in the text, not hidden or pushed aside, and therefore, blending in with the background. We want to highlight in a bold, distinguishable manner characters and stories that unveil and promote the beauty of diverse literature written/illustrated by

DOI: 10.4324/9781003321941-13

and for Native Nations and all other marginalized groups. First, we must review the demographics around Indigenous people and the impact it has in education.

In the U.S. Census of 2020, the Indigenous population (3.7 million) accounted for 1.1% of all people living in the United States. Of that, Indigenous students make up 1.2% of public-school students nationally, equating to approximately 90% of all Indigenous students attending regular public schools and about 8% attending schools administered by the Bureau of Indian Affairs through the Bureau of Indian Education (NIES, 2019). What is important about this figure is the fact that 90% of Indigenous students are in everyday classrooms and not just in highly populated Indigenous schools on or near reservations. Additionally, in the school year 2018–19, the national adjusted cohort graduation rate for public high school students was 86%. More specifically, Asian/Pacific Islander students had the highest rate (93%), followed by White (89%), Hispanic (82%), Black (80%), and American Indian/Alaska Native (74%) students, *the lowest of all groups* (NCES, 2022). Brayboy, Faircloth, Lee, Maaka, and Richardson (2015) note that Native education has been "a battle for the hearts and minds of Indigenous nations" (p. 1). Yazzie (1999) supports the notion and believes that in order to serve Indigenous students better, teachers must make the cognizant connection to match culturally relevant teaching materials and instructional strategies to the values and ideologies of their students.

While the overall Indigenous population is small in comparison to the rest of the U.S. population, the cultural variance is vast. Today, there are currently 574 federally recognized and 60 state-recognized tribal nations in the United States and within this diversity over 260 unique Indigenous languages spoken. Geographic representation ranges from the Aleut of St. Paul Island, Alaska to Native Hawai'ians in O'ahu, Hawai'i, from the Mashpee Wampanoag in Massachusetts to the Seminole Tribe in Florida, and everywhere in between. Each Tribal nation has its own culture and traditions (e.g., varying religious practices, ceremonies, festivals, and spiritual beliefs).

With this much diversity, it would be difficult to know every cultural nuance that exists among our people. Even I, as an enrolled Mohawk Tribal citizen (Haudenosaunee), am unaware of traditions and histories held by my Indigenous brothers and sisters of other tribes; however, it is said that books harbor the power to inspire critical thinking, heighten social sensitivity, and make a child feel proud to be who they are. My mother left the reservation in New York in hopes of raising a family away from the poverty that plagued our tribe. I was always told not to stay out in the sun too long as it would darken my skin too much, which could reflect negatively on me as a "person of color," but it was never really explained why. My grandfather would tell me during our walks together to "stay 10 steps behind the White man," so I would not draw too much attention to myself. We were raised believing we were inferior to White people and that's how it was. It wasn't until I was a teenager before I knew I needed and wanted more information on where I came from and who I was. According to Sir Francis Bacon (1597), "Knowledge is power." Native author, Joseph Bruchac (1998), believes, "We all share a deep respect for the power, a power that often can only be described as sacred, of stories. Language, in the living shape of a song or a story, makes things happen" (p. viii). We want to encourage young people to be curious and seek to build knowledge that exists within their own lineage while also being open to learn from others through stories as a power source. Bringing this knowledge to the classroom can expand the mindset of children and adults and create a space to remember. Kaler-Jones (2021) posits, "the act of remembering taps into what students know from their communities, elders and ancestors" (p. 21). It is a reminder of what we know that has been passed down to us, despite oppressive acts or forgotten history. In addition to knowing the unique cultural experiences both in a historical sense and current times, there is also the issue of understanding the preferred terminology.

Appropriate terminology is a critical factor when discussing themes surrounding indigenous populations in the Americas. When discussing issues related to native peoples, the common terms that have emerged include Native American, American Indian, Indigenous or aboriginal people, Alaska Native, and Native Hawai'ian. The terms Native American and American Indian are often interchanged and are broadly used in professional literature. However, their use is not consistent among native people as many do not consider either term appropriate, and there are some who do not prefer one way over the other. One universal point where agreement seems consistent is the use of the traditional name of their people. Whenever possible, it is most appropriate to identify a person from their tribal group or tribal name. Since this chapter spans across Tribal Nations, Native Hawai'ians, and Alaskan villages, the term "Indigenous" will be used most widely.

Historical Context

History tells a story of civilization. Learning and appreciating historical events can offer an educated perspective into the culture and history of a group of people, often seen as invisible and forgotten. For Indigenous people, this perspective uncovers a unique (and troubled) tribal-federal relationship with the United States government through treaties. These treaties represented formal recognition of the government-to-government relationship between the federal government and Indian tribes that serve as the foundation for tribal sovereignty and self-determination found in contemporary federal Indian law" (Mackey, 2017, p. 787). The trust agreement acknowledged the expectation that the federal government would attend to the physical, educational, social, economic, and community needs while also upholding promises made to Indigenous people within the U.S. to ensure their survival, economic welfare, and social/cultural wellbeing *as long as* Tribal nations relinquished their land, resources, and other assets (Bowman, 2015). The keystone of this tribal-federal relationship is known as *tribal sovereignty*: the right of a people to self-government, self- determination, and self-education. Indigenous people are the only minority group in the United States with a legal relationship to the government based on sovereignty. While Tribal sovereignty continues to be the overarching goal, it remains in a contentious state.

Federal law recognizes tribal sovereignty is inherent; it is not something that another government "gives" to tribes, yet there exists hundreds of unfulfilled treaties and broken promises between tribal governments and the federal government to this day (Sabis-Burns, 2011). Tribal governments pre-date the state and federal government. Although government and education have changed and evolved, the origins continue to be deeply rooted in history, tradition, and culture that still play an important role today but is not always in a fair and equitable manner.

The federal government's responsibility to educate Indian students and the methods of education delivery has varied with federal policies toward Indian tribes. Federal treatment of tribes throughout various periods of federal-tribal policy has been a strong determinant of the type and quality of education Indigenous students received. Table 11.1 provides a brief, historical summary of how federal policy influenced educational policy. These time periods are important not just in historic terms but because each era has a significant and lasting impact on the continued education issues affecting Indigenous students.

Indigenous students have their roots in history unlike other minority groups in the United States. For centuries, Indigenous children suffered with inequitable policies and procedures that have oppressed a population of people into a "sink or swim" method of survival (McCarty, 1993). While these key milestones move to make a more equitable learning landscape for Indigenous children, within this history of education in the United States, there exists a dark period. This is especially important for teachers and pre-service teachers to know in order to fully grasp the neglect, oppression, and massacre the children endured to Captain Pratt's "Kill the Indian, save the man" heinous mantra when he established the first boarding school for Indigenous children, the Carlisle Boarding School in Pennsylvania.

Boarding Schools

Beginning with the Indian Civilization Act of 1819, the United States enacted laws and implemented policies establishing and supporting

Table 11.1 American Indian educational policies created by the federal government.

Federal Government Policy	Description/Definition
Indian Civilization Act of 1819	Defined the goal of Indian education as "civilizing" Indians. This act funded mission schools aimed at assimilating Indians into western culture.
General Allotment Act of 1887 ("Dawes Severalty Act")	Moved Indigenous American lands from communal ownership to individual allotments that could then be sold. Part of the larger goal of assimilating and "civilizing" Indians. Destroyed culture and language transmission.
The Problem of Indian Administration, better known as the Meriam Report of 1928	The first government study to demonstrate with extensive data that federal Indian policy in the 19th century had resulted in a travesty of social justice to Indigenous Americans. It described the poverty and poor living conditions on the reservations, terrible disease and death rates, and grossly inadequate care of the Indigenous children in the boarding schools.
Indian Reorganization Act of 1934 ("Indian New Deal")	Reversed the Allotment Act of 1887 and enabled Tribes to organize for their common welfare, adopt federally approved constitutions and bylaws, and make education decisions locally.
Johnson O'Malley Act of 1934	Provides supplementary funding for Indigenous education at schools that are on or near Indian reservations.
Impact Aid Act of 1950	Provides funding to local school districts in lieu of property taxes for schools that are on or near Indigenous reservations.
Elementary and Secondary Education Act of 1965: Title IX	Signaled the beginning of building federal infrastructure to accommodate Indigenous participation in decision-making. Directed formation of the National Advisory Council on Indian Education (NACIE).
Title VII Indian Education Act of 1972	Provides funding for three major areas: a formula grant for PK-12 Indigenous student services, Demonstration grants for new and innovative projects, and professional development grants for Indigenous teachers and educational leaders.
Indian Self-Determination & Education Assistance Act of 1975	Provides a mechanism for the federal government to contract with Tribes for the administration of programs that were formerly administered by the Secretary of the Interior.

Federal Government Policy	Description/Definition
Native American Languages Act of 1990	Allows for exceptions to teacher certification requirements for federal programs, for teachers of Native American languages, encourages state and territorial governments to do the 35 same.
No Child Left Behind Act of 2001 (reauthorization of ESEA)	Addresses Native American education in all 10 title sections; provides for unprecedented levels of data reporting and accountability for all subgroups, including Native American students.
The Esther Martinez Native American Languages Preservation Act (2006)	Provided grant funding for a range of language and culture initiatives: Native American language nests, language survival schools, restoration programs, Native American language immersion programs, and Native American language and culture camps.
Executive Order 13592 of 2011	Authorized a White House initiative on American Indian and Alaska Native education intended to help expand educational opportunities and improve educational outcomes for all Indian students.
The Every Student Succeeds Act (ESSA) of 2015	Articulated provisions aimed "to ensure that Indian students gain knowledge and understanding of Native communities, languages, tribal histories, traditions, and cultures." In addition, it provided the establishment of language immersion programs and "activities that recognize and support the unique cultural and educational needs of Indian children and incorporate appropriately qualified tribal elders and seniors."
Executive Order 14049—White House Initiative on Advancing Educational Equity, Excellence, and Economic Opportunity for Native Americans and Strengthening Tribal Colleges and Universities (2021)	To advance equity, excellence, and justice in our Nation's education system and to further Tribal self-governance, including by supporting activities that expand educational opportunities and improve educational outcomes for all Native American students.

Note: Adapted from *American Indian policy scan: PK-12 education policies impacting American Indian students in Wisconsin* by N. Bowman & M. Reinhardt (2014); Midwest Comprehensive Center at American Institutes for Research, and R. M. Lowery & D. Sabis-Burns (2019).

boarding schools for the Indigenous children across the nation. The purpose of these boarding schools was to assimilate Indigenous children by forcibly removing and relocating them far away from their families and communities to distant residential facilities where their Native American, Alaska Native, and Native Hawaiian identities, languages and beliefs were stripped and replaced with the intent to "Christianize" them to a Western American culture. Children lost their Native-given names and were forced to take on Euro-American names. The hair of the children was drastically cut (keep in mind the cultural significance of hair in the Indigenous culture) or shaved, and their tribal clothes were removed, burned, and replaced with Western clothing. Unsanitary and overpopulated living conditions, sexual abuse, and starvation led to the spread of disease to which many students did not survive (Blakemore, 2021). Bounties were sometimes offered for students who tried to run away and return to their families hundreds of miles away, and many students ultimately took their own lives.

This dark era continues to haunt us today. In 2021, discoveries of mass graves have been found on old boarding school grounds. Jumping forward to the twenty-first century, great strides have been made to right these horrific wrongs. In 2022, Secretary of the Interior, Deb Haaland (Pueblo of Laguna), announced a Federal Indian Boarding School Initiative, a comprehensive review of the troubled legacy of federal boarding school policies. This initiative serves as an investigation about the loss of human life and the lasting consequences of residential Indian boarding schools in the hopes that repatriation and healing can begin for the survivors and their families. The primary goal is to identify boarding school facilities and sites; the location of known and possible student burial sites located at or near school facilities; and the identities and Tribal affiliations of children interred at such locations, so families of those lost and those who survived can perhaps begin the healing process (U.S. Department of Interior, 2021). Today, we emerge in a much better place with a better understanding of cultural representation in schools than the boarding school era, but the work is far from complete.

Culturally Responsive Teaching

One of the primary ways teachers share information with their students is through reading; however, sadly, the 2019 National Indian Education Study collected data from a survey of fourth and eighth-grade teachers of Indigenous students on how often they integrate Indigenous materials on culture and history into their reading/language arts lessons. Approximately 52% of fourth-grade teachers and 73% of eighth-grade teachers reported doing it once a year or never at all. When asked the same about how often they integrated history and culture into their mathematics materials, 85% of fourth-grade teachers and 88% of eighth-grade students reported doing it once a year or never at all. Teachers can be better equipped to inspire curiosity in the topic of Indigenous culture by participating in professional development on instructional practices specifically designed for Indigenous students. Culturally specific instructional practices include assignment of reading and other activities that are contextualized in Indigenous cultural information (Apthorp, et al., 2002), and using such strategies can lead Indigenous students to develop interest in exploring the topic further (NIES, 2019).

It is important to understand that indigenous worldview is different from the mainstream, dominant Western worldview. Yazzie (1999) pointed to the growing body of research suggesting better learning occurs when teachers transform their educational practices and curriculum to reflect the children's home culture. Many scholars found the current curriculum, pedagogy, student support, resources, and lack of Native American role models add up to a culturally inappropriate education for many public-school students, including Native American students (Bowman, 2003; Butterfield, 1994; Reyhner & Eder, 2004). As history paints a clearer picture, Indigenous people have faced unmet educational needs, substandard educational conditions, and voices for change, which have been widely ignored. This means that children of indigenous communities may not perceive things the same way as their counter parts perceive them. Therefore, the "one size fits all" does not work in education, especially for children of indigenous communities (Singh & Espinoza-Herold, 2014). For example. Kawagley, et al. (2010) argue that the worldview of Native Alaskans is unique: "They have their own terminology for constellations and have an understanding of the seasonal positioning of these constellations, the behavior of ice and snow, and the meaning of different cloud formations" (pp. 224–225). Barnhardt and Kawagley (2005) agree there is a mismatch between the processes of mainstream schooling and educational needs of Indigenous children in the United States. They note the teaching methods of mainstream schools have not recognized or appreciated knowledge systems such as those of Indigenous students that focus on inter-relationships and interconnectivity. Au (2009) argued teachers should build on the background knowledge and experiences gained in the home and community in order to "close the achievement gap between students of diverse backgrounds and their mainstream peers" (p. 179). In other words, educators who do not recognize and value the cultural background of Indigenous and other culturally diverse students can instigate a vicious cycle of self-doubt that leads their students to discount their home and community learning experiences, capacities, and gifts (Battiste, 2002).

In addition to sharing Indigenous cultural information, teachers have the opportunity to share cultural knowledge in the context of teaching core subjects. For example, when teachers integrate information about Indigenous culture and history into reading/language arts and mathematics lessons, Indigenous students have an additional opportunity to consider the importance of their people's traditions and ideas (NIES, 2019). In addition, the NIES asked fourth and eighth-grade teachers in both low and high-density populated schools with Indigenous students how many times they attended professional or community-based development programs aimed at developing culturally specific instructional practices for Indigenous students. An average of 82% reported either have never attended or attended once in two years any type of professional development training. For teachers of language and literacy, culturally relevant training is vital to remain informed and able to provide a quality and equitable education for all students. Children's literature becomes a bridge to that responsibility by sharing both the history and contemporary culture and traditions of children of color that make up the classroom population. The reader's sense of truth in how a specific cultural experience has been represented within a book, particularly when the reader is an insider to the culture portrayed in that book, is probably the most common understanding of cultural authenticity (Fox & Short, 2004).

Stereotypes and Indigenous People

I would like to share a story when I encountered negative stereotype merchandise while shopping with my daughter. While this experience is a bit dated, the message is still the same:

> *One summer day, my daughter and I were walking through a very crowded shopping center in the middle of a downtown, metropolitan center when something caught my eye. A poster with a light teal background and dark brown lettering was hanging in the store front window. This poster was posed with the intent of advertising the store's merchandise– beer. At first glance the earth-tone colors blended with the other posters on display. The surrounding posters displayed statements (I believe they were intended to be humorous) regarding drinking too much beer, the promotion of a certain type of beer, and how beer is "good for life." However, this poster was unique in its kind. As I read it, my immediate response was to shuffle my 18-year-old daughter away from where she was standing and move her past the window. After she quickly reminded me of her newly attained adulthood status, I explained to her the anger, humiliation, and embarrassment I felt, and it ran quite deep at that moment. On the front of this poster in bold, dark letters read, "My Indian name is Runs with Beer." I immediately and carefully studied the other posters displayed near this particular one. No other comments or statements referenced any other racial or ethnic group, those posters simply sported statements about beer. Many questions began to cloud my mind ... What message is this sending to the hundreds of thousands of people who pass by this window? What message does it send about the Native American people in general? What about the respect for their beliefs, ideals, or culture? What message does this send to the Indigenous people? More importantly, what is this saying to the children? My daughter begged me not to engage with the store manager, but I couldn't help myself. While he listened (uncomfortably I might add), I used this as an unexpected teachable moment and explained the importance of this negative stereotype.*

I share this to say that negative stereotypes, no matter if in a book, a poster, or on a t-shirt, have no place in our world. According to Barton and Brophy-Herb (2006), within the first 18 months of life, most infants who have explored shared books and environmental print with adults show a uniquely human understanding that pictures and images symbolize things in the real world. If a child is exposed to literature with incorrect representations of race and culture repeatedly throughout their youth, it is safe to say they will most likely associate these inaccurate pictures as truth. Historically, children's literature includes a predominance of stereotyped representations, both positive and negative, and in inaccurate ways (Hirschfelder, et al., 1999). While dated, Mo and Shen (1997) speak to these issues in their report, *"Reexamining the Issue of Authenticity in Picture Books."* These authors present definite distinctions between cultural inauthenticity and stereotypical representation in texts, highlighting the presence of racism and cultural inaccuracies, which stands over the test of time. Moreover, stereotyping, caricature, and marginalization of minoritized groups have been persistent problems in children's literature throughout the field's long history (Bradford, 2001; Forest, et al., 2015). As a former early childhood teacher, I witnessed the effect of an inaccurate or stereotyped book on students. Those students do not feel they have a voice, do not feel included, and may not know how to articulate that feeling of marginalization, especially at a young age.

According to Fox and Short (2004), every child reserves the right to see themselves positively and accurately portrayed in stories and to find truth based on their own experiences instead of negative stereotypes and misrepresentation. Historically, literature involving multicultural characters or events written from a European American perspective tends to perpetuate the European American dominance within society (Lim & Ling, 1992). What makes a good story? It includes accurate portrayals of history, representation of contemporary issues, a display of authentic cultural values, and no negative stereotypes. As children gain the knowledge to critically approach books that involve these events, it is believed that children become able to challenge the status quo and seek more meaningful experiences as they learn their culture or culture that is different than their own (Sabis-Burns, 2009).

Like many cultures, Indigenous culture is rich and deeply embedded in ancient traditions among its people. Their values, ideas, government, traditions, foods, clothing, music, art, and recreation have been well documented over the past few centuries. However, stereotypical images of young children in headdresses, passive girls in long, black braids, and the portrayal of Native people as savage beasts are reported in many children's books today (McMahon, et al., 1996). By definition, a stereotype is a "fixed image, idea, trait or convention, lacking in originality or individuality, most often negative" (Dowd, 1992, p. 220), which takes away the human qualities of individuals and promotes an unclear understanding of social realities (Verrall & McDowell, 1990). Books with such presentations are deemed inaccurate and disrespectful and are said to deny the rich diversity among specific Native tribes (Lindsay, 2003; Reese, 1999; Stewart, 2002). As Norton (1990) specified, literature is identified as a key component to increasing cultural awareness. It must be carefully selected to accurately reflect customs and values of other Native cultures while heightening students' understanding of their beliefs and lifestyles. Furthermore, "using literature that gives inaccurate information can be more harmful than the failure to represent other cultures at all" (Hilliard, 1995, p. 729). Lastly, along dimensions of the stereotype content model (Fiske et al. 2002), Indigenous were viewed as less competent, less competitive, and lower in social status than Asian Americans and less competent and lower in social status than African Americans (Erhart & Hall, 2019). As a result, the need to recognize the stereotypes that are often identified in books featuring Indigenous themes in the classroom becomes essential.

The earliest stereotypes of Indigenous came from missionaries and explorers who portrayed Native people as uncivilized, superstitious, simplistic, perfect for conversion to Christianity, and dependent on the European influences. When the landing of Christopher Columbus took place and the European rivalries over land began in North America, Indigenous became known as "blood thirsty savages" greatly feared by their enemies (Reese, 1998). For the most part, children are influenced by these stereotypes of Indigenous people, which lead them to believe that either our people cease to exist after 1890 or Indigenous people are exotic people who wear feathers and smoke peace pipes (Caldwell-Wood & Mitten, 1991; Reese, 1998). Because children's books play an important role in shaping children's perception of various cultures, books are more than just entertainment; they are vehicles that transfer cultural knowledge, awareness, and thought and bear the responsibility of upholding the truth of our nation's past.

Howard (1991) posited an authentic book contains a story set within the distinctiveness of characters and settings and reflects the universality of experience throughout the pages. The broad and specific combine to create a story where "readers from the culture will know that it is true, will identify, and will be affirmed, and readers from another culture will feel that it is true, will identify, and learn something of value" (p. 92). If the story is not accurate or wrongly portrays a history or culture, Howard argued that children can not only walk away with inaccurate information, but this erroneous information can follow them throughout their schooling. One of our most important responsibilities as teachers is to continually seek truths and empower our students as they search for truths both within and about themselves, their cultures, and the worlds outside themselves (Susag, 1998). Teachers can be that source of cultural knowledge for Indigenous students by learning how to select appropriate material and to foster a safe learning environment.

Selection Criteria

Kaiwi and Kahumoku (2006) found the introduction of a Native Hawaiian approach to examine literature, by acknowledging and validating students' perspectives, empowers them by demonstrating a constant connection to ancestors, develops a greater respect for parents and grandparents, and increases intrinsic learning. Because there is a strong relation between books we choose to read and critical literacy (Leland, et al., 2012), the way that teachers select and choose texts matters, for this "underpins our goals of growing literate beings who are competent and confident readers and writers, who think critically, and who have a commitment to making the world an equitable place for all" (p. 60). Further, diversifying our lenses for text selection matters because children's literature can "enable children to see representations of social cooperation and the interconnectedness of humanity while also fostering critical discernment and empathetic sensibilities about the ways in which difference is often produced by inequality" (Ghiso, et al., 2012, p. 21).

Selecting texts that students will find culturally relevant can be a challenge for teachers (Tatum, 2008). Since Indigenous lifestyles may not be well known across the country, it is prudent for educators to refer to existing resources that can assist in evaluating books about Native peoples. One of the most comprehensive resources for evaluating children's literature featuring Native peoples is *Through Indian Eyes: The Native Experience in Books for Children* by Beverly Slapin and Doris Seale (1998). Taken directly from their list of selection criteria (and adding a couple of extra questions), when selecting books or materials that include Indigenous people, one should begin by asking the questions shown in Table 11.2.

The Good News

The University of Wisconsin's Cooperative Children's Book Center (CCBC) has compiled statistics on the percentage of multicultural children's literature over the past two decades. Data taken from their reports shows that over the last four years, there is an increase in books by and/or about Indigenous people. In 2018, children's books *by* Indigenous authors went from 27 to 47 in 2021, and books *about* Indigenous people rose from 32 to 64 respectively. In the past when a new Indigenous-themed book was published, it stood alone on the shelf. Today, however, there are many beautifully talented illustrators and authors with Indigenous roots being discovered every day.

Conclusion

History is truly in the eyes of the beholder (and the ones who have written language to document their perspective). Indigenous people used oral

Table 11.2 Guide to selecting children's books representing Indigenous populations.

Selection Criterion	Questions to consider
General considerations	• What was the author's purpose in writing it and what perspectives does the author bring to it? Are his/her ethnic affiliations identified? • Is there appropriate identification of a specific tribe or tribes? • What do Native American reviewers or readers say about this book? (www.oyate.org) • Does the student shares cultural markers with the main character, such as race, ethnicity, or religion (Ebe, 2010)?
Look at picture books	• Are children shown "playing Indian"? • Are animals dressed as "Indians"? • Do "Indians" have ridiculous names, like "Indian Two Feet," or "Little Chief"?
Look at stereotypes—Is there anything in this book that would employ stereotypical thinking in a non-Native child? Is there anything in this book that would embarrass or hurt a Native child?	• Are Native peoples portrayed as savages, or primitive craftspeople, or simple tribal people, now extinct? • Are Native peoples shown as human beings, members of highly defined and complex societies? • Are Native people all one color, one style? • Does the author avoid a generalized portrayal of American Indian peoples as being all alike?
Look for loaded words	• Are there insulting overtones to the language? • Is the language respectful?
Look for tokenism	• Are Native people depicted as stereotypically alike, or do they look just like White people with brown faces? • Are Native people depicted as genuine individuals?
Look for distortion of history	• Is the story truthful? • Is the book respectful? • Is history put in the proper perspective: the Native struggle for self-determination and sovereignty against the Euro-American drive for conquest? • Does the story show the ways in which Native people actively resisted the invaders?
Look at lifestyles	• Are Native cultures presented in a condescending manner? • Is the focus on respect for Native peoples and understanding of the sophistication and complexity of their societies? • Are Native peoples discussed in the past tense only, supporting the "vanished Indian" myth? Is the past unconnected to the present? • Are Native religions, Creation stories, and traditions described accurately, in the context of their civilizations?

Selection Criterion	Questions to consider
Look at the dialogue	• Do the People speak in either a sort of "early jawbreaker" or in the oratorical style of the "noble savage"? • Do the People use language with the consummate and articulate skill of those who come from an oral tradition?
Look for standards of success	In modern times, are Native peoples portrayed as childlike and helpless? Does a White authority figure—pastor, social worker, teacher—know better than Native people themselves what is "good for them?" Are Indian children "better off" away from their families? • Does it take "White" standards for Native people to get ahead? • Are Native values of cooperation, generosity, sharing, honesty, and courage seen as integral to growth and development?
Look at the role of women	• Are women completely subservient to men? Do they do all the work, while the men look around, waiting for the next hunt? • Are women portrayed as the integral and respected part of Native societies that they really are?
Look at the role of elders	• Are elders treated as a dispensable burden upon their People to be abandoned in times of trouble or famine; querulous, petulant, demanding, nagging, irritating, and boring?
Look for the effects on a child's self-image	• Is there anything in the story that would embarrass or hurt a Native child? • Are there one or more positive role models with whom a Native child can identify?
Look at the author's or illustrator's background	• Is the background of the author and illustrator devoid of the qualities that enable them to write about Native peoples in an accurate, respectful manner? Is there an ethnocentric bias which leads to distortions or omissions? • Is there anything in the author's and illustrator's background that qualifies them to write about native peoples? Do their perspectives strengthen the work?

language and storytelling to communicate, so when history happened, their side of the story was often never told. When we teach history, or any topic for that matter, we must be aware and informed of who makes up our classrooms. We must ask, who are the students in front of us? It takes time to go through curriculum folders and research family background, but it is an imperative function of what makes a truly culturally responsive teacher. There is a plethora of resources available to parents, educators and librarians to make informative, responsible choices on what and how to teach all children. As mentioned in the beginning of this chapter, the bar has been elevated by offering a deeper focus and expanded landscape for celebrating the intricacies that storytelling brings to the table. We hope to keep the bar moving. Joseph Bruchac (1998) believes:

> The lessons taught by so many Native American stories, both traditional and contemporary, have never been more needed in our classrooms. The stories remember histories that others have forgotten. They teach us again the importance of community and generosity, the importance of the individual and the balancing of virtues of courage and compassion, self-respect and self-control. The strength of women, the true values of family, the recognition that we human beings are not alone in the world but part of a complex and interdependent web of life are themes easily found—not once, but again and again.
>
> (Bruchac, 1998, p. ix)

We need to open a space for children to learn truthfully, to provide them with critical thinking tools to learn to push back against negative stereotypes, and to critique and share the narrative through their eyes. This will help us keep the forward momentum.

Reflection Questions

1. The author states that 90% of Indigenous students attend public schools. Why is this statistic important for you and your teaching?
2. Reread the section on Culturally Responsive Teaching. What are two specific items you should consider adding to your current teaching (or future teaching) practices to support all students?
3. Using one of the books in Table 11.3, critique the book using the questions posed in Table 11.2.
4. Review the Appendix. Look specifically at one resource provided. What did you learn and share with your colleagues/classmates?

Table 11.3 Recommended pieces multicultural literature for elementary aged classrooms.

Book Information:	Summary
Title: *We Are Water Protectors* **Author and Illustrator:** Written by Carole Lindstrom (Anishinabe/Métis) and illustrated by Michaela Goade (Tlingit) **Awards:** Caldecott Award-Illustrator; Kirkus Prize Finalist **Grade Level Band:** K-3	**Summary:** Carole Lindstrom and Michaela Goade have given the world a gift in this powerful story of protecting water rights on the reservation. Breathtaking illustrations and thoughtful and provocative text share the voice of a young girl who takes on the social justice fight to protect her environment.

Book Information:	Summary
Title: *Fry Bread* **Author and Illustrator:** Written by Kevin Noble Maillard (Seminole Nation of OK) and illustrated by Juana Martinez-Neal **Awards:** 2020 Robert F. Sibert Informational Book Award; Picture Book Honor choice for the 2020 American Indian Youth Literature award **Grade Level Band:** K-3	**Summary:** A wonderful depiction mixing a modern-day Indigenous family and the timeless culture and tradition of making fry bread into a delightful story. Using lively verse and beautifully-crafted illustrations from a Caldecott-winning illustrator, Kevin Maillard's debut picture book is full of fun, wonderment, and yumminess as he takes you through the importance of fry bread (and includes a recipe in the back!).
Title: *Ancestor Approved: Intertribal Stories for Kids* **Author and Illustrator:** Edited by Cynthia Leitich Smith (Muscogee Nation); Cover art by Nicole Neidhardt **Awards:** 2022 ILA Notable Books for a Global Society; 2022 ALA Notable Children's Books; Kirkus Reviews Best Middle-Grade Anthologies of 2021 **Grade Level Band:** 3–5	**Summary:** Entries from some of the best Indigenous writers featuring Joseph Bruchac, Art Coulson, Christine Day, Eric Gansworth, Dawn Quigley, Carole Lindstrom, Rebecca Roanhorse, David A. Robertson, Andrea L. Rogers, Kim Rogers, Cynthia Leitich Smith, Monique Gray Smith, Traci Sorell, Tim Tingle, Erika T. Wurth, and Brian Young. In a backdrop of a local powwow, these intersecting stories and poems reflect joy, resilience, strength in and around community, and exude Native pride.
Title: *Herizon* **Author and Illustrator:** Daniel Vandever (Diné) and Illustrated by Corey Begay (Diné) **Awards:** Picture Book Winner for the 2022 American Indian Youth Literature award **Grade Level Band:** 2–5	**Summary:** This wordless picture book details the journey of a Diné girl as she helps retrieve her grandmother's sheep with the aid of a magical headscarf, a symbol of ancestral knowledge and support. The author wrote *Herizon* for his nieces to reflect self-advocacy, empowerment, and something that spoke to a brighter future for young women. *Herizon* is an ode to Missing and Murdered Indigenous Relatives (MMIR) and in honor of those without a voice.
Title: *Bowwow Powwow* **Author and Illustrator:** Written by Brenda Child (Red Lake Ojibwe) and illustrated by Jonathan Thunder (Red Lake Ojibwe) **Awards:** 2020 American Indian Youth Literature Award winner for Picture Book; 2019 American Library Association Notable Children's Book; 2019 Cooperative Children's Book Center Best of the Year **Grade Level Band:** K-2	**Summary:** This story is about a girl and her dog, making their way to a powwow. She sees veterans in a Grand Entry, a visiting drum group, and traditional, grass, and jingle-dress dancers. She shares the moments with friends and family. The story is translated into Ojibwe by Gordon Jourdain (Lac La Croix First Nation) and offers an imaginative lens to a central tradition of powwow, but with an imaginative and whimsical dream sequence.

Book Information:	Summary
Title: *Birdsong* **Author and Illustrator:** Written and illustrated by Julie Flett (Cree Métis) **Awards:** 2020 TD Canadian Children's Literature Award; 2020 American Indian Youth Literature Award **Grade Level Band:** K-2	**Summary:** After moving to a new town, Katherena befriends an elderly neighbor, Agnes, who helps her navigate her new surroundings through the shared passion of art and the love of being outdoors. Flett offers the reader warmth and vibrancy through a powerful story of intergenerational relationships.
Title: *Classified: The Secret Career of Mary Golda Ross, Cherokee Aerospace Engineer* **Author and Illustrator:** Written by Traci Sorell (Cherokee Nation) and illustrated by Natasha Donovan (Métis) **Awards:** 2022 American Indian Youth Literature Picture Book Honor Book **Grade Level Band:** 2–5	**Summary:** Since a teenager in the 1920s, Mary Golda Ross, a Cherokee woman, excelled at math and attended college at age 16, majoring in engineering. Eventually she was selected to be part of a secret team researching orbiting satellites for the space race, which was classified, much of it remains classified today. Mary became a role model for young women, as well as becoming a beacon supporting Native people across the country.
Title: *We Are Still Here! Native American Truths Everyone Should Know* **Author and Illustrator:** Traci Sorell (Cherokee Nation) and illustrated by Frané Lessac **Awards:** 2022 American Indian Youth Literature Picture Book Honor Book; 2022 Robert F. Sibert Honor Book **Grade Level Band:** 2–5	**Summary:** Twelve Indigenous kids present historical and contemporary history through laws, policies, struggles, and resiliencies in being a Native American, each with a powerful refrain: We are still here! This non-fiction book takes on topics that are often missing, untruthful, or not accurate in books found in schools and transforms them into a precise, honest approach to history of Indigenous people. This is a companion book to the award-winning *We Are Grateful: Otsaliheliga*. It presents topics including: forced assimilation (such as boarding schools), land allotment and Native tribal reorganization (tribal sovereignty), termination (the U.S. government not recognizing tribes as nations), Native urban relocation (from reservations), self-determination (tribal self-empowerment), Native civil rights, the Indian Child Welfare Act (ICWA), religious freedom, economic development (including casino development), Native language revival efforts, cultural persistence, and nationhood (less).

Book Information:	Summary
Title: *Healer of the Water Monster* **Author and Illustrator:** Brian Young (Diné) **Awards:** 2022 American Indian Youth Literature Award Winner: Best Middle Grade Book **Grade Level Band:** 3–6	**Summary:** Nathan visits his grandmother on the Navajo reservation in New Mexico. With no internet or cell service, he finds ways to explore and keep himself busy. While lost in the desert, he stumbles upon a Navajo Creation story Holy Being, a Water Monster, needing help. Nathan is determined to help his friend while discovering his strength to overcome adversity even he wasn't expecting to find.
Title: *Sisters of the Neversea* **Author and Illustrator: Cynthia Leitich Smith (Muscogee Nation);** **Front Cover by** **Awards:** 2021 Best Books in Publishers Weekly, Kirkus Reviews, Chicago Public Library, American Indians in Children's Literature and more. **Grade Level Band:** 3–8	**Summary:** A reimagined story of the fairytale, Peter Pan, with a whimsical and contemporary twist. Native American Lily and English Wendy navigate the island of *Neverland* and engage with Merfolk, Fairies, wild animals, and kidnapped children. It explores and challenges the original story's colonial undertones, prejudice, and racist depictions of Native American people, making it a breath of fresh air for the old-fashioned tales of the past.

References

Au, K. (2009). Isn't culturally responsive instruction just good teaching? *Social Education*, 73(4), 179–183.

Apthorp, H. S., D'Amato, E. D., & Richardson, A. E. (2002). Effective standards-based practices for Native American students: A review of research literature (ED469297). https://files.eric.ed.gov/fulltext/ED469297.pdf.

Apthorp, H. S. (2016). *Where American Indian students go to school: Enrollment in seven Central Region states* (REL 2016-2113). Washington, DC: U.S. Department of Education, Institute of Education Sciences, National Center for Education Evaluation and Regional Assistance, Regional Educational Laboratory Central. http://ies.ed.gov/ncee/edlabs.

Bacon, F. (1597). *Meditationes sacrae.* Excusum impensis Humfredi Hooper.

Barnhardt, R., & Kawagley, A. O. (2005). Indigenous Knowledge Systems and Alaska Native Ways of Knowing. *Anthropology & Education Quarterly*, 36(1), 8–23.

Battiste, M. (2002). *Indigenous knowledge and pedagogy in First Nations education: A literature review with recommendations.* Ottawa, ON: Indian and Northern Affairs Canada.

Barton, L. R., & Brophy-Herb, H. E. (2006). Developmental foundations for language and literacy from birth to three years. In S. E. Rosenkoetter & J. Knapp-Philo (Eds.), *Learning to read the world: Language and literacy in the first three years* (15–60). Zero to Three.

Blakemore, E. (2021). A century of trauma at U.S. boarding schools for Native American Children in the United States. www.nationalgeographic.com/history/article/a-century-of-trauma-at-boarding-schools-for-native-american-children-in-the-united-states.

Bowman, N. R. (2003). Cultural differences of teaching and learning: A Native American perspective on participating in educational systems and organizations. *American Indian Quarterly*, 27(1 & 2), 91–102.

Bowman, N. R. (2015). Wunj iin Daaptoonaakanum Niiloona Eelaachiimwuyeengwu [Our story from my voice]: Indigenous educational policy development with Tribal governments: A case study (Doctoral dissertation). Retrieved from University of Wisconsin-Madison/ProQuest/UMI.

Bowman, N. R., & Reinhardt, M. (2014). *American Indian policy scan: PK-12 education policies impacting American Indian students in Wisconsin*. Washington, DC: American Institutes for Research.

Bradford, C. (2001). *Reading race: Aboriginality in Australian children's literature*. Melbourne University Press.

Brayboy, B., Faircloth, S., Lee, T., Maaka, M., & Richardson, T. (2015). Sovereignty and education: An overview of the unique nature of Indigenous education. *Journal of American Indian Education*, 54(1), 19.

Bruchac, J. (1998). Forward. In D. M. Susag, *Roots and branches: A resource of Native American literature themes, lessons, and bibliographies* (pp. vii–ix). Washington, DC: National Council of Teachers of English. https://eric.ed.gov/?id=ED423543.

Butterfield, R. A. (1994). *Blueprints for Indian education: Improving mainstream schooling*. Charleston, WV: ERIC Clearinghouse on Rural Education and Small Schools. (ERIC Document Reproduction Service No. ED372898).

Caldwell-Wood, N. & Mitten, L.A. (1991). *"I" is not for Indian: The portrayal of North Americans in books for young people*. Compiled for the American Indian Library Association.

Cooperative Children's Book Center. (2022). *Books by and about Black, Indigenous and People of Color 2018*. School of Education, University of Wisconsin-Madison. https://ccbc.education.wisc.edu/literature-resources/ccbc-diversity-statistics/books-by-and-or-about-poc-2018/.

Dowd, F.S. (1992). "We're not in Kansas anymore": Evaluating children's books portraying Native American and Asian cultures. *Childhood Education*, 68(4), 219–224.

Ebe, A. E. (2010). Culturally relevant texts and reading assessment for English language learners. *Reading Horizons: A Journal of Literacy and Language Arts*, 50(3). Retrieved from https://scholarworks.wmich.edu/reading_horizons/vol50/iss3/5

Erhart, R.S., & Hall, D.L. (2019). A descriptive and comparative analysis of the content of stereotypes bout Native Americans. *Race and Social Problems*, 11, 225–242.

Fiske, S. T., Cuddy, A. C., Glick, P., & Xu, J. (2002). A model of (often mixed) stereotype content: Competence and warmth respectively follow from perceived status and competition. *Journal of Personality and Social Psychology*, 82(6), 878–902.

Forest, D. E., Garrison, K. L., & Kimmel, S. C. (2015). "The university for the poor": Portrayals of class in translated children's literature. *Teachers College Record*, 117(2), 1–40.

Fox, D. L., & Short, K. G. (2004). *Stories matter: The complexity of cultural authenticity in children's literature*. National Council of Teachers of English.

Gay, G. (2010). *Culturally responsive teaching: Theory, research, & practice* (2nd ed.). Teachers College Press.

Ghiso, M. P., Campano, G., & Hall, T. (2012). Braided histories and experiences in literature for children and adolescents. *Journal of Children's Literature*, 38(2), 14–22.

Hilliard, L.L. (1995). Defining the "multi" in "multicultural" through children's literature. *The Reading Teacher*, 48(8), 728–729.

Hirschfelder, A., Molin, P.F., Wakim, Y., Dorris, M.A., and Beamer, Y. (1999). *American Indian stereotypes in the world of children: A Reader and bibliography.* The Scarecrow Press.

Howard, E. F. (1991). Authentic multicultural literature for children: An author's perspective. In M. V. Lindgren (Ed.), *The multicolored mirror: Cultural substance in literature for children and young adults* (pp. 91–99). Fort Atkinson, WI: Highsmith Press.

Kaiwi, M. K., & Kahumoku, W. (2006). Makawalu: Standards, curriculum, and assessment for literature through an indigenous perspective. *Hülili: Multidisciplinary Research on Hawaiian Wellbeing*, 3, 182–206.

Kaler-Jones, C. (2021). Through the lens of those we love: Uplifting oral histories and finding common threads. *Rethinking Schools*, 36(1), 20–27.

Kawagley, A. O., Norris-Tull, D., & Norris-Tull, R. (2010). The Indigenous world-view of Yupiaq culture. In R. Barnhardt & A. O. Kawagley (Eds.), *Alaska Native education: Views from within* (219–235). Alaska Native Knowledge Network, Center for Cross-cultural Studies, University of Alaska.

Khubba, S., Heim, K. and Hong, J. (2022). 2020 Post-enumeration survey estimation report, PES20-G-01, National census coverage estimates for people in the United States by demographic characteristics. www2.census.gov/programs-sur veys/decennial/coverage-measurement/pes/census-coverage-estimates-for-people-in-the-united-states-by-state-and-census-operations.pdf.

Kottak, C. P., & Kozaitis, K. A. (2012). *On being different: Diversity & multiculturalism in the North American mainstream* (4th Ed.). McGraw-Hill.

Leland, C., Lewison, M., & Harste, J. (2012). *Teaching children's literature: It's critical!* Routledge.

Lim, S. G., & Ling, A. L. (1992). *Reading the literatures of Asian Americans.* Philadelphia, PA: Open University Press.

Lindsay, N. (2003). 'I' still isn't for Indian: A look at recent publishing about Native Americans. *School Library Journal*, 49(11), 42–43.

Mackey, H. (2017). The ESSA in Indian country: Problematizing self-determination through the relationships between federal, state, and tribal governments. *Educational Administration Quarterly*, 53(5), 782–808.

McCarty, T. (1993) Federal language policy and American Indian education. *Bilingual Research Journal*, 17(1–2), 13–34.

McMahon, R., Saunders, D, and Bardwell, T. (1996). Increasing young children's cultural awareness with American Indian literature. *Childhood Education*, 73, 105–108.

Mo, W., & Shen, W. (1997). Reexamining the Issue of Authenticity in Picture Books. *Children's Literature in Education*, 28, 85–93.

Myers, W. D. (2014). Where are the people of color in children's books?www.nytim es.com/2014/03/16/opinion/Sunday/where-are-the-people-of-color-in-childrens-books.html.

NCES. (2022). Public high school graduation rates. https://nces.ed.gov/programs/coe/indicator/coi.

Nieto, S. (2010). *Language, culture, and teaching: Critical perspectives* (2nd ed.). Taylor & Francis Group.

Norton, D. E. (1990). Teaching multicultural literature in the reading curriculum. *The Reading Teacher, 44*(1), 28–40.

Rampey, B. D., Faircloth, S. C., Whorton, R. P., and Deaton, J. (2021). *National Indian Education Study 2019* (NCES 2021–018). Institute of Education Sciences, National Center for Education Statistics.

Reese, D. (1998). "Mom, Look! It's George, and he's a TV Indian!": *The Horn Book Magazine, 74*(5), 636–644.

Reese, D. (1999). Authenticity and sensitivity: Goals for writing and reviewing books with Native American themes. *School Library Journal, 45*(11), 36–37.

Reyhner, J., & Eder, J. (2004). *American Indian education: A history.* University of Oklahoma Press.

Sabis-Burns, D. (2009). Once upon an encounter: A content analysis of selected children's literature portraying the encounter of Christopher Columbus and the Taino people. Retrieved from www.proquest.com/dissertations-theses/once-upon-encounter-content-analysis-selected/docview/304878743/se-2

Sabis-Burns, D. (2011). Taking a critical look at Native Americans in children's literature. In L. A. Smolen, & R. A. Oswald (Eds.), *Multicultural literature and response: Affirming diverse voices* (pp. 131–152). Libraries Unlimited.

Sabis-Burns, D., & Lowery, R. M. (2019). YOUR LAND! MY LAND! OUR LAND!: American Indian/Alaska Native students in schools. In R. M. Lowery, R. M. Pringle, & M. E. Ellen Oslick (Eds.), *Land of opportunity: Immigrant experiences in the North American landscape* (pp. 9–18). Rowman & Littlefield.

Singh, N.K., & Espinoza-Herold, M.M. (2014). Culture-Based Education: Lessons from Indigenous Education in the U.S. and Southeast Asia. *NABE Journal of Research and Practice, 5*(1), 7–39.

Slapin, B., & Seale, D. (1998). *Through Indian eyes: The Native experience in books for children.* Los Angeles, CA: American Indian Studies Center.

Slapin, B., Seale, D., & Gonzales, R. (2000). *How to tell the difference: A guide to evaluating children's books for anti-Indian bias.* Oyate.

Stewart, M. P. (2002). Judging authors by the color of their skin? Quality Native American children's literature. *School Library Journal, 49*(11), 42–43.

Susag, D. M. (1998). *Roots and branches: A resource of Native American literature—themes, lessons, and bibliographies.* National Council of Teachers of English.

Tatum, A. W. (2008). Toward a more anatomically complete model of literacy instruction: A focus on African American male adolescents and texts. *Harvard Educational Review, 78*(1), 155–182.

Thomas, E. E. (2016). Stories still matter: Rethinking the role of diverse children's literature today. *Language Arts, 94*(2), 112–119.

U.S. Department of Interior. (2021, June 22). Secretary Haaland announces federal Indian boarding school initiative. Press release. www.doi.gov/pressreleases/secretary-haaland-announces-federal-indian-boarding-school-initiative.

Verrall, C., & McDowell, P. (1990). *Resource reading list 1990: Annotated bibliography of resources by and about Native people*. Canadian Alliance in Solidarity with the Native Peoples.

Yazzie, T. (1999). Culturally appropriate curriculum. In K. Swisher, & J. Tippeconnic (Eds.), *Next steps: Research and practice to advance Indian education* (pp. 84–106). Appalachia Educational Laboratory.

Appendix: What Can You Do Now?

The chart listed below provides a list of resources that any parent, educator, or librarian can reference when making appropriate choices for quality literature by and about Indigenous authors and illustrators. The list is not exhaustive, but it highlights resources for learning more about various topics such as Indigenous educational organizations, educational resources, publishers, and literature sources.

Resource		URL (If applicable)	Description
Indigenous Literature Resources	American Indian Library Association		Information Resources for Communities Serving Native Peoples. AILA provides a plethora of resources listing programs to assist in the continuation of culture, tradition and language, a repository to collect resources that document tribal history, inspire reading, writing, research, and scholarship, and provide an educational resource for achieving a greater understanding of the Indigenous way of life
	Cynthia Leitich Smith's Native American Children's and Young Adult Book Bibliographies and Educator Resources	https://cynthia leitichsmith. com/lit-re sources/read/ diversity/na tive-am/	These bibliographies and resources are drawn largely from articles and books published between 1995 and 2021. While award-winners and best-sellers are included, part of the goal is to feature underappreciated gems.
	Ongoing Coverage of Native Books at Cynsations	https://cynthia leitichsmith. com/tag/na tive-america n-first-nations/	Leitich Smith is a one-stop shop of current and up and coming Indigenous authors and illustrators. Know when new books are being published by following her page.

Resource	URL (If applicable)	Description
Home and Classroom Teaching: Native American Children's Teens' Books & Resources	https://cynthialeitichsmith.com/2020/04/home-classroom-teaching-native-americans-teens-books-resources/	Leitich Smith also manages and offers a plethora of resources for home and classroom education. Access this resource when lesson planning on topics that engage in Indigenous knowledge sharing.
American Indian Youth Literature Award	https://ailanet.org/activities/american-indian-youth-literature-award/	Awarded biennially, the AIYLA identifies and honors the very best writing and illustrations by Indigenous people and Indigenous peoples of North America. Books selected to receive the award present Indigenous North American peoples in the fullness of their humanity. In odd-numbered years, nominations are encouraged in fiction or nonfiction and may include graphic novels; for picture books, the award is for both author and illustrator. Awards are granted in even-numbered years. Authors/illustrators may win the American Indian Youth Literature Award in the categories Best Picture Book, Best Middle Grade Book, and Best Young Adult Book. In addition, up to five awards may be selected as Honors books in each category.
American Indians in Children's Literature (AICL)	www.americanindiansinchildrensliterature.net/	Debbie Reese's American Indians in Children's Literature Blog. "Established in 2006, provides critical perspectives and analysis of indigenous peoples in children's and young adult books, the school curriculum, popular culture, and society."
If I Can Read, I Can Do Anything	www.ala.org/news/news/pressreleases2010/march2010/readergrlz_yalsa	A family literacy program led by AILA member Loriene Roy from 2008–2010 to assist the libraries serving Native American children in increasing reading skills while preserving Native identity.
YALSA Teen Book Finder	http://booklists.yalsa.net/	Includes recent AILA Youth Literature Award winners and honor books.
Talk Story: Sharing stories, sharing culture	www.talkstorytogether.org/	A joint literacy program that reaches out to Asian Pacific American and American Indian/Alaska Native children and their families. The program celebrates and explores their stories through books, oral traditions, and art to provide an interactive, enriching experience.

Resource		URL (If applicable)	Description
American Library Association Office for Diversity Inclusive Booklists,		www.ala.org/a boutala/offices/ diversity/litera cy/inclusive-booklist	These booklists highlight diverse voices including racial diversity and sexuality and can be used in the classroom and when ordering collections. There are many booklists in the world that are categorized by topic, but these booklists ensure that underrepresented voices are being heard as well.
Reading While White		http://reading whilewhite. blogspot.com/ 2016/07/revie wing-while white-there-is-tribe-of. html	White library workers organizing to confront and dismantle racism in the field of children's and young adult literature. They are committed to working for authenticity and visibility in books, and to supporting opportunities for Black, Indigenous and People of Color (BIPOC) in all aspects of the children's and young adult book world. They resolve to examine their own white racial experiences without expecting BIPOC to educate them.
Rich in Color		http://richinco lor.com/	Rich in Color is dedicated to reading, reviewing, talking about, and otherwise promoting young adult books (fiction and non-fiction) starring or written by BIPOC.
We Need Diverse Books		https://diverse books.org/blog/	A non-profit and a grassroots organization of children's book lovers that advocates essential changes in the publishing industry to produce and promote literature that reflects and honors the lives of all young people.
Hawai'ian book publisher		https://bessp ress.com/col lections/p icture-books	Hawai'ian Book Collections.
Hawai'ian Children's Literature		www.encyclop edia.com/chil dren/academic-a nd-educationa l-journals/hawa iian-children s-literature	The contributions of Hawaiian authors to and the depiction of Hawaiian history, culture, and mythology in the children's literature genre.
Biography Clearinghouse		www.thebio graphyclearing house.org/tra ci-sorell.html	Many great websites exist like this one that offers quality texts about Indigenous people and provides teaching ideas as well.

Resource	URL (If applicable)	Description
	Milestones in Children's Literature and Indigenous people	https://america nindiansinchil drensliterature. blogspot. com/p/milesto nes-indigen ous-peoples-in. html	Its focus is on Indigenous Peoples of the Tribal Nations in the United States, who have done something that is about Native peoples, specifically in literature for children and young adults.
	Children's Literature Hawai'i	www.children slithawaii.org/	Promote interest in and appreciation of children's literature through community activities such as storytelling, educational workshops, presentations, and events for children.
Indigenous Organizations	Generation Indigenous	https://genindi genous.com/	launched by President Obama on December 3rd, 2014. Gen I is a Native youth initiative focused on removing the barriers that stand between Native youth and their opportunity to succeed.
	UNITY	https://unityinc. org/	a national network organization promoting personal development, citizenship, and leadership among Native American youth.
	Project 562	www.pro ject562.com/	develops a body of imagery and cultural representations of Native Peoples to counteract the relentlessly insipid, one-dimensional stereotypes circulating in mainstream media, historical textbooks and the culture industry
	American Indian Science and Engineering Society (AISES)	www.aises.org/	A non-profit professional association with the goal of substantially increasing American Indian, Alaskan Native, Native Hawaiian, Pacific Islander, First Nation and other indigenous peoples of North America representation in the fields of science, technology, engineering, math (STEM) and other related disciplines.
	National Congress of American Indians	www.ncai.org/ about-tribes.	Free resources online that can help you become more knowledgeable on Tribal Nations and the United States:
Resources on Indigenous Education	U.S. Department of Education, Office of Indian Education	https://oese.ed. gov/offices/ office-of-india n-education/	Meets the unique educational and culturally related academic needs of Indian students, so that such students can meet the challenging State academic standards

Resource		URL (If applicable)	Description
	Bureau of Indian Education	www.bie.edu/	Provides quality education opportunities from early childhood through life in accordance with a tribe's needs for cultural and economic well-being
	Indian Education Curriculum Development & Implementation	https://opi.mt. gov/Educators/ Teaching-Learning/ Indian-Education-for-All	Montana Office of Public Instruction provides schools and staff with knowledge, skills, and content to ensure Indian Education for All means cultural enrichment, academic engagement, and equitable pedagogy for students.
	Heard Museum Educational Resources for the Classroom	https://heard. org/education/ teacher resources/	Art and cultural resources for the classroom
	Native American Heritage Month	www.nativeam ericanheritagem onth.gov/for-teachers/	The Library of Congress, National Archives and Records Administration, National Endowment for the Humanities, National Gallery of Art, National Park Service, Smithsonian Institution and United States Holocaust Memorial Museum join in paying tribute to the rich ancestry and traditions of Indigenous people.
	Native Knowledge 360	www.nmai.si. edu/nk360 https://america nindian.si.edu/ nk360/informa tional/native-am erican-literatur e-in-your-cla ssroom	Provides educators and students with new perspectives on Native American history and cultures. Created by Smithsonian National Museum of the American Indian
	National American Indian Education Association	www.niea.org/	Resources for educators, students, and advocates to learn about effective strategies, innovative programming, and professional learning opportunities aligned with creating a safe, successful, and supportive learning environment.
Book Publishers of Indigenous books by Indigenous authors and illustrators	Wisdom Tales	www.wisdomta lespress.com/ index.shtml	Based in Bloomington, Ind., is a small press that publishes books from traditions across the world, including recent books on Persian, Jain, and American Indian history and traditional stories.

Resource	URL (If applicable)	Description
Orca Book Publishers	www.orcabook.com/	Based on the west coast of Canada, also makes a strong effort to represent First Nations authors and illustrators.
Lee and Low	www.leeandlow.com/	Is the largest multicultural children's book publisher in the United States.
Little, Brown & Company	www.littlebrown.com/?s=native+american	Publishes children's literature by and about Indigenous people.
Kegedonce Press	www.kegedonce.com/books/	Has been crafting books that involve Indigenous Peoples at all levels of production.
Heartdrum	www.harpercollins.com/collections/heartdrum-books-by-native-american-authors	A new imprint by Native American authors for kids 8+! These children's books emphasize the present and future of Indian Country and the strength of young Indigenous heroes.

12 Using LGBTQ+ Children's Literature to Create a Sense of Belonging for All Within Elementary Classrooms

Aimee Frier and Stephanie Branson

Rationale

Around the time anti-LGBTQ+ legislation referred to as "Don't Say Gay" (2022) passed in the state of Florida, my (Aimee's) class of pre-service teachers had been assigned to read Alex Gino's book *Melissa's Story* (formerly published as *George*) for their literature circle meeting. *Melissa's Story*, frequently found on the list of banned and challenged books because it focuses on a transgender character, has facilitated interesting conversations in previous courses. I expected this conversation to be no different. I looked out across the room of preservice teachers, each one of them preparing to intern in local classrooms. "Well, what did you think of the book?" I asked my preservice students. After a few moments, one student offered, "It was good! I liked reading about Melissa's experience." Then another student asked hesitantly the question I expected; "Can I read this book in my class?"

Similarly, Stephanie's (second author) pre-service teachers were discussing LGBTQ+ books as part of their children's literature class, and the same types of questions inevitably came up during discussion. In addition to asking about whether they could read books with LGBTQ+ characters, they also grappled with what the new legislation meant for them personally (as members of the LGBTQ+ community and parents of children who identify as LGBTQ+ and as future teachers).

Books deemed to have controversial topics, particularly those with LGBTQ+ themes and characters, tend to generate questions related to "appropriateness" within the classroom space. In both of our courses, we address concepts such as representation and inclusivity throughout the semester, so students understood the need for all children and their families to be "seen" within classroom books and feel as if they belong in their classroom community. Yet, working with preservice teachers, we understand there will be trepidation with content viewed as controversial.

As a professor of children's literature, a member of the LGBTQ+ community, and a mother of two elementary-aged children, I (Aimee)

DOI: 10.4324/9781003321941-14

find myself in an interesting position. I understand preservice teachers' hesitation to integrate so-called controversial topics in order to avoid potential conflicts, particularly in light of recent legislation. However, each child within the classroom deserves to see themselves, and their families, within the read-alouds and on bookshelves in the classroom. For my family, my children deserve and have the right to see their family represented as much as any other child in class. My answer is simple and straightforward: Which children do you choose to include, and which do you want to exclude? Hopefully, that seemingly simple question means my children and every child within the classroom can find themselves represented within the classroom space and feel a sense of belonging.

Historical Perspective

The history of LGBTQ+ people in the United States has had a tumultuous path. We use the acronym LGBTQ+ as a broad, encompassing abbreviation for "lesbian, gay, bisexual, queer, and/or questioning." As recently as the 1950s, the American Psychiatric Association's manual listed homosexuality as a sociopathic personality disorder, and an executive order was enacted to ban homosexuals from working for the federal government. While there has been progress in the last decade with the repeal of "Don't Ask, Don't Tell" (a 1994 discriminatory ban on gay and lesbian service members), antidiscrimination laws to protect LGBTQ+ workers from discrimination, and the passage of marriage equality, LGBTQ+ people and their families still face discrimination (Public Broadcasting Service, N.D.).

According to the GLSEN website, "No Promo Homo" and "Don't Say Gay" laws emerged in the 1990s to "prohibit positive and affirming representations of LGBTQ+ identities in schools" (www.glsen.org). The laws were first intended to restrict content and discussions in sex education courses, although they were further applied to other curricular areas and activities as well. Since that time, many states eliminated harmful anti-LGBTQ+ curricular laws, but others have either kept existing legislation or adopted new versions of the law under the guise of "parental rights," which prohibits classroom instruction in primary grades or any manner that is not "age or developmentally appropriate" at any grade.

In stark contrast, other states have instituted protective laws to counter LGBTQ+ discriminatory practices and included curricular standards requiring the inclusion of the "histories and contributions" of marginalized people that embrace LGBTQ+ communities (www.glsen.org). Across the United States, there are current laws and policies that either support or prohibit teaching LGBTQ+-inclusive topics (see Chapter 4 for more information). Recent anti-LGBTQ+ legislation in our state, (Florida) directed at what teachers can discuss or share and what is age appropriate, prompted us to consider how to continue approaching a humanizing curriculum and how to include inclusive texts to affirm many voices, experiences, and identities. Simply put, we want all students to feel as if they are valued and they belong. We offer the social construct of "belongingness" as a way to advocate for the inclusion of LGBTQ+ characters in the elementary classroom. While we acknowledge teachers need to be aware of the laws, and language within those laws that impact their teaching and student safety, we want to offer solutions and suggestions for a range of books for classroom consideration.

Book Banning and Censorship

Censorship is a centuries-old issue for the United States. There are many examples of censorship and attempts to censor, which is often viewed as a violation of the First Amendment and the right to free speech (Steele, 2020). According to the American Library Association (ALA) website, censorship is a "change in the access status of material, based on the content of the work and made by governing authority or its representatives. Such changes include exclusion, restriction, removal, or age/grade level changes" (ALA, 2016, para. 2). While many definitions of censorship exist, "the general sentiment behind most definitions is that something is withheld from access by another" (Oppenheim & Smith, 2004, p. 160; see Chapter 5 for more information about censorship).

One commonly cited reason behind book challenges and censorship in the United States are claims of obscenity (Steele, 2020). Censorship in public libraries is "as old as the public library movement itself" (Thompson, 1975, p. 1). While the Supreme Court has heard many cases related to First Amendment rights and censorship, a pivotal ruling in 1975 sided with students challenging an attempt to remove access to books deemed as inappropriate. In the ruling, Justice William Brennan stated, "local school boards may not remove books from school library shelves simply because they disliked the ideas contained in those books and seek by their removal to 'prescribe what shall be orthodox in politics, nationalism, religion, or other matters of opinion'" (*Board of Education, Island Trees Union Free School District No. 26 v. Pico* 1982, p. 872).

Despite the 1982 ruling regarding the removal of materials, censorship of children's books has increased in the twentieth century. Kidd (2009) states, "as censorship of adult materials became less acceptable, and childhood [is] imaged more and more as a time of great innocence and vulnerability" (p. 199), which has meant an increased scrutiny for books labeled for children. Parent and religious groups often challenge books related to LGBTQ+ themes under the guise that they are not suitable for the child's age group. This makes finding access to these materials difficult for LGBTQ families.

Lesléa Newman's (1989) book, *Heather Has Two Mommies*, illustrated by Diana Souza, was one of the first positive portrayals in children's literature to show two same sex parents engaged in normal, everyday experiences. Originally published in 1989, the story centers around a little girl with two "mommas" and sends the message that family is about the people who love each other. Soon after it was originally released, the book made headlines, but for all the wrong reasons. While some people hailed it as a positive step forward and a catalyst for change, others challenged, vilified, and criticized it for attacking what some people called traditional family values. *Heather Has Two Mommies*, a story of a loving, happy family, ended up on the most challenged list, alongside books such as *The Catcher in the Rye* (Salinger, 1951), for not being suitable or appropriate for young audiences. If we, as teachers, are to promote an inclusive environment, where everyone belongs, what message are we sending children when we censor books that show a depiction of their family or a classmate's family?

While a segment of the population would argue that censoring materials from young people is a means of protection, this is in direct opposition to the ALA's Freedom to Read Statement. According to their 2010 statement, "There is no place in our society for efforts to coerce the taste of others, to confine adults to the reading matter deemed suitable for adolescents, or to inhibit the efforts of writers to achieve artistic expression" (ALA, 2010, p. 203). Parents, teachers, and librarians bear the responsibility of ensuring young people are prepared for the diversity of human life they are sure to encounter. This means including diverse people and experiences within the curriculum. This chapter is a call to action for current and future classroom teachers to move beyond a general awareness of different people and perspectives and move towards a stance of inclusion and belonging.

Recommended Literature as a Basis for Teaching and Learning about Belonging

Children's literature is a fundamental aspect for teaching literacy, and books and read-alouds often serve as the centerpiece for instruction. A well-crafted story is key to maintaining sustained engagement while learning about a topic. A compelling story allows students to grapple with new areas of learning and wrestle with difficult questions without a single "right" answer. During the read-aloud, skilled teachers can facilitate deep conversation about meaningful, authentic topics, in a supportive classroom environment (Ahiyya, 2022).

Beyond the shared-reading space, students interact with children's literature through the classroom library. During independent reading, students explore a selection of books curated by the classroom teacher. While the texts chosen for a read-aloud are often dictated by curriculum adoption and/or state standards, the classroom library is a space where teachers can ensure that all students have access to books representative of themselves, their families, and the world around them. Explicitly stated in the International Literacy Association's (ILA) position statement on Children's Right to Read (2018) is a child's right to choose what they read and have access to read books that "mirror their experiences and language, provide windows into the lives of others, and open doors into diverse worlds" (Bishops, 1990, as cited in ILA, 2018). Providing these windows and mirrors through children's literature creates a sense of belonging for all students.

Inclusion of materials in your personal library collection and within your curriculum begins with considering books that promote a sense of belonging and acceptance. Belonging is the fundamental social need to be accepted and acknowledged and to feel that "one fits in" (Raman, 2014). It includes feeling seen, connected, valued, supported, and needed by others in a group or community. While acceptance is related to belonging, it is a part of identity and includes the desire for validation and respect. Within the elementary school, teachers strive to create a classroom community that promotes belonging and acceptance, and one way a teacher can accomplish this is through carefully selected books and read-alouds. With the right book and a knowledgeable teacher, read-alouds can promote kindness, empathy, and inclusion, while celebrating the beauty of diversity (Ahiyya, 2022). Characters and stories can help children understand different perspectives and different ways of experiencing life, which may be different from their own (Bishops, 1990, as cited in ILA, 2018).

Belonging and Identity

Michael Hall created *Red: A Crayon's Story* to share his personal experience labeled with a disability, but the story can apply to anyone who has felt misunderstood or mislabeled. The story begins with Red, a mislabeled crayon, who tries to be the color that others want him to be and perceive him to be. A friend, who accepts him, shares a different point of view and asks him to try a new approach. Red finds acceptance and belonging once he realizes who he really is. Michael Hall wrote several other books in his collection that affirm self-awareness, belonging, and being true to oneself, including *Little i*, a playful story about self-discovery, as told through the alphabet.

Jessica Love depicts identity and belonging through her picture book, *Julian is a Mermaid*. This beautifully illustrated story follows Julian and his Abuela and what happens when he encounters three "mermaids" in sweeping gowns on the subway. He wonders if maybe he could be a mermaid as well, but what would his Abuela think? This story has an impactful message of belonging within your own family and honoring what you feel inside. The simple, yet powerful words, are paired with exquisite illustrations that represent the beauty of diverse human experiences.

Other books that talk about belonging in terms of recognizing and embracing differences include *Not Your Typical Dragon* by Dan Bar-el and illustrated by Tim Bowers and *The Different Dragon* by Jennifer Bryan and illustrated by Danamarie Hosler. Both stories emphasize the apprehension that sometimes comes with feeling different from others but ultimately highlight the significance of recognizing the value of differences in a community. These stories model belonging and inclusion through the love and respect shown by community members and friends, even when they seem a little different from each other.

Belonging as Part of a LGBTQ+ Family

Classroom book collections need to contain representation of many different types of family units. Oftentimes, a "traditional" family unit of a mom, dad, sister, and brother are represented between the covers, whether explicitly discussed as part of the storyline or shown in the illustrations on the pages. Where does that leave other family units? By definition, a family unit is the adults and children in a household, and that unit can be formed in different ways, whether by birth, marriage, choice, or through adoption (Law Insider Dictionary, 2022). Therefore, books should reflect different family compositions. When children see and read about family structures similar to their own, it sends a message their families belong and are worth reading about in the pages of books.

As teachers, we want to locate books that represent and share the storylines of multifaceted family units. Newman's book, *Heather Has Two Mommies* and *Momma, Mommy, and Me*, paved the way for other LGBTQ + family stories and perspectives. *The Girl with Two Dads* by Meg Elliott features a story about friendship and celebrating the differences and similarities of family structures. In *My Maddy*, illustrated by Violet Tobacco, Gayle Pitman introduces children to gender non-conforming parents through a loving parent-child relationship and relatable experiences. Parnell and Richardson's award-winning book, *And Tango Makes Three*, is the true story of two penguins, Roy and Silo, who hatch and raise a penguin chick. The story emphasizes love and what is considered a family. *The Different Dragon* by Jennifer Bryan shares the nighttime storytelling routine of a LGBTQ+ family, with themes of imagination, adventure, and embracing differences. Each of these stories introduce and embrace the everyday experiences of families.

Other books about families are broader concept books and share the diversity of what makes a family. *The Great Big Book of Families* by Mary Hoffman, illustrated by Ros Asquith uses simple text and detailed scenes to reinforce "families come in all shapes and sizes". The book shows similarities and differences between families through their everyday activities and traditions. *One Family* by George Shannon is a simple, rhythmic counting book celebrating diversity in the type and size of any one family. *Love Makes a Family* by Sophie Beer approaches diverse family units through loving actions such as baking a cake or lending a helping hand. Each of these books help children look beyond their own families and experiences, to understand others and develop pride in their own unique family unit.

However, some family books have come under fire for depicting non-traditional families. A district in Florida challenged *Everywhere Babies* by Susan Meyers and illustrated by Marlee Frazee for depictions of diverse family units within various scenes; one scene presents two dads with their baby, and another scene exhibits two moms rocking their baby to sleep. The book was written after the birth of the author's grandchild as a simple ode to the adoration and blessings of babies in the world rather than promoting any perceived agenda. This brings forward questions about what contradictory messages we are sending to children if we omit books reflective of many families.

Belonging in History

An emerging genre in LGBTQ+ Literature is the representation of historical perspectives that explore legislation, historical figures and events, and other nonfiction topics that have shaped our country. Belonging in history means to recognize and highlight the many people and events that paved the way for basic human rights. Holidays and monthly recognitions are another way to show how people or groups of people belong in this world. Age appropriate, LGBTQ+ non-fiction books are few and far between, but there are a few that teachers can include within their collections to meet reading standards, while also sharing historical figures and events.

Rob Sanders, an author and former elementary school teacher in Florida, published a number of books during and after his time in the classroom, addressing many different topics and themes. Two nonfiction picture books in particular were written about pivotal moments in LGBTQ+ history. *Pride: The Story of Harvey Milk and the Rainbow Flag*, illustrated by Steven Salerno, is a beautiful representation of hope, equity, love, and justice as told through the origins of the Pride Flag. Another called *Stonewall. A Building. An Uprising. A Revolution*, illustrated by Jamey Christoph, is a story based on the 1969 events of the Stonewall Uprising as narrated and witnessed by the Stonewall Inn. Told from the building's perspective, the author weaves in facts and details from the events and shares the bravery and fortitude of the people who advocated for equality and protected a place where they felt they belonged.

Gayle Pitman is another notable author who made her mark through LGBTQ+ non-fiction picture books. Similar to Sanders, Pitman wrote a book, called *Sewing the Rainbow: The Story of Gilbert Baker and the Rainbow Flag*, illustrated by Holly Clifton-Brown, about Gilbert Baker's journey and legacy, celebrating the origins of the Pride Flag. This book is a great compliment to her other book, *When You Look Out the Window: How*

Phyllis Lyon and Del Martin Built a Community, illustrated by Christopher Lyles. This untold story shares the transformational impact of two community activists and their contribution to LGBTQ+ rights. In Pitman's other book, *This Day in June*, illustrated by Kristyna Litten, she honors Pride month and teaches children about respect, inclusion, joy, and a united human spirit. The bright illustrations and rhythmic verse are a great introduction for young children.

As teachers, we know it's important to include children's books and texts that show diverse groups of people as part of historical and everyday experiences across genres. Suggestions are available for evaluating cultural authenticity in children's literature that can be adapted and applied when considering how to evaluate books with LGBTQ+ stories and characters. A general starting question might be: *How do you know the children's book you chose authentically portrays the characters or experiences?* You can use the following reflection questions, based on the content in this chapter, to start conversations about the inclusion of LGBTQ+ stories and characters and to evaluate books to bring into the classroom.

Reflection Questions

1. What role has censorship in the United States played in education policy and practice?
2. In what ways can you create a sense of belonging for all children within your classroom?
3. Review the selected texts in the table. How might you incorporate these within the curricular standards?
4. Critical Questions for Evaluating Your Classroom Literature and Library:

    - In practice—Evaluate your read-alouds:

      a. What families are represented in my classroom, school, and community?
      b. What questions can I ask? What should I consider in advance?
      c. What voices do my students hear most often?
      d. What can I do to diversify my classroom read-alouds?
      e. What cultural stereotypes are present in the books I read to my students?

    - In practice—Evaluate your own classroom library:

      a. What can I do to diversify my classroom library?
      b. What cultural stereotypes are present in the books available to my students?
      c. Who and what is represented on my bookshelf? What authors? What characters? What topics?
      d. What voices and topics are missing from my bookshelf?
      e. What books promote belonging? Acceptance? Inclusivity?

Table 12.1 Recommended pieces LGBTQ+ and gender identity for elementary aged classrooms.

Book Information	Summary
Title: Red: A Crayon's Story **Author and Illustrator:** Michael Hall (Author and Illustrator) **Awards:***Rainbow Project Book List*; *E.B White Read-aloud Honor* **Grade Level Band:** K-2	**Belonging and Identity:** In this humorous and lighthearted story, a mislabeled crayon tries very hard to live up to its label, but with the help of a friend realizes it's more important to be true to yourself. Although the author wrote this story to depict his own disability, it really reflects any person who finds themselves incorrectly labeled.
Title: George (AKA Melissa's Story) **Author:** Alex Gino **Awards:** 2016 Stonewall Book Award; 2016 Lambda Literary Award **Grade Level Band:** 3–5	**Belonging and Identity:** This chapter book follows Melissa, a young trans girl, trying to be herself and show others around her who she is becoming. Melissa is an endearing character that wants to belong and be accepted by her family and peers. From vying for the lead role of Charlotte in the school play to finding just the right outfit for a special occasion, Melissa is just like everyone else. Alex Gino crafts a relatable story that emphasizes inner strength, yearning to belong, acceptance, and allyship.
Title: Morris Micklewhite and the Tangerine Dress **Author and Illustrator:** Christine Baldacchino (Author), Isabelle Malenfant (Illustrator) **Grade Level Band:** 1–3	**Belonging and Identity:** Morris loves to dress up in all sorts of things, especially the tangerine dress. This wonderful story about imagination, natural curiosity, courage, and vulnerability, will capture the attention of children and send a message of acceptance and being who you are even when others try to put you down.
Title: Peanut Goes for the Gold **Author and Illustrator:** Jonathan Van Ness (Author) Gillian Reid (Illustrator) **Grade Level Band:** K-2	**Belonging and Identity:** This upbeat picture book features a lovable, non-binary guinea pig who just wants to have fun and give it their all in everything they choose to do. This hilariously charming story by Jonathan Van Ness encourages self-acceptance, inclusion, and positivity.

Book Information	Summary
Title: Pride: The Story of Harvey Milk and the Rainbow Flag **Author and Illustrator:** Rob Sanders (Author), Steven Salerno (Illustrator) **Grade Level Band:** 1–5	**Belonging in History:** Covered in bright rainbows throughout, this beautifully illustrated, non-fiction story traces the beginnings of the Pride Flag, through activist Harvey Milk and designer Gilbert Baker. This age-appropriate introduction to a historical symbol, embraces and celebrates "Equality. Pride. Hope. Love." The end pages include biographical notes, a timeline, and photographs, and resources.
Title: Stonewall: A Building. An Uprising. A Revolution **Author and Illustrator:** Rob Sanders (Author), Jamey Christoph (Illustrator) **Grade Level Band:** 3–5	**Belonging in History:** Stonewall tells the true story of events that happened at the Stonewall Inn during the 1960s, sparking a civil rights movement. Narrated by the Inn itself, the illustrations present the scenes unfolding from the perspectives of the buildings. The end pages include historical information, photographs, an interview with a participant, a glossary, and resources.
Title: The Different Dragon **Author and Illustrator:** Jennifer Bryan (Author), Danamarie Hosler (Illustrator) **Grade Level Band:** K-3	**Belonging and Family:** This fantasy story shares a magical bedtime read-aloud as told by Go-Ma and Noah. Families will relate to the chaos of bedtime and the ritual of storytelling. The imaginative bedtime tale explores the differences that make us unique and learning to embrace who we are. The story and illustrations showcase another type of family unit and normalize experiences for all types of families.
Title: My Family, Your Family **Author and Illustrator:** Lisa Bullard (Author), Renee Kurilla (Illustrator) **Grade Level Band:** K-2	**Belonging and Family:** Families units are all different and all beautiful. This introductory book to all types of families talks about what makes a family and how they are the same and different for everyone. Follow Makayla as she goes on a "treasure hunt" in her community to find other families that are just as special as her own.

Resources

The following resources are meant to support you in your thinking and provide you with resources to use in your classroom:

Podcasts

- Cult of Pedagogy—Uncovering Your Implicit Bias: https://podcasts. apple.com/us/podcast/188-uncovering-your-implicit-biases-an-exercise-for/id900015782?i=1000556099337
- What I Want to Know with Kevin P. Chavous—How Do We Encourage Diversity in Children's Literature: https://whatiwanttoknow.libsyn.com/ 30-how-do-we-encourage-diversity-in-young-adult-literature

Videos

- Ezra Jack Keats Foundation—Tell Me Another Story: www.ezra-jack-keats.org/tell-me-another-story/
- Webinar: LGBTQ+ Children's Books: https://youtu.be/8LDg3fw4C3E

Blogs

- NCTE Incorporating LGBTQ Students and Texts in the Classroom: https://ncte.org/blog/2018/10/incorporating-lgbtq-students-texts-classroom/
- How to Make Your Classroom More LGBTQ-Friendly: https:// itgetsbetter.org/blog/lesson/how-to-make-your-digital-classroom-more-lgbtq-friendly/
- Lee and Low Checklist for Creating a Diverse Book Collection https://blog.leeandlow.com/2014/05/22/checklist-8-steps-to-creating-a-diverse-book-collection/

Websites

- Gay, Lesbian, and Straight Education Network: www.glsen.org.
- GSLEN Educator Resources: www.glsen.org/resources/educator-re sources GLSEN is an organization founded by teachers, providing support, research, materials, and resources for students, families, educators, and advocates.
- Reading LGBTQ+ Inclusive Children's Books in Schools: https:// welcomingschools.org/resources/using-lgbtq-inclusive-childrens-books.
- Learning for Justice: www.learningforjustice.org/.
- Learning for Justice: Gender and Sexual Identity www.learningforjus tice.org/topics/gender-sexual-identity.
- It Gets Better Project: https://itgetsbetter.org/education/.
- Lee and Low LGBTQ+ Book List and Resources: www.leeandlow.com/ uploads/loaded_document/697/LeeandLow_LGBTQBookListResources. pdf.

Books

- Booklist from Welcoming Schools: https://hrc-prod-requests.s3-us-west-2.amazonaws.com/welcoming-schools/documents/WS-Diverse-

Picture-Books-Transgender-Non-Binary.pdf?mtime=20210501080020& focal=none.
- Ryan, C. L., & Hermann-Wilmarth, J. M. (2018). Reading the rainbow: LGBTQ-inclusive literacy instruction in the elementary classroom. Teachers College Press.
- Learning For Justice Reading Diversity Tool for text selection: www.learningforjustice.org/magazine/publications/reading-diversity.

Author-Curated List of Children's LGBTQ+ Literature

Gender Spectrum

Gale, H. (2019). *Ho'onani: Hula warrior*. Tundra Books.
Hirst, J. (2018). *A house for everyone: A story to help children learn about gender identity and gender expression*. Jessica Kingsley Publishers.
Benedetto, N. (2016). *It's me*. CreateSpace Independent Publishing Platform.
Baldacchino, C. (2020). *Morris micklewhite and the tangerine dress*. Groundwood Books.
Stewart, S. (2022). *My shadow is purple*. Larrikin House US.
Anderson, A. (2018). *Neither*. Little, Brown Books for Young Readers.
Parr, T. (2011). *It's okay to be different*. Little, Brown Books for Young Readers.
Van Ness, J. (2020). *Peanut goes for the gold*. HarperCollins.
Love, J. (2018). *Julian is a mermaid*. Candlewick Press.

Transgender Representation

Ford, J.R. (2021). *Calvin*. G.P. Putnam's Sons Books for Young Readers.
Gino, A. (2015). *George (Scholastic Gold)*. Scholastic.
Patterson, J. (2021). *Born ready: The true story of a boy named Penelope*. Crown Books for Young Readers.
Walton, T. (2016). *Introducing Teddy*. Bloomsbury.

Families

Elliot, M. (2019). *The girl with two dads*. Farshore
Hoberman, M. A. (2009). *All kinds of families!*. Little, Brown Books for Young Readers.
Hoffman, M. (2011). *The great big book of families*. Dial Books.
Lukoff, K. (2019). *When aidan became a brother*. Lee & Low Books.
Meyers, S. (2004). *Everywhere babies*. Clarion Books.
Newman, L. (2009). *Mommy, mama, and me*. Tricycle Press.
Newman, L. (2011). *Donovan's big day*. Random House Digital.
Newman, L. (2015). *Heather has two mommies*. Candlewick Press.
Parr, T. (2003). *The family book*. Little, Brown Books for Young Readers.
Pitman, G. E. (2020). *My maddy*. Magination Press.
Beer, S. (2018). *Love makes a family*. Penguin.
Bryan, J. (2006). *The different dragon*. Two Lives Publishing.

Carney, J. (2021). *The accidental diary of BUG*. Puffin.
Polacco, P. (2009). *In our mother's house*. Philomel Books.
Schiffer, M. (2015). *Stella brings the family*. Chronicle Books.

Self-Acceptance/Embracing Differences/Inclusiveness/Pro Humanity

Bar-el, D. (2013). *Not your typical dragon*. Viking Books for Young Readers.
Hall, M., & Miles, R. (2015). *Red: A crayon's story*. Greenwillow Books.
Hall, M. (2017). *Little i*. Greenwillow Books.
Tharp, J. (2020). *It's ok to be a unicorn*. Imprint.
Sima, J. (2017). *Not quite narwhal*. Simon and Schuster.
Alexander, C. (2021). *A little bit different (The ploofers)*. Happy Yak.

Historical Perspectives

Sanders, R. (2018). *Pride: The story of Harvey Milk and the rainbow flag*. Random House Books for Young Readers.
Sanders, R. (2019). *Stonewall: A building, an uprising, a revolution*. Random House Books for Young Readers.
Pitman, G. E. (2014). *This day in* June. Magination Press.
Pitman, G. E. (2017). *When you look out the window: How Phyllis Lyon and Del Martin built a community*. Magination Press.
Pitman, G. E. (2018). *Sewing the rainbow: A story about Gilbert Baker*. Magination Press.

References

Ahiyya, V. (2022). *Rebellious read-alouds: Inviting conversations about diversity with children's books*. Corwin Literacy.
ALA. (2010). *Intellectual freedom manual*. American Library Association.
ALA. (2016). Challenge Support. www.ala.org/tools/challengesupport.
ILA. (2018). *The case for children's rights to read*. International Literacy Association.
Kidd, K. (2009). "Not Censorship but selection": Censorship and/as prizing. *Children's Literature in Education*, 40(3): 197–216.
Law Insider Dictionary. (2022). Family unit definition: 262 samples. www.lawinsider.com/dictionary/family-unit.
Newman, L. (1989). *Heather has two mommies*. Alyson Books.
Oppenheim, C., & Smith, V. (2004). Censorship in libraries. *Information Services & Use* 24(4), 159–170.
Public Broadcasting Service. (n.d.). Milestones in the American gay rights movement. www.pbs.org/wgbh/americanexperience/features/stonewall-milestones-american-gay-rights-movement/.
Raman, S. (2014). Sense of belonging. https://link.springer.com/referenceworkentry/10.1007/978-94-007-0753-5_2646.
Salinger, J. D. (1951). *The catcher in the rye*. Little, Brown and Company.
Steele, J. E. (2020). A history of censorship in the United States. *Journal of Intellectual Freedom & Privacy*, 5(1), 6–19.
Thompson, A. H. (1975). *Censorship in public libraries in the United Kingdom during the twentieth century*. Epping: Bowker.

Appendix: Foundational Teaching Tips

Read-alouds are a valuable tool in the elementary classroom, and choosing a book involves knowing students (i.e. their backgrounds, interests, and needs), understanding curricular goals, and understanding what is considered a quality text, free of bias and stereotypes. The following are some helpful tips to get you started with read-alouds, reflective of many children and experiences:

1. Get to know your students and who they are. Ask them questions about their interests and hobbies, their families, their community, and types of books they gravitate towards.
2. Choose stories and characters that are around the same age as your students.
3. Choose inclusive stories that portray diverse positive and affirming examples of many different people.
4. Read the story and read it again. Practice the story with appropriate voice, expression, and pacing that matches the intended tone of the story.
5. Plan your questions in advance. What is your goal for reading? What questions are best aligned to that goal? Make sure to plan the right number of questions. Too many questions can take away from the enjoyment of reading and the flow of the read-aloud.
6. Consider how much time you need for the read-aloud. A read-aloud typically takes between 10–20 minutes and not every book needs to be finished in one sitting.
7. Allow enough time for a discussion.
8. Ask questions that get students thinking and talking (see prompts and starters).
9. Monitor your audience as you read.
10. Self-assess and ask yourself what went well and what you'd do differently next.

13 Children/YA Literature that Represents Disabilities and the Special Child

David Allsopp, Aimee Frier, and Margaret Krause

Rationale

People with disabilities/exceptionalities (D/E), like many marginalized populations, have experienced a long history of discrimination, brutal treatment, and exclusion from the rest of society and access to major life activities. Along with other marginalized populations, education is a major life activity to which people with D/E have historically been denied equal access. Kindergarten through 12th (K-12) students with D/E comprise 14% of the total K-12 student population (NCES, 2022). Although progress has been made with respect to the inclusion of students with D/E, educational outcomes for K-12 students with D/E continue to be stagnant and are far below their peers without D/E. For example, the latest report from the National Assessment of Educational Progress (NAEP) shows that 63% of 4th and 8th grade students with D/E performed below the basic level in reading compared to 22% of 4th and 8th grade students without D/E, a 41% discrepancy (National Center for Education Statistics, 2022).

Students with D/Es also experience significant social and emotional difficulties due to how the individual academic and social characteristics/symptoms of their D/E impact their ability to interact successfully in social situations, often resulting in social exclusion. The negative impact of these experiences can lead to emotional difficulties, some that can be observed both through externalizing behaviors (acting out, verbal outbursts, aggression, defiance, etc.) and internalizing behaviors, which are more difficult to "observe" (depression, anxiety, eating disorders, etc.). These behaviors can lead to poor relationships with both peers and adults.

Importantly, students with D/E also have strengths that oftentimes go unnoticed because society and educators focus solely on perceived deficits. Like all of us, students with D/E have areas of strengths that educators should seek to find and understand with respect to their student's educational success (see www.viacharacter.org for further information about character strengths). Since the passage of the Education for All Handicapped Children's Act (EAHCA) of 1975, the first Federal law

DOI: 10.4324/9781003321941-15

mandating a free and appropriate education for all students with D/E, research exploring teacher attitudes toward including students with D/E in their classrooms suggest that a myriad of factors can impact how teachers perceive the inclusion of students with D/E, including factors such as age and teaching experience, grade level taught, level of preparation, the types of behaviors students with D/E engage in, and perceived adequacy of supports, among others (e.g., MacFarlane & Woolfson, 2013; Monsen, et al., 2014; Noreen et al., 2019).

Historical Perspectives

In this section historical foundations of people with disabilities and special education are summarized. Also, intersections between this history and the rise of the field of positive psychology are discussed.

Foundations Related to People with Disabilities and Special Education

The history of the treatment of people with D/E by society has threads that run through culture, economics, religion, science, medicine, and education. This history spans the world's geographic and cultural regions with differing levels of documentation. It is not possible to recount such a long and wide-ranging history; therefore, the historical focus of this chapter will be a summary of how people with D/E have been treated in western society and the evolvement of the education of people with D/E in the United States. In western society, "Disability" as a construct has been used to discriminate against people with D/E along with other marginalized populations (e.g., women, African Americans, immigrants, etc.). Since the eighteenth century, when issues of societal inclusion arose, "disability" has been used as a lens for determining who should and who should not be included in society (Baynton, 2013). Historically in the U.S., women, African Americans, and immigrants have been viewed as possessing deficient traits or characteristics when considering their "rights" with respect to citizenship, voting rights, education, employment, etc. For example, one of the most used rationales for slavery was that African Americans lacked the level of intelligence to participate in society equally with Whites (Baynton, 2013).

Therefore, it is no surprise that, historically, a deficit perspective has been applied to people with D/E (Winzer, 2009). Preindustrial societies (before the mid 1700s) were particularly harsh toward infants with D/E at birth, particularly infants with physical differences. During this time, it was common practice to commit infanticide when the infant was deemed to be unable to live normally in society (Renz-Beaulaurier, 1998). Biblical and classical sources indicate ancient societies attributed demonic possession or supernatural causes toward people with D/E, due to the wrath of god(s)/God (Neubert & Cloerkes, 1987). Preindustrial societies, regardless of type of D/E, categorized people with D/E into one broad term, "idiot", and as idiots, people with D/E were perceived to be inferior beings, absent of any rights or privileges (Winzer, 2009). Indeed, during this time, society believed that most people with D/E were incapable of benefitting from any type of instruction because God or the devil had inflicted them and only divine intervention could cure people with D/Es (Winzer, 2009).

During the age of European Enlightenment (the late seventeenth and eighteenth centuries) a change in how western civilization viewed the world and society emerged. Reason and the scientific method began to challenge the longstanding societal belief that the absolute monarchy and church were the primary sources of knowledge and information (Foun-toulakis, 2022). Several social reforms in the eighteenth and nineteenth centuries, driven by political and religious advocates, such as Dorothea Dix and Horace Mann, acknowledged that "people were more than the sum of their 'defects'" (Mostert, 2011, p. 23).

It was during this time in history that Europe and Britain began to consider the possibilities of educating people with D/E. John Locke's theory of *tabula-rasa* (blank slate) challenged the idea that human capacity was inborn, rather that one's environment supplied knowledge through all the senses (Rekret, 2018). Locke's philosophy was widely accepted and led to efforts toward the education of deaf people. Influenced by Locke and French philosophers like Diderot and Rousseau, Epee created a silent language of the hands, using sign language to teach the deaf (Winzer, 2007). Epee's work promoted innovations by himself and others in education for other D/E groups including those with blindness, those who were deaf and blind, and those with intellectual disabilities (Winzer, 1993).

Despite these advances, asylums for the insane, also known as "lunatic hospitals", became commonplace in Europe during the late eighteenth century. These asylums were "catch all" institutions for people who were deemed to disrupt society or the religious order including people with mental illness, intellectual disabilities, albinism, epilepsy, and those considered to be dissenters or heretics (Doermer, 1969). Asylum inmates were treated harshly including being chained naked in rat-infested cubicles below ground, whipped, and starved (Winzer, 2009). However, French physicians such as Phillippe Pinel, Jean Marc Gaspard Itard, and Edouard Seguin, pushed forward in developing humane and methodological ways to treat people with disabilities. The French psychiatrist Phillipe Pinel used his "moral treatment" approach to treat people with mental illness through kindness, minimal restraint, structure, consistency, and constructive activity (Kauffman, 1976). Jean Marc Gaspard Itard's work with Victor, known as the Wild Boy of Aveyron, was the first recorded attempt to educate a feral child, and his work led towards efforts to educate people with intellectual disabilities. Itard's student,

Edouard Seguin, built upon his mentor's work and established insights to further develop approaches to educate people with intellectual disabilities and make the education of people with intellectual disabilities legitimate (Flugel & West, 1964). In fact, Edouard Seguin strongly believed that education was a universal right for all people and it was society's responsibility to improve the lives of all (Winzer, 2009).

In the United States during this time period, institutions for the "mentally ill" began to be developed as places to treat those thought to have mental illness; however, many were plainly people with a variety of D/E (Martin & Rodriquez, 2022). In 1882, the Undesirables Act was passed to ensure mechanisms were put in place to exclude immigrants from entering the country if they were deemed to be a burden to society, or an "undesirable" (Martin & Rodriquez, 2022). Also, positive sentiment grew toward the "science" of eugenics and using sterilization to ensure people with undesirable traits who lived in the U.S. did not procreate and continue their burden on society through the inherited traits of their children (Selden, 2000).

Despite these realities, progress in the U.S. regarding society's need to educate people with D/E began to develop the acceptance that people with D/E were not criminals or useless to society. In the nineteenth and early twentieth centuries, the notion that people with D/E could be "normalized" away from asylums and institutions started to take hold by such individuals as Samuel Gridley Howe, Dorothy Dix, and Anne Sullivan, the teacher of Helen Keller (Mostert, 2011). Compulsory education for all students evolved during the late 1800s into the early 1900s, and it was then that educators began to observe the dramatic differences in learning between students with D/E and students without D/E, leading to the belief students with D/E were best educated in segregated settings (Mostert, 2011). This practice continued into the 1950s and 1960s when families and advocates began to press for greater levels of access to public education and educational supports leading to legislation, such as the Education of Mentally Retarded Children Act of 1958, the Secondary Education Act of 1965, The Elementary and Secondary Education Act of 1965, and The Early Education Assistance Act of 1968. Finally, in 1975, Congress passed the Education for All Handicapped Children's Act (EAHCA), which provided a free and appropriate public education for all students with D/E (Mostert, 2011). Since that time, the law has been reauthorized and amended multiple times and is more widely known today as the Individuals with Disabilities Education Act (IDEA).

Since the early 1900s, the field slowly evolved from a deficit-first lens regarding people with D/E and their education to a wider social-ecological lens. Through this lens, people with disabilities are recognized as people first, and their abilities can be developed to learn and lead to fulfilling lives. However, the notion of *how* students with disabilities should be included in public education has been a point of contention and advocacy.

Initially, the focus was on *normalization*, a human service perspective that certain individuals with "deviancy" could be brought into society to function as normally as possible. Over time, the notion of *mainstreaming*, a broad term suggesting that students with D/E should be educated in general education classrooms as much as possible, became the educational goal. The notion of mainstreaming evolved into a focus on *inclusion*, a construct advocating that students with D/E should receive their educational services in settings with their peers without D/E with appropriate supports. An important principle included in the IDEA is *least restrictive environment*, which mandates students with D/E receive education alongside their peers without D/E to the maximum extent appropriate and remain in the general education classroom, unless learning cannot be achieved even with the use of supplementary aids and services (IRIS Center, 2019). There has been much debate over how the least restrictive environment should be operationalized both generally and in individual student cases. It is beyond the scope of this chapter to fully synthesize the nature and outcomes of these debates. The courts have attempted to recognize the multifaceted nuances of this mandate: balancing the intent of the law with respect to students with D/E being educated as much as reasonably possible with their peers without D/E, schools demonstrating students with D/E are making educational progress, and affirming a continuum of educational services (whereby educational services may be provided in an array of contexts based on the needs of the student) (Willis, et al., 2020).

Intersections Between the Fields of Disabilities/Exceptionalities and Psychology

Alongside shifts away from a deficit-based model of D/E to a more social-ecological model of human functioning in the field of education, shifts in psychology also occurred, particularly during the past few decades. During Martin Seligman's term as the president of the American Psychological Association in the late 1990s, he emphasized that "psychology has moved too far away from its original roots, which were to make the lives of all people more fulfilling and productive, and too much toward the important, but not all-important area of curing mental illness" (Seligman, 1999, p.559). Thus, the notion of "positive psychology" emerged amongst scholars, creating a new paradigmatic lens through which to view human functioning. A central goal of positive psychology aims to identify, develop, and enhance well-being (Wood & Johnson, 2016). These include setting valued goals, imagining one's best possible self, using strengths, being grateful for positive experiences, developing optimism, strengthening relationships, developing grit, being courageous, among several other indicators (Carr, et al., 2021). Essentially, the goal of positive psychology and associated interventions is to enhance overall well-being and happiness for the individual.

While positive psychology has faced criticism for adopting a "Pollyanna" view, or essentially ignoring the negative issues in life (Lazarus, 2003), Diener (2009) rejects this notion. Diener suggests "positive psychologists do not ignore the negative in life … they maintain that often one form of solution to problems, and in some cases the more effective one, is to build on the positive rather than directly work on the problem" (Diener, 2009, p. 10).

Understanding the intersections between the movements in the fields of education and psychology related to notions of supporting people with D/E enables us to better serve students with D/E. Merging elements of positive psychology constructs and social-ecological models of human functioning allow us to recognize disability is impacted by many factors that are both internal and external to the individual (Buntinx, 2013). Given the multi-dimensional interaction between diverse capabilities and environmental demands for individuals with D/E (and arguably, all individuals), there is a call to find ways to optimize functioning within a variety of contexts and promote subjective well-being, inclusive of quality of life (Schalock et al., 2010).

Understanding these historical perspectives can provide educators with a practical frame for application within inclusive classrooms. One example of an application that underscores these connections between perspectives stemming from the fields of D/E and psychology involves the use of bibliotherapy. As described in Chapter 2, Bibliotherapy is defined as "the use of reading for emotional change and personality development" (Mehdizadeh & Khosravi, 2019, p. 285). For children with D/E, bibliotherapy provides a practical application for teachers to demonstrate to the child that they are not the only one facing challenges, to engage children in conversation regarding a variety of life circumstances, to develop problem-solving skills, to improve personal self-concept, to remove mental and emotional pressures, to foster realistic self-evaluation, to create a way of empathizing with others, and to increase personal understanding of human behavior and motivation (Mehdizadeh & Khosravi, 2019). This practical application connects to a more social-ecological model of human functioning and positive psychology because there is potential to upregulate positive emotions in children with D/E, in order to promote productivity and subjective well-being, leading to a better quality of life and happiness. In addition to supporting students with D/E, Kurtts and Gavigan (2008) suggest ways that bibliography can be used to help all students develop empathy and understanding about diversity, as well as help pre-service teachers to inform their practice about supporting the individual needs of students in their classroom. We outline specific examples of how to use bibliotherapy with selected texts for these purposes in the next section.

Recommended Children's Literature and Practice

Table 13.1 provides a summary of recommended children's literature related to disability/special education.

Table 13.1. Recommended literature for elementary and middle-aged children in inclusive classrooms.

Book Information	Summary
Title: *Fish in a Tree* **Author and Illustrator:** Lynda Mullaly Hunt (Author) **Awards:** Schneider Family Book Award, New York Times Bestseller, ALSC Notable Book of 2016 **Grade Level Band:** Grades 4–7	**Summary:** Ally, a mathematically and artistically talented adolescent, has managed to hide her inability to read as she moves from school to school through creating clever disruptions. Her perspective changes as she works with her new teacher, Mr. Daniels. For the first time, she experiences a teacher who believes in her and all of her potential. Through this journey, her confidence grows, and she discovers there is much more to individuals than a label.
Title: *The Boy with Big, Big Feelings* **Author and Illustrator:** Britney Winn Lee (Author), Jabob Souva (Illustrator) **Awards:** **Grade Level Band:** Preschool–3	**Summary:** Meet the boy with big feelings! He tries to hide his emotions by stuffing them away inside. With a little help he learns that his feelings are something to be celebrated.
Title: A Walk in the Words **Author and Illustrator:** Hudson Talbot **Awards:** Schneider Family Award **Grade Level Band:** Preschool–3	**Summary:** When he was young, Hudson Talbott loved to draw and tell stories. As he got older, he found that reading became a challenge. His love of reading wouldn't allow him to give up and he gave himself permission to read at his own pace. Everyone is unique in their own way, and that is okay!
Title: Charlotte and the Quiet Place **Author and Illustrator:** Deborah Sosin (Author) and Sarah Woolly (Illustrator) **Awards:** Independent Publisher Book Award **Grade Level Band:** Preschool–3	**Summary:** Charlotte likes quiet, but the world around her is a noisy place. Charlotte discovers a quiet place in the park that allows her to have a break from an overstimulating world. The book shows children how Charlotte practices mindfulness through a message of self-discovery and empowerment.
Title: Thank you, Mr. Falker **Author and Illustrator:** Patricia Polacco **Awards:** Parents Choice Award **Grade Level Band:** 2–5	**Summary:** Author Patricia Polacco is a well-known children's book author, but reading wasn't always easy. This book tells the story of a very caring teacher who recognized her dyslexia and helped her to overcome her reading difficulties.
Title: The Girl Who Thought in Pictures: The Story of Dr. Temple Grandin **Author and Illustrator:** Julia Finley Mosca (Author) and Daniel Rieley (Illustrator) **Awards:** NSTA Best STEM Books for K-12 Selection and A Mighty Girl Book of the Year **Grade Level Band:** K-3	**Summary:** Temple Grandin saw the world differently than other children. Many people didn't understand that being autistic made Temple "different, not less." In order to escape bullying, Temple's mom sent her to her aunt's ranch. This is where Temple first developed empathy towards cows, which ultimately led her to revolutionize livestock science into a more humane practice.

Book Information	Summary
Title: El Deafo **Author and Illustrator:** Cece Bell **Awards:** Newberry Honor **Grade Level Band:** 3–7	**Summary:** Cece is moving from a school where everyone is deaf into a new school where she will be part of a general education setting. This author tells the story of Cece's childhood in a humorous manner through her creation of an alternate identity as a superhero named El Deafo. Cecelearns to cope with a sense of loneliness that followed her first years of hearing loss.
Title: As Brave as You **Author and Illustrator:** Jason Reynolds **Awards:** Coretta Scott King Author Honor Book, Schneider Family Book Award, and Kirkus Award Finalist **Grade Level Band:**5–7	**Summary:** Genie and his brother Earnie are traveling for the first time from Brooklyn to rural Virginia to spend the summer with their grandparents. When meeting his grandpop for the first time, Genie discovers his grandpop is blind. This is just one of the many secrets he discovers during his time with his grandparents. This powerful book leads to a journey of discovery of bravery Genie and Grandpop both need.

Teaching Using Disability/Special Education Related Children's Literature

The use of the bibliotherapy process in conjunction with children's literature for diverse students was discussed in Chapter 2. In this section we focus on how to extend this instructional process to students with D/E specifically. As mentioned in the Historical Perspectives section, bibliotherapy is one avenue for upregulating positive emotions and productive problem-solving for children with and without D/E. Bibliotherapy is a "projective indirect intervention that uses carefully selected thematic books or reading materials of any kind, such as biographies, novels, poems, short stories, that fit children's emotional needs, and their unique background and characteristics" (Lucas, et al., 2019, p. 201; Lucas & Soares, 2013). The use of children's literature focused on D/E in bibliotherapy is grounded in the premise that people identify themselves with similar characters. As children engage in reading (or listening) and empathize with the characters of the book, they gain insight into challenges children may also be experiencing (Lucas & Soares, 2013).

In the context of children's literature related to D/E, bibliotherapy is an intentional reading activity that combines reading with targeted reflection on the selected reading about the lived experiences of individuals with D/E. A defining characteristic of bibliotherapy is the dialogue and activities surrounding the story. The purpose of these activities is to allow children to "co-create the story and build new meanings about the situation" in positive ways (Lucas, et al., 2019, p. 202). Lucas et al. (2019) suggest bibliotherapy occurs through the following stages: (1) identification with the characters, (2) the catharsis—the child becomes emotionally involved with the struggles and with the emotional release as the character successfully solves the problems, and (3) the insight—the child thinks about what happened in the story and connects with their own life. As the character finds solutions to a problem, the child gains hope in finding solutions to the difficulties faced and (4) universalism—the child gains a broader perspective of his/her own challenges and is able to understand that others may have similar problems, losing the sense of isolation and alienation, and also finding him/herself in a better position to access personal resources and coping skills (Heath et al., 2005; Wilson & Thornton, 2006).

We suggest five basic phases or steps in a bibliotherapy lesson when using children's literature related to issues of D/E specifically:

1. lesson goal/objectives;
2. pre-reading;
3. guided reading or read aloud;
4. post-reading; and
5. closure/problem-solving-reinforcement activities.

These lesson plan phases closely align with those introduced in Chapter 2. One notable area of emphasis is on ensuring that teachers consider reading instructional practices that support students with D/E to successfully read and gain meaning from the text (see Appendix A).

Supporting SEL among All Students Related to Individuals with D/E

These bibliotherapy phases/steps can support SEL among all students, whether a student does or does not have a D/E. Because Chapter 2 provides a thorough discussion of the important role that bibliotherapy using children's literature can play in the development of SEL among students towards individuals and issues of diversity, we will not repeat this important discussion in this chapter. However, we do believe it is important to note that the use of bibliotherapy with D/E children's literature can be productive for all students, contributing to a wider lens of students developing greater levels of awareness about self, other, and social-political dynamics within a diverse world. As discussed earlier, the historical context of individuals with D/E contextualizes their marginalized status, a context similar to other marginalized sub-groups but also unique to the experiences of individuals with D/E and subsequent intersections between D/E and culture (race, ethnicity, linguistic differences, poverty, etc.,).

Connecting Bibliotherapy and D/E Children's Literature to Academic Instruction for Students with D/E

Another instructional adaptation we suggest for bibliotherapy using D/E related children's literature for students with D/E occurs during Step 5: *Closure/Problem-solving-Reinforcement Activities.* The focus of this adaptation is to connect the D/E bibliotherapy children's literature process to promoting academic success specifically for students with D/E. Below, we summarize a framework for accomplishing this important goal. This teaching strategy/framework incorporates critical SEL related constructs and practices discussed in Ch. X (i.e., the Collaborative for Social and Emotional Learning (CASEL) SEL areas/categories and framework) in addition to character strengths.

To create a memorable way to think about this framework, we have captured the essential steps of this instructional adaptation using the acronym, WISE. The four steps in WISE can be used to explicitly connect Social Emotional Learning (SEL) to academics within the bibliotherapy process using D/E related children's literature.

WISE describes four steps we suggest teachers use to explicitly connect Social Emotional Learning (SEL) to academics within the bibliotherapy process using D/E related children's literature:

W-What's the theme?
I-Identify a connected SEL skill category.
S-Select an associated character strength.
E-Establish connection(s) to the target academic skill.

To implement WISE within the process of bibliotherapy, teachers should first determine what the theme(s) are with respect to the targeted D/E related children's literature text (What's the theme?). Second, teachers identify which Collaborative for Social and Emotional Learning (CASEL) SEL area/category (CASEL, 2022) to which the selected theme connects (Identify a connected SEL skill category.). These SEL categories include *self-awareness, self-management, relationship skills, social awareness, relationship skills, responsible decision-making.* Third, teachers can use the research and practice base related to character strengths (Park, Peterson, & Seligman, 2006; Peterson & Seligman, 2004; see also www.viacharacter.org) to select one or more character strengths students possess that align with the identified SEL category (Select an associated character strength.). Teachers can gain access to the VIA character strengths inventory at the website above for their students to complete at the beginning of the school year and results can be used and integrated to support academic learning during the year. The fourth step of WISE (Establish connection to the target academic skill.) cues teachers to reflect on how the selected character strength can be applied with students to support the targeted academic skill area. Teachers should spend time considering one or more particular academic skill areas in which the student's identified strength can be used to support success.

Title of Text: A Walk in the Words
Relevant Theme(s): Overcoming fear; Finding one's own path
Storyline in One Sentence: A boy who struggles with reading discovers his own pathway toward finding the joy in reading and becoming a better reader.

CASEL Social Emotional Learning Areas ➡	Self-awareness	Self-management	Responsible Decision-making	Relationship Skills	Social Awareness
	X	X			
Virtue ↓ Character Strength					
Wisdom					
Creativity	X				
Curiosity	X				
Judgement					
Love of Learning	X				
Perspective	X				
Courage					
Bravery		X			
Perseverance		X			
Honesty					
Zest					
Humanity					
Love					
Kindness					
Social Intelligence					
Justice					
Teamwork					
Fairness					
Leadership					
Temperance					
Forgiveness					
Humility					
Prudence					
Self-Regulation		X			
Transcendence					
Appreciation of Beauty and Excellence					
Gratitude					
Hope					
Humor					
Spirituality					

Focus Academic Area: *Reading Comprehension – Making sense of a reading passage*
Target Character Strength(s): *Self-regulation & Perseverance*
Strength-based Academic Support Plan Summary (one to two sentences each):

 Academic Skill Area – Comprehension-paraphrasing text

 Goal(s)–*Use the RAP-Q strategy to paraphrase reading text (**R**ead the passage/text; **A**sk myself, what is the main idea?; **P**ut the main idea in my own words; **Q**uestions I have.*

 Teaching approach –*Explicitly teach RAP-Q and provide opportunities for guided practice and discuss the meaning of "self-regulation" and "perseverance" and the role these character strengths can support using RAP-Q successfully.* Monitoring plan –*Daily/Weekly "check ins" with student about 1) how often did they used the RAP-Q strategy when reading?; 2) which character strength(s) did they use and why?; 3) how did it go? (a simple checklist/form can be developed to track student responses)*

Figure 13.1 Tool for implementing the WISE framework with D/E related children's literature.
Note: The virtues and character strengths included come from VIA Character Strengths Institute, 2022

Figure 13.1 shows a tool that teachers can use to reflect upon and document the decisions made when incorporating the WISE framework within Bibliotherapy using D/E children's literature. In this example, the teacher identifies two CASEL SEL areas and three possible character strengths in each SEL area that they could focus on with students for the text *A Walk in the Words*, a story about a boy with reading difficulties/disabilities. This tool provides a structure for use with individual D/E related children's literature texts. Teachers identify the title of the text, relevant themes in the storyline, and a brief one sentence description of the text's storyline. Then, teachers use the matrix to identify potential character strengths that align with the identified theme or themes. Last, the teacher uses the planning tool to identify the academic skill area of focus, which targeted character strength(s) will be emphasized to support academic skill development, and a brief strength-based academic support plan including goal(s), teaching approach, and monitoring plan. In this plan, the teacher selects teaching the RAP-Q Strategy (Allsopp & Minskoff, 2003), a research-supported learning strategy that promotes students' ability to paraphrase text passages and texts to enhance reading comprehension:

R-Read the passage/text.
A-Ask myself what is the main idea?
P-Put the main idea in my own words.
Q-Questions I have.

Teachers can consider the extent to which using the WISE framework could be done collaboratively with student(s) whole class, in small groups, or one-to-one dependent upon the particular instructional context. Engaging students in all or part of the WISE framework can empower then to take ownership for their academic development in connection with D/E related children's literature, enhancing the relevance of D/E children's literature to students related to their academic achievement. Appendix B shows practical examples of bibliotherapy using D/E relevant children's literature including integration of the WISE framework.

Reflection Questions

1. How does a historical perspective of people with D/E impact your thinking about your role in supporting the educational needs of students with D/E?
2. How might current and historical intersections of D/E and culture, particularly marginalized cultures (based on race, ethnicity, linguistic diversity, poverty, sexual/gender identity, etc.) impact persons/students with D/E similarly and differently today?

3. How might you think about integrating the four stages of bibliotherapy in your classroom practice?
4. How has your perspective of the use of children's literature in your classroom changed or expanded after considering the role of D/E related children's literature?
5. How might the use of D/E related children's literature positively impact the culture of your classroom and upregulate positive emotions among all of your students?
6. After selecting a recommended text in Table 13.1, how would you plan an instructional read aloud?
7. After reviewing the resources provided below, identify one or more that you find thought provoking and share why.

Resources

Podcasts

- Disability Representation in Literature: www.icantstandpodcast.com/post/disability-representation-in-literature
- Must Haves for an Inclusive Classroom: https://anchor.fm/caroline-collier

Videos

- Ted Talk—The Windows and Mirrors of Your Child's Bookshelf: www.youtube.com/watch?v=_wQ8wiV3FVo
- Ted Talk by Dr. Martin Seligman: www.ted.com/talks/martin_seligman_the_new_era_of_positive_psychology
- TedTalk: I'm Not Your Inspiration, Thank You Very Much: www.ted.com/talks/stella_young_i_m_not_your_inspiration_thank_you_very_much?language=se
- The Decemberists—Once in My Life: www.youtube.com/watch?v=bHFbaF9_kpI

Websites

- 5 Things Every Kid Should Know About Disability: https://booksforlittles.com/disability-empowerment/.
- Disability—Social Justice Books: https://socialjusticebooks.org/booklists/disabilities/.
- Diverse Book Finder: https://diversebookfinder.org/content/disability/page/10/.
- Positive Psychology Center University of Pennsylvania: https://ppc.sas.upenn.edu/.
- VIA Institute on Character: www.viacharacter.org/.
- Understood: www.understood.org/.

Articles

- Exploring Issues of Disability in Children's Literature: https://dsq-sds. org/article/view/3865/3644.
- The Future of Positive Psychology and Disability: www.ncbi.nlm.nih. gov/pmc/articles/PMC8696272/.

References

Allsopp, D. H. & Minskoff, E. (2003). The learning toolbox: An on-line instructional resource for students with learning disabilities & ADHD, their teachers, and parents. *Journal of International Special Needs Education*, 6, 43–45.

Avramidis, E., & Norwich, B. (2002). Teachers' attitudes towards integration/inclusion: a review of the literature. *European journal of Special Needs Education*, 17(2), 129–147.

Baynton, D. C. (2013). Disability and the justification of inequality in American history. *The Disability Studies Reader*, 17(33), 33–57.

Berry, R. A. (2011). Voices of experience: General education teachers on teaching students with disabilities. *International Journal of Inclusive Education*, 15(6), 627–648.

Buntinx, W. H. (2013). Understanding disability: A strengths-based approach. In M. L. Wehmeyer (Ed.), *The Oxford Handbook of Positive Psychology and Disability* (pp. 7–18). Oxford University Press.

Cameron, D. L. (2017). Teacher preparation for inclusion in Norway: a study of beliefs, skills, and intended practices. *International Journal of Inclusive Education*, 21(10), 1028–1044.

Carr, A., Cullen, K., Keeney, C., Canning, C., Mooney, O., Chinseallaigh, E., & O'Dowd, A. (2021). Effectiveness of positive psychology interventions: a systematic review and meta-analysis. *The Journal of Positive Psychology*, 16(6), 749–769.

Casebolt, K. M., & Hodge, S. R. (2010). High school physical education teachers' beliefs about teaching students with mild to severe disabilities. *Physical Educator*, 67(3), 140.

CASEL. (2022). What Is the CASEL framework?https://casel.org/fundamentals-of-sel/what-is-the-casel-framework/

Cook, B. G. (2001). A comparison of teachers' attitudes toward their included students with mild and severe disabilities. *The Journal of Special Education*, 34(4), 203–213.

Diener, E. (2009). Subjective well-being. *The Science of Well-Being*, 37, 11–58.

Doermer, K. (1969). *Madmen and the bourgeoisie*. Basil Blackwell. (English translation, 1981)

Flugel, J. C., & West, D. J. (1964). *A hundred years of psychology* (3rd ed.). Duckworth.

Fountoulakis, K. N. (2022). *Psychiatry: From its historical and philosophical roots to the modern face*. Springer.

Heath, M. A., Sheen, D., Leavy, D., Young, E., & Money, K. (2005). Bibliotherapy: A resource to facilitate emotional healing and growth. *School Psychology International*, 26(5), 563–580. doi:10.1177/0143034305060792.

IRIS Center. (2019). *Information brief: Least restrictive environment*. Vanderbilt University.

Kahn, S., & Lewis, A. R. (2014). Survey on teaching science to K-12 students with disabilities: Teacher preparedness and attitudes. *Journal of Science Teacher Education*, 25(8), 885–910.

Kauffman, J. M. (1976). Nineteenth century views of children's behavior disorders: Historic contributions and continuing issues. *Journal of Special Education*, 10, 335–349.

Kurtts, S. A., & Gavigan, K. W. (2008). Understanding (dis) abilities through children's literature. *Education Libraries*, 31(1), 23–31.

Lazarus, R. S. (2003). Does the positive psychology movement have legs? *Psychological Inquiry*, 14(2), 93–109.

Lucas, C. V., & Soares, L. (2013). Bibliotherapy: A tool to promote children's psychological well-being. *Journal of Poetry Therapy*, 26(3), 137–147.

Lucas, C. V., Teixeira, D., Soares, L., & Oliveira, F. (2019). Bibliotherapy as a hope-building tool in educational settings. *Journal of Poetry Therapy*, 32 (4), 199–213.

Martin, E. & Rodriquez (2022). Historical foundations of special education law: A civil rights movement. In J. A. Rodriquez & W. W. Murawski (Eds.), *Special education law and policy from foundation to application*. Plural Publishing.

MacFarlane, K., & Woolfson, L. M. (2013). Teacher attitudes and behavior toward the inclusion of children with social, emotional and behavioral difficulties in mainstream schools: An application of the theory of planned behavior. *Teaching and Teacher Education*, 29, 46–52.

Mehdizadeh, M., & Khosravi, Z. (2019). An inquiry into the effectiveness of bibliotherapy for children with intellectual disability. *International Journal of Developmental Disabilities*, 65(4), 285–292.

Monsen, J. J., Ewing, D. L., & Kwoka, M. (2014). Teachers' attitudes towards inclusion, perceived adequacy of support and classroom learning environment. *Learning Environments Research*, 17(1), 113–126.

Mostert, M. P. (2011). A journey from awareness and advocacy to action: Special education in the United States. In M. A. Winzer & K. Mazurek (Eds.), *International practices in special education*. Gallaudet University Press.

National Center for Education Statistics. (2022). Students with disabilities. https://nces.ed.gov/programs/coe/indicator/cgg.

Neubert, D., & Cloerkes, G. (1987). *Behinderung und Behinderte in verschiedenen Kulturen*. Eine vergleichende Analyse ethnologischer Studien.

Noreen, H., Intizar, F., & Gulzar, S. (2019). Teachers' multidimensional attitude towards inclusive education. *UMT Education Review*, 2(2), 72–89.

Park, N., Peterson, C., & Seligman, M. E. (2006). Character strengths in fifty-four nations and the fifty U.S. states. *The Journal of Positive Psychology*, 1(3), 118–129.

Peterson, C., & Seligman, M. E. (2004). *Character strengths and virtues: A handbook and classification* (Vol. 1). Oxford University Press.

Rekret, P. (2018). The posthumanist tabula rasa. *Research in Education*, 101(1), 25–29.

Renz-Beaulaurier, R. (1998). Empowering people with disabilities: The role of choice. In *Empowerment in social work practice: A sourcebook* (pp. 73–84). Brookes/Cole.

Schalock, R. L., Borthwick-Duffy, S. A., Bradley, V. J., Buntinx, W. H., Coulter, D. L., Craig, E. M., ... & Yeager, M. H. (2010). *Intellectual disability: Definition, classification, and systems of supports*. American Association on Intellectual and Developmental Disabilities.

Selden, S. (2000). Eugenics and the social construction of merit, race and disability. *Journal of Curriculum Studies, 32*(2), 235–252.

Seligman, M. E. (1999). The president's address. *American Psychologist, 54*(8), 559–562.

van Steen, T., & Wilson, C. (2020). Individual and cultural factors in teachers' attitudes towards inclusion: A meta-analysis. *Teaching and Teacher Education, 95*, 103–127.

Willis, C. B., Bruno, L. P., Scott, L.A., & Bateman, D. F., (2020). Identifying the least restrictive environment. In J. A. Rodriquez & W. W. Murawski (Eds.), *Special education law and policy from foundation to application.* Plural Publishing.

Wilson, S., & Thornton, S. (2006). *To heal and enthuse: Developmental bibliotherapy and pre-service primary teachers' reflections on teaching and learning mathematics.* Mathematics Education Research Group of Australasia.

Winzer, M. A. (1993). *The history of special education: From isolation to integration.* Gallaudet University Press.

Winzer, M. A. (2007). Confronting difference: An excursion through the history of special education. In *The Sage handbook of special education,* 21–33.

Winzer, M. A. (2009). *From integration to inclusion: A history of special education in the 20th century.* Gallaudet University Press.

Wood, A. M., & Johnson, J. (2016). *The Wiley handbook of positive clinical psychology.* Wiley.

Children's Literature Cited

Bell, C. (2014). *El Deafo.* Harry N. Abrams.

Hunt, L. M. (2015). *Fish in a tree.* Penguin.

Lee, B. W. (2019). *The boy with big, big, feelings.* Beaming Books.

Mosca, J. F. (2019). *The girl who thought in pictures: The story of Dr. Temple Gradin.* The Innovation Press.

Polacco, P. (2012). *Thank you, Mr. Falker.* Philomel Books.

Reynolds, J. (2017). *As brave as you.* Atheneum.

Sosin, D. (2015). *Charlotte and the quiet place.* Plum Blossom.

Talbot, H. (2021). *A walk in the words.* Nancy Paulsen Books.

Appendix A: Foundational Teaching Tips

1. Incorporate pre-reading, during-reading, and post-reading strategies with your students when introducing a new children's literature text to support comprehension and student engagement.
2. Determine the extent to which the readability level of a selected children's literature text is developmentally appropriate for your students and plan supports as needed.
3. Consult with a professional at your school who has expertise in disabilities/special education to learn more about a particular disability represented within your classroom to appropriately engage students in discussion and reflection, particularly when a student in your class may be experiencing the D/E within a selected text.
4. Consider how disability/special education children's literature connects across content areas and current grade level standards.
5. Critically reflect on the extent to which a selected children's literature text accurately and positively portrays individuals with disabilities.

Appendix B: Practical Examples of Bibliotherapy Using D/E Relevant Children's Literature Including Integration of the WISE Framework

A *Walk in the Words* by Hudson Talbot

Bibliotherapeutic Strategies

Pre-reading (Identification with Character)

- When introducing the book, discuss how each person has unique strengths. Ask students to think of examples of what they consider a personal strength. Share a personal strength as an example, then solicit examples from the students.
- Show the students the front cover of the book. Point to the words overwhelm, persevere, curiosity, and determination. Write the three words on an anchor chart and provide a student friendly definition. With a partner, have the students examine the book cover and take into consideration the vocabulary words to make a prediction about the story.

Guided Reading OR Read Aloud (Catharsis)

Prior to reading the story, choose instances where the main character demonstrates perseverance, curiosity, and determination and mark the pages with a sticky note. While reading the story, stop at the preselected pages to consider the following questions:

- Why is the main character feeling overwhelmed? How do the illustrations show that the boy is overwhelmed? (books flying at him, hiding under his notebook, etc.)
- How does he use his strength (art) to help him not feel overwhelmed?
- Post Reading Discussion:(Insight)
- With the whole group, facilitate discussion surrounding the following questions:
- In the beginning, the boy loved drawing and creating stories through pictures. As he got older, the pictures in books disappeared and were

replaced with more words. Why didn't he want his classmates to know he was struggling to read the words on the page?
- How did the boy demonstrate perseverance when learning to read?
- How did his strengths (art, curiosity, and determination) help him overcome his challenges?

Problem-Solving/Reinforcement Activities (Universalism)

Ask the students to do the following:

- In the book the author writes (show page) "I could tell a story with pictures. Or I could tell it with words." How have you worked to solve a problem in the past? Create your own comic of a time when you had difficulty in the past and how you worked to solve the problem using both images and words.

Problem	Solution

Ask volunteers to share comics and discuss their problem-solving strategies in difficult situations.

Teach Academic Skills Using the WISE framework:

- Use the Tool for Implementing the WISE Framework with D/E Related Children's Literature (Figure 1) to document and structure instructional decisions.
- Follow the WISE steps to identify the text's theme(s), SEL area/category, relevant character strength, and to establish connection(s) to a target academic skill.
- Create a brief plan for using the target character strength to support development of the target academic skill including identifying the academic skill area of focus, goal(s), teaching approach, and monitoring plan).

The Boy with Big, Big Feelings by Britney Winn Lee

Bibliotherapeutic Strategies

Pre-reading (Identification with Character)

- Introduce the book by emphasizing that everyone has feelings- big and small. Take a picture walk with the children and ask children to show a "thumbs up" when they see images that represent different emotions the character is feeling.

- Consider descriptive vocabulary to introduce: sad, angry, frustrated, happy, sensitive, alone, reeling. Create an anchor chart with the vocabulary list to remind children of descriptive language they can use to precisely represent their emotions.

Guided Reading OR Read Aloud (Catharsis)

Carefully choose moments where the boy experiences different emotions. Mark these pages with sticky notes as a reminder to pause. When you pause, consider the following questions:

- Give me a thumbs-up if you have ever felt this emotion.
- What colors do you see that represent what the boy is feeling? What does his face look like? What about his body?
- How do the emotions of the people around him make him feel?
- What does his artwork tell us about his emotions?

Post Reading Discussion (Insight)

With the whole group, facilitate discussion surrounding the following questions:

- Why was the boy scared for the other children to see his big emotions?
- How did the boy and girl who cried demonstrate kindness to one another?
- What did the boy realize about the girl and the other children? What did this help him understand about his big, big feelings?

Problem-Solving/Reinforcement Activities (Universalism)

Ask students to do the following: Think of a time you had big, big feelings. Draw a picture that shows what you felt like when you experienced this feeling. You can also write words to describe your illustration.

Share illustrations in pairs or small groups. Provide a format for sharing where students ask each other the following questions to discuss their illustrations:

- How does your illustration show your big feeling? Was your feeling really big, or was it medium or small?
- Why can it be scary sometimes to show our feelings?
- How can we be kind to each other when we feel this feeling- like the boy and girl in the story?

Teach Academic Skills Using the WISE framework:

- Use the Tool for Implementing the WISE Framework with D/E Related Children's Literature (Figure 1) to document and structure instructional decisions.
- Follow the WISE steps to identify the text's theme(s), SEL area/category, relevant character strength, and to establish connection(s) to a target academic skill.
- Create a brief plan for using the target character strength to support development of the target academic skill including identifying the academic skill area of focus, goal(s), teaching approach, and monitoring plan.

14 Religious Diversity through Children's Literature

Connie R. Green

Rationale

Religion connects people to one another, provides comfort in difficult times, guides the moral decisions of followers, and assures cultural continuity. For many American families, religion is a way to find meaning in their lives (Corbett-Hemeyer, 2016). Through churches, synagogues, temples and mosques, religious adherents serve their communities and people around the world. Learning about the world's religions in a factual way supports students' understanding of humanity (Carroll, 2021), both past and present, and prepares them to be informed citizens in a democratic country.

What Is Religion?

Religion addresses the ultimate questions about life, such as: What is our purpose on earth? How should we live? What happens to us when we die? (Carroll, 2021). These are questions that humans have asked for millennia. Religion, however, does more than answer difficult questions or provide a set of beliefs for people to follow. Religion is also about behavior and the creation of moral communities (Sacks, 2020). Religions are immensely powerful social institutions (Dennett, 2006) that influence culture through sacred stories, rituals, and moral codes. Durkheim (1995, as cited in Sacks, 2020) asserted that religion is primarily about behaviors, rather than beliefs; "A religion is a unified system of beliefs and practices relative to sacred things ... which unite into one single moral community ... all those who adhere to them" (p. 285).

Religions are dynamic and evolving systems (Carroll, 2021; Dennett, 2006), adapting to science, culture and historical events. When Muslims, Hindus, and Buddhists emigrate to the U.S., their practices change to fit in with their new culture. For example, Muslims in Nashville, Tennessee have Sunday school where children learn Arabic letters and study the Qur'an. It is not uncommon for Catholics, Protestants, and Jews in the U.S. to practice a form of Buddhist meditation alongside their primary faith traditions.

DOI: 10.4324/9781003321941-16

Learning about Religion

The study of religion encourages students to continue the American ideal of respecting people of all faith traditions and prepares them to live in a country with the most religious diversity in the world (Eck, 2001; Patel, 2018). As students learn about the many contributions of religious communities, they will develop respect for these traditions. Positive attitudes and relationships can develop as students focus on resonance among religions, rather than differences (Patel, 2018).

Pew Research Center researchers found that Americans who had a personal connection with someone who practiced a certain religion had warmer feelings toward the religion (Masci, 2019). For example, study participants who knew someone of the Hindu faith, rated themselves as having warmer feelings toward Hindus in general. Similarly, Americans who had a high level of knowledge about a certain religion felt warmer toward practitioners of that religion. For example, those who answered correctly 65% or more questions about Judaism, felt 16% warmer toward Jews than those who answered only 49% or fewer questions about Judaism. This is significant information for educators. Teaching students about different religions is likely to influence their attitudes and acceptance of others. Inviting guest speakers or visiting houses of worship can engender positive attitudes toward members of various faith groups.

If we fail to address teaching factual information about religions in our pre-kindergarten to twelfth grade curriculum, we are leaving out a major segment of history, literature, music, and art. For hundreds of years, European artists painted and sculpted characters from the bible. Likewise, during the same period, most classical music was written to celebrate events in the liturgical calendar. Masterpieces of Islamic architecture can be found all over Asia and Europe, including the Taj Mahal in India and the Dome of the Rock in Jerusalem. Studying the music of Jewish cantor or the poetry of the Talmud will enrich a study of Jewish life in the past or present.

Children in pre-kindergarten to twelfth grade schools today will invariably live and work with people from many cultural and religious backgrounds in the future. Reading and discussing books about people with various traditions will prepare them to engage with neighbors and colleagues with different backgrounds. Knowledge of religious and spiritual traditions can also help to eliminate stereotyping and prejudice (Green & Oldendorf, 2011).

Historical Perspectives

This section provides a brief overview of the history of the religions addressed in this chapter. Our focus is on religions in the United States, therefore it will address the five religions with the most adherents. Although Sikhism is the fifth largest world religion, we do not have space to address it in this chapter. We begin our historical perspective with the arrival of Europeans and the belief systems they found in the new world.

When Europeans first arrived in what is now the United States, they encountered native people who had well developed spiritual traditions. The spirituality of Native Americans was not a set of beliefs, but rather an understanding of the relationship between humans, nature, and supernatural forces (Butler, 2000). Shamans often mediated between the life on earth and the spiritual realm.

Judaism

During colonial times, the few Jews who lived in America resided in port cities, such as New York, Newport, Charleston, and Savannah, where they engaged in commerce and trade. There was one synagogue in each city, which became the center of religious and social life for Jews (Sarna & Golden, 2000). Orthodox Jews, originally emigrating from Eastern Europe, hold to traditional practices such as the dietary (kosher) laws and separation of genders in the synagogue. Ultra-Orthodox Jews, such as the Hasidic sect, are religiously and socially conservative, and live in separate communities, mainly in New York. Conservative Jews include Hebrew in their services and are committed to Jewish traditions, but believe that laws and practices must change with the times (Green & Oldendorf, 2011). In the nineteenth century, young Jews concerned about the future of their faith, started the first breakaway Reform Jewish congregation in Charleston. This is a uniquely American type of Judaism, adapted to the free spirit of their new country. The new Reform services are shorter and include a sermon in English. Today, 41% of young Jews (age 18–29) say they belong to no particular branch of Judaism (Alper & Cooperman, 2021).

Judaism is also sometimes separated into "religious Jews," those who attend synagogue, pray and study the wisdom writings of Judaism, and "cultural Jews." The latter are Jews by ethnicity and may enjoy the foods, traditions, and music of Judaism. Jews originally emigrated to the U.S. from many countries and cultures, bringing different practices and traditions. Also, about 10,000 non-Jews convert to Judaism each year (Corbett-Hemeyer, 2016). There are about 5.8 million Jewish adults, or 2.4% of the U.S. population. Additionally, 2.3 million adults, 1.1% of U.S. adults have at least one parent who is Jewish, or were raised Jewish, but now claim another religion (Pew Research Center, 2021a, 2021b).

Christianity

European colonists brought Christianity to what is now the United States in the sixteenth and seventeenth centuries. Many Protestants left Europe because of religious persecution and settled along the east coast in the Massachusetts Bay Colony, New Netherland (part of New York, New Jersey, Pennsylvania, Connecticut, and Delaware), the Virginia Colony and the Carolina Colony. Pennsylvania was founded by William Penn, a religious thinker and writer who was a member of the Religious Society of Friends (Quakers). The Puritans, settled in New England, hoping to "purify" doctrine and practices of the Church of England. Maryland began as a haven for Roman Catholics escaping persecution in England (Corbett-Hemeyer, 2016).

There are many denominations of Protestantism in the U.S., including Baptists, Methodists, Lutherans, Presbyterians, and Episcopalians, all originating in Europe. There are also a number of denominations that originated in the U.S.: Latter-day Saints (Mormons), Christian Scientists, Seventh-day Adventists, and Jehovah's Witnesses. The most noteworthy trends in Protestantism are Evangelical Christianity, megachurches, and the religious-political right. Christian television stations, contemporary Christian music and best-selling books, such as the *Left Behind* series of novels by Timothy LeHaye and Jerry Jenkins are evidence of the popularity of these movements (Corbett-Hemeyer, 2016).

It is likely that the first people to arrive in what is now the United States were Catholic. Within decades of the arrival of early explorers in the Americas, Catholic missionaries from Spain arrived in Florida and later the Southwest. English Catholics were among the early settlers but were not missionaries. During the colonial period, fewer than one percent of the population was Catholic (Corbett-Hemeyer, 2016).

Immigrants from Ireland arriving between 1820 and 1930 increased the number of Catholics by 4.5 million (Library of Congress, n.d.). Catholicism has long been the faith of many immigrants, in the early 20th century those from Italy and other European countries and later immigrants from Central and South America.

Christianity is rapidly declining in the U.S., according to an extensive interview study in 2018–2019 conducted by the Pew Research Center (2019). In 2009, 78% of Americans identified themselves as Christian. In 2019, only 65% identified as Christian. Protestantism is down from 51% in 2009 to 43% in 2019. Catholicism had a 3% loss in population during that time period. Most of this decline can be attributed to younger Americans who report having no religious affiliation. Recent generations (Millennials and Gen X) are an increasingly large proportion of the population and have little interest in joining religious organizations (Jones, 2021).

Islam

The first wave of Muslims came to America from West Africa aboard slave ships, beginning in the seventeenth century. It is estimated that between 10 and 20% of African slaves were followers of Islam. Because of family separation and forced adoption of Christianity, the enslaved people were unable to maintain their home religion (Melman, 2010).

Muslims voluntarily immigrated to the United States in two waves. The first wave occurred between 1870 and the beginning of World War I. These people were mainly Arabs from the Mediterranean region and worked as peddlers, miners, and migrant farmworkers in the U.S. After World War II, another wave of immigration brought Muslims from the Middle East and Eastern Europe to settle in large urban areas such as Chicago and New York. These immigrants tended to be better educated or sought to pursue higher education when they arrived in the United States.

Starting in the late 1960s, political unrest around the world contributed to more and more Muslims fleeing oppression or revolution and emigrating to the United States. In recent decades, Muslims arrived as refugees from South Asia, Somalia, Sudan, and Bosnia, to name a few countries (Melman, 2010). These immigrants brought traditions from their countries of origin and different ways of practicing Islam. Muslims in the U.S. hail from over 75 different countries. There are about 3.45 million Muslims living in the U.S., or 1.1% of the population (Pew Research Center, 2017).

Hinduism and Buddhism

Trade between the U.S. and Asia began in 1784, bringing some artifacts and ideas from that part of the world. Emerson, Thoreau, and other Transcendentalists studied Eastern thought and introduced it in the U.S. (Corbett-Hemeyer, 2016). During the 1893 World Parliament of Religions, held in Chicago, many Americans were introduced to people from Japan and China and learned about their religions, primarily Hinduism and Buddhism (Mann, Numrich & Williams, 2001).

The Immigration Act of 1965 opened the door for immigrants from Asia and other non-Europeans to become permanent residents and eventually U.S. citizens. Many of the immigrants from India were graduate students or professionals in the fields of technology and medicine. Since 80% of the population of India was Hindu, most of the immigrants from India practiced the Hindu faith. Coming from different geographic areas in India, their particular practices could be quite different, emphasizing different deities, texts, and festivals. There are about 2.5 million Hindus living in the U.S., or about 0.7% of the population (World Population Review, 2022).

The first Buddhists from China, emigrated to the U.S. between 1840 and 1900, mainly to try their luck in the California gold rush or to work on the railroad. Between 1868 and 1912, many Japanese immigrants came to the U.S. Both Chinese and Japanese immigrants experienced discrimination, and laws passed to limit immigration from Asia. During the

1920s and 1930s, second generation Japanese Buddhists, influenced by their Protestant neighbors, built temples and held services similar to those of local Christian churches (Mann, Numrich, & Williams, 2001).

The 1960s saw an increased interest in Eastern religions, particularly Zen Buddhism. Meditation and yoga became popular with young people during this period and increased over the decades that followed. For example, some celebrities and sports stars became Buddhists or were at least influenced by Buddhist teaching and meditation practices. Today there are around 1,000 Buddhist temples in the U.S. Approximately 1%, between 3 and 4 million Americans, are Buddhist (Public Religion Research Institute, 2021).

Other Belief Systems

As mentioned earlier, the number of American adults who identify as Christian decreased dramatically in recent years. At the same time, those who identify as atheist, agnostic or "nothing in particular" rose from 17% in 2009 to 26% in 2019. Atheism refers to people who do not believe in a God, and agnosticism refers to those who doubt whether or not a God exists. Although neither of these belief systems emphasize a belief in a supernatural being or god, they do advocate living a moral life and honoring all humanity. The term Humanism derives "values from the experience of human life in this world, without reference to God … or anything else supernatural" (Corbett-Hemeyer, 2016, p. 223). They affirm the goodness of human life and nature and the importance of leading a moral life.

Unitarianism had its roots in Christianity and the transcendentalist movement. The name Unitarian refers to the unity of God, in contrast to trinitarians who believe in three aspects of God. Universalists believe that a loving God would reject no one; all are saved. The two traditions merged in 1965, becoming Unitarian Universalism, one of the most liberal religious traditions in the U.S.

Reflection Questions

1. What was your religion or belief system as you were growing up? How have those beliefs influenced your life as an adult?
2. How do you think children's religions influence their behaviors in school?
3. What can elementary school students learn about United States history by reading books mentioned in this chapter?
4. What can be learned about different storytelling traditions from reading children's literature from different religions, such as books referencing a great flood?

Table 14.1 Recommended books on religious diversity.

Book Information	Summary
Books about Many Religions	
Title: *What Do You Believe? Big Questions about Religion* **Author and Illustrator:** NA **Grade Level Band:** 4–6	**Summary:** Using a variety of text features, DK Publishing presents content about many religions in a question & answer format. Textboxes, maps, timelines, photographs and drawings enhance this busy, yet informative, informational book.
Title: *First Light, First Life: A Worldwide Creation Story* **Author and Illustrator:** Paul Fleishman (Author), Julie Paschikis (Illustrator) **Grade Level Band:** 2–5	**Summary:** Drawing on creation stories from 24 different cultures, Fleishman and Paschikis combine phrases and sentences to show similarities in the myths of life's beginning and the story of the great flood.
Title: *The Enduring Ark* **Author and Illustrator:** Gita Wolf (Author), Joydeb Chitrakar (Illustrator) **Grade Level Band:** K-3	**Summary:** Flood stories are found in many cultures and religious traditions around the world. *The Enduring Ark* is an Indian version with accordion pages and the Patua style of scroll painting, using bold colors.
Books about Judaism	
Title: *Stones for Grandpa* **Author and Illustrator:** Renee Londner (Author), Martha Avilés (Illustrator) **Grade Level Band:** Pre-K-2	**Summary:** A young boy remembers his grandfather as he and his parents live through the year following his death: building the sukkah, celebrating Hanukkah, and joining the Purim parade. At the end of the year family and friends gather to share memories and place stones on Grandpa's tombstone.
Title: *The Christmas Mitzvah* **Author and Illustrator:** Jeff Gottesfeld (Author), Michelle Laurentia Agatha (Illustrator) **Grade Level Band:** Pre-K-3	**Summary:** Al, a Jew, felt sorry for his Christian neighbors who had to work on Christmas. For three decades he volunteered to pump gas, serve meals, sort male, bag groceries, and park cars so others could spend the holiday with their families. (Inspired by a true story)
Title: *Noah's Ark* **Author and Illustrator:** Jerry Pinkney (Author & Illustrator) **Awards:** Caldecott Honor **Grade Level Band:** K-3	**Summary:** Pinkney's exquisite watercolor and pencil illustrations take us back to the time of the great flood. This story is found in all the Abrahamic faiths: Judaism. Islam, and Christianity.

Book Information	Summary
Title: *It's a...It's a...It's a Mitzvah* **Author and Illustrator:** Liz Suneby & Diane Heiman (Authors), Laurel Molk (Illustrator) **Grade Level Band:** Pre-K-2	**Summary:** To Jews, good deeds or mitzvot are part of God's commandments. With animal characters and lots of humor, the authors teach children about finding joy in kindness, for giver and receiver.
Title: *This Is the Matzah* **Author and Illustrator:** Abby Levine (Author), Paige Billin-Frye (Illustrator) **Grade Level Band:** Pre-K-3	**Summary:** With repetition and cartoon-style illustrations, the author-illustrator pair present a modern story of Passover from a child's perspective.

Books about Christianity

Book Information	Summary
Title: *What's Given from the Heart* **Author and Illustrator:** Patricia C. McKissick (Author), April Harrison (Illustrator) **Awards:** Coretta Scott King **Grade Level Band:** K-3	**Summary:** James Otis has lost his father, his home, and the family farm. He and his mother find that, poor as they are, they are able to give to others and receive kindness and gifts from the members of their church.
Title: *A Church for All* **Author and Illustrator:** Gayle E. Pitman (Author), Laure Fournier (Illustrator) **Awards: Stonewall** **Grade Level Band:** Pre-K-2	**Summary:** Based on the story of the Glide Church in San Francisco, the book's cheerful illustrations depict a diverse congregation of GLBT families and singles, old, young, rich and poor congregants. The banners in the church and sparse text describe an accepting, connected, welcoming church.
Title: *Preaching to the Chickens: The Story of Young John Lewis* **Author and Illustrator:** Jabari Asim (Author), E. B. Lewis (Illustrator) **Grade Level Band:** K-3	**Summary:** Young John Lewis grew up on a farm in the rural south helping with the animals, especially the chickens. He loved attending church with his family and admired the pastor's speaking style, which he practiced among the chickens.
Title: *By and By: Charles Albert Tindley the Father of Gospel Music* **Author and Illustrator:** Carol Boston Weatherford (Author), Bryan Collier (Illustrator) **Grade Level Band:** 1–4	**Summary:** Born in 1851, Charles Tindley worked as a sharecropper, teaching himself to read from scraps of newspaper. His first encounter with the Bible was through spirituals he heard in the field. As an adult he penned "I'll Overcome Some Day," on which the civil rights anthem was based.

Books about Islam

Book Information	Summary
Title: *In My Mosque* **Author and Illustrator:** M. O. Yuksel (Author), Hatem Aly (Illustrator) **Grade Level Band:** Pre-K-2	**Summary:** Yuksel and Aky present a lyrical introduction to Islam. Playful illustrations create a child-like perspective on the love, peace and security youngsters feel in the mosque. Illustrations and endnotes depict architecture found in world mosques.

Book Information	Summary
Title: *The Proudest Blue: A Story of Hijab and Family* **Author and Illustrator:** Ibtihaj Muhammad with S. K. Ali (Authors), Hetem Aly (Illustrator) **Grade Level Band:** K-3	**Summary:** Faizah is excited about the first day of school, her new backpack and light-up shoes. She is also proud of her older sister, Asiya for wearing her sky blue hijab to school for the first time. Asiya shows her little sister how to stand strong when a classmate teases her about her hijab.
Title: *Bakara Beats* **Author:** Maleeha Siddiqui **Grade Level Band:** 5–7	**Summary:** The novel begins at Nimra's Ameen, a celebration to honor her memorization of the Qur'an. The focus of the story is on a Muslim girl's transition to a public middle school.

Books about Hinduism

Book Information	Summary
Title: *Priya Dreams of Marigolds & Masala* **Author and Illustrator:** Meenal Patel (Author and Illustrator) **Grade Level Band:** K-3	**Summary:** When Priya returns from school, she helps Babi Ba (her grandmother) make rotli, Indian bread. Priya asks Babi Ba to tell her about her native India.
Title: *Grandfather Gandhi* **Author and Illustrator:** Arum Gandhi and Bethany Hegedus (Authors), Evan Turk (Illustrator) **Grade Level Band:** K-5	**Summary:** Arum Gandhi recounts summers he spent at an ashram service village, learning life lessons that his famous grandfather shared through stories and example.
Title: *The Night Diary* **Author and Illustrator:** Veera Hiranandani **Awards:** Newbery Honor **Grade Level Band:** 5–7	**Summary:** Written as letters to her late mother, Nisha tells the story of the partition of India from the perspective of a child whose father is Hindu and whose mother was Muslim. *The Night Diary* is historical fiction at its best.

Books about Buddhism

Book Information	Summary
Title: *Under the Bodhi Tree: A Story of the Buddha* **Author and Illustrator:** Deborah Hopkinson (Author). Kailey Whitman (Illustrator) **Grade Level Band:** K-3	**Summary:** The story of the Buddha has been told in many picture books. This telling is unique in that it addresses the reader in places, such as acknowledging that they, too, will want to leave home and explore the world someday.
Title: *The Seed of Compassion* **Author and Illustrator:** His Holiness the Dalai Lama (Author), Bao Luu (Illustrator) **Grade Level Band:** 1–4	**Summary:** Part autobiographical and part lessons on compassion, the Dalai Lama's message will help children to treat other with kindness and become more peaceful.

Book Information	Summary
Other Belief Systems	
Title: *I Wonder* **Author and Illustrator:** Annaka Harris (Author), John Rowe, Illustrator **Grade Level Band:** K-3	**Summary:** As Eva and her mother take a walk, the child asks questions about the moon, gravity, butterflies and other mysteries. Eva learns that her mother's answer to questions is "I don't know," and wondering about the universe is a good thing.
Title: *Humanism for Kids* **Author and Illustrator:** Devin Carroll (Editor), Marion Young (Illustrator) **Grade Level Band:** 4–6	**Summary:** Written by children and parents in Humanist families, this informational book explains beliefs and principles through examples of how humanists live in the world.

Resources for Teachers

- May, C. M. (undated). Religion's legal place in the schoolhouse. American Association of School Administrators. www.aasa.org/SchoolAdm inistratorArticle.aspx?id=7730
- Learning for Justice. www.learningforjustice.org/?gclid=CjwKCAjw3c SSBhBGEiwAVII0Z8lRdRjDzq1m8yEQAva0C0akWy3KQIMQnlpE m81oUhrfK8sjwF-imxoCaf8QAvD_BwE
- Pew Research Center (2019, April). Being Muslim in the U.S. [Video]. www.pewresearch.org/religion/2018/04/17/video-being-muslim-in-the-u-s/
- Religion and Ethics Newsletter. https://unctv.pbslearningmedia.org/ collection/awr09/
- Religion in America. https://religioninamerica.org/
- Religious landscape study. www.pewforum.org/religious-landscape-study/
- Religious Tolerance. www.religioustolerance.org/
- Teaching American History. https://teachingamericanhistory.org/

References

Alper, B. A. & Cooperman, A. (2021, May). 10 key findings about Jewish Americans. Pew Research Center. www.pewresearch.org/fact-tank/2021/05/11/ 10-key-findings-about-jewish-americans/.

Butler, J. (2000). *Religion in colonial America*. Oxford University Press.

Carroll, J. (2021). *World religions: A beginner's guide*. Rockridge Press.

Corbett-Hemeyer, J. (2016). *Religion in America* (7th ed.). Routledge.

Dennett, D. (2006, February). "Let's teach religion—all religion—in schools. TED. [Video]. TED Conferences. www.pewforum.org/2017/07/26/findings-from-pew-research-centers-2017-survey-of-us-muslims/.

Eck, D. (2001). *A new religious America*. HarperCollins.

Green, C. R., & Oldendorf, S. B. (2011). *Religious diversity and children's literature: Strategies and resources*. Information Age Publishing.

Library of Congress. (n.d.). Irish-Catholic Immigration to America. loc.gov/cla ssroom-materials/immigration/irish/irish-catholic-immigration-to-america/#:~: text=It%20is%20estimated%20that%20as,all%20immigrants%20to%20this% 20nation.

Jones, J. (2021). U.S. church membership falls below majority for first time. https:// news.gallup.com/poll/341963/church-membership-falls-below-majority-first-time. aspx.

Mann, G. S., Numrich, P. D., & Williams, R. B. (2001). *Buddhists, Hindus, and Sikhs in America*. Oxford University Press.

Masci, D. (2019). In U.S., familiarity with religious groups is associated with warmer feelings toward them. www.pewresearch.org/fact-tank/2019/10/31/in-u-s-familiarity- with-religious-groups-is-associated-with-warmer-feelings-toward-them.

Melman, A. (2010). *Islam in America*. Mason Crest Publishers.

Patel, E. (2018). *Out of many faiths: Religious diversity and the American promise*. Princeton University Press.

Pew Research Center. (2017, July). U.S. Muslims Concerned about their Place in society but continue to believe in the American Dream. www.pewforum.org/ 2017/07/26/findings-from-pew-research-centers-2017-survey-of-us-muslims/.

Pew Research Center. (2019a, April). Being Muslim in the U.S. www.pewresearch. org/religion/2018/04/17/video-being-muslim-in-the-u-s/.

Pew Research Center. (2019b, October). In U.S., decline of Christianity con- tinues at rapid pace. www.pewresearch.org/religion/2019/10/17/in-u-s-decline-of- christianity-continues-at-rapid-pace/.

Pew Research Center. (2021, May). Jewish Americans in 2020. www.pewresearch. org/religion/2021/05/11/the-size-of-the-u-s-jewish-population/.

Public Religion Research Institute. (2021, July). The 2020 census of American reli- gion. www.prri.org/research/2020-census-of-american-religion/#:~:text=identify% 20as%20independent.-,Buddhist,the%20San%20Francisco%20Bay%20Area.

Ragan, N. (2018). *Major world religions: Hinduism*. Mason Crest.

Sacks, J. (2020). *Morality: Restoring the common good*. Hatchette Book Group.

Sarna, J. D. & Golden, J. (2000). The American Jewish experience through the nineteenth century: Immigration and acculturation. http://nationalhumanities center.org/tserve/nineteen/nkeyinfo/judaism.htm.

World Population Review. (2022). Hindu countries. https://worldpopulationre view.com/country-rankings/hindu-countries.

Children's Literature Cited

Asim, J. (2016). *Preaching to the chickens: The story of young John Lewis*. Nancy Paulsen Books.

Carroll, D. (2020). *Humanism for kids*. Family of Humanists.

Dalai Lama (2020). *The seed of compassion*. Penguin Random House.

Dorling Kindersley. (2011). *What do you believe? Big questions about religion*. DK Publishing.

Fleischman, P. (2016). *First light, first life: A worldwide creation story*. Henry Holt and Company.

Gandhi, A. (2014). *Grandfather Gandhi*. Atheneum Books for Young Readers.

Gottesfeld, J. (2021). *The Christmas mitzvah*. Creston Books.

Harris, A. (2013). *I wonder*. Four Elephants Press.

Hiranandani, V. (2018). *The night diary*. Dial Books.

Hopkinson, D. (2018). *Under the Bodhi tree: A story of the Buddha*. Sounds True.

Levine, A. (2005). *This is the matzah*. Albert Whitman & Company.

Lodner, R. (2015). *Stones for Grandpa*. Kar-Ben Publishing.

McKissack, P. C. (2019). *What is given from the heart*. Schwartz & Wade Books.

Muhammad, I. (with Ali, S.K.) (2019). *The Proudest Blue*. Little Brown.

Pinkney, J. (2002). *Noah's ark*. N North-South Books.

Pitman, G. E. (2018). *A church for all*. Albert Whitman & Company.

Siddiqui, M. (2021). *Barakah beats*. Scholastic.

Suneby, L. & Heiman, D. (2012). *It's a…It's a…It's a Mitzvah*. Jewish Lights Publishing.

Weatherford, C. B. (2020). *By and by: Charles Albert Tindley the father of gospel music*. Atheneum Books for Young Readers.

Wolf, G. (2013). *The enduring ark*. Tara Books.

Yuksel, M. O. (2021). *In my mosque*. HarperCollins.

Appendix: Lesson Ideas

1. **Heroes.** Standards in many states suggest a study of heroes in elementary schools, which typically include people such as Martin Luther King, Jr., Rosa Parks, George Washington Carver, Amelia Earhart, and Oprah Winfrey. Expand children's knowledge of heroes by including religious heroes, such as Saladin, the Muslim leader from the Middle Ages, Hindu's Mahatma Gandhi, or Buddhism's 14th Dalai Lama.
2. **The African-American Church in the Civil Rights Movement.** Teachers often address various aspects of the civil rights movement with their elementary students, but rarely address the role of the church in bringing people together and organizing for demonstrations. Focusing on the importance of religion to the leaders of the movement, the musicians, and the ordinary people who stood up for their rights, will open a new perspective for students.
3. **Musical Instruments.** From the Jewish shofar, the Hindu pungi, and Buddhist flutes to contemporary Christian rock, the music of various religious traditions can provide insights into beliefs and practices.
4. **Storytelling Traditions.** All religions have stories that for the basis of some of their followers' behaviors and beliefs. Comparing and contrasting creation stories or flood stories can provide insights about the religions and their practitioners.

15 Supporting Children and Families Impacted by Incarceration Through Multicultural Children's Literature

Susan V. Bennett, Emily McConnaughy, Jessica N. Szempruch, and AnnMarie Alberton Gunn

Rationale

Although incarceration rates in the United States have declined since 2008, the U.S. maintains the highest incarceration rate in the world and holds racial disparities within prisons (Gramlich, 2021; Warren, et al., 2019). According to Turney (2019), since 1970, the number of individuals in prison increased by five times, in particular men of color from low socioeconomic backgrounds who most likely have not received a diploma. Black and Hispanic people comprise 25% of the population in the U.S., yet within the correctional institutions in 2016, the population consisted of 71% Hispanic and Black (Love, 2019). Despite the smaller population size for children of color, the percentage of these children who have a parent in prison mirrors this imbalance (see Table 1). Due to the surge in incarceration rates, children with a parent who is incarcerated (CPI) also continues to rise, and of the individuals in criminal justice systems, 50–75% disclosed they had one or more children under 18 (Martin, 2017; Turney, 2019).

A parent, whether present or not present in a child's life, impacts their experiences and possibly their success in academics and successful adult outcomes. When a parent is incarcerated, this experience has the potential to cause trauma to the child, and these traumatic experiences are

Table 15.1 2018–2019 children with a parent who was ever incarcerated.

Race or Ethnicity	Population Number	% of Population
American Indian	52,823	20%
Asian and Pacific Islander4	34,963	1%
Black or African American	1,269,509	13%
Hispanic or Latino	1,157,507	6%
Non-Hispanic White	2,298,204	6%

Note: Based on data from the Annie E. Casey Foundation (2022)

DOI: 10.4324/9781003321941-17

often neglected in research, as well as avoided in classroom discussion (Sykes & Pettit, 2014). In the U.S., approximately 2.6 million children have experiences with parents in the criminal justice system (Pochlmann-Tynan & Turney, 2021; Sykes & Pettit, 2014). According to Martin (2017) these experiences can adversely impact those children in numerous ways, resulting in these children becoming "hidden victims." They are more likely to be children of color, from a lower socioeconomic area, and with a parent with low educational attainment. African American children with a parent in prison occurs 7.5 times more often than for White children and for Hispanic children 2.3 times more often (Martin, 2017; Turney, 2019; Warren, et al., 2019).

The impact on CPI can result in social-emotional, behavioral, psychological, academic or physical problems (Kjellstrand & Eddy, 2011; Martin, 2017; Reimer, 2019; Warren, et al., 2019). When a parent becomes incarcerated, children experience emotional stress as this parent is no longer in their home to nurture and care for them, and the families might experience financial problems as they now live in a single parent home. Children might feel isolated, alone, and embarrassed due to the stigma of having a parent in prison. This can also have the potential for low academic performance, behavior problems, truancy, or substance abuse. CPI are at greater risk of becoming incarcerated themselves, six times more likely as an adult or juvenile (Martin, 2017). Not every child will endure these adverse outcomes; however, teachers must develop an awareness and understanding to support CPI.

Historical Perspectives

Although we could examine and recognize how Jim Crow laws and postwar eras impacted incarceration rates, for the purpose of this chapter, we focus on the excessive surge that occurred between 1970 and 2010 (Thompson, 2010). In the 1960s and 1970s, incarceration rates began to rise as legislation, politicians, and government maintained strong boundaries toward crime, which included the war on drugs, harsher sentencing, and police officials fixated disproportionately on communities of color and low socioeconomic areas (Mauer, 2013; Thompson, 2010). In addition, at the height of social justice movements (civil rights, American Indian, women's rights, LGBTQ, etc.), activists who fought for social justice and equity were arrested for protesting and speaking up. The number of individuals in prison or jail in 1972 increased 500% by 2010 (Mauer, 2013).

Due to this immense growth, from 1991 to 2007, children with a parent in prison increased by 80% (Warren, et al., 2019). Today, there are over 2 million children (approximately 1 in 28) with a biological parent in jail or state or federal prison (Martin, 2017; Turney, 2019). Some children have a parent who experienced the criminal justice system but might not

be in jail or prison, such as parents who were released or being super-
vised; coupling these two populations means approximately 11% of children under 18 in the U.S. have been affected (Kjellstrand & Eddy, 2011).

Women and Men

As stated previously, the war on drugs greatly impacted incarceration and
even more so for women; women on average were incarcerated for non-
violent crimes. Since the 1980s, children with a mother in prison
increased 100% and fathers 75% (Martin, 2017). From1980–2010, the
number of women in prison escalated 646%, rising from 4% to 7% of
the entire population in federal and state prisons, where men in prison
grew 419% (Mauer, 2013). For many decades, women continued to
become incarcerated at higher rates than men; from 2000 to 2009, women
climbed 21.6% and men 15.6 % (Mauer, 2013). In urban areas, where a
larger number of people of color live and are in a lower socioeconomic
bracket, by the age of nine, 1/3 of the children have a father in prison and
1/10 a mother (Turney, 2019).

Race and Ethnicity

African American, Hispanic, and Native American individuals are at
greater risk of being incarcerated, and their children are more likely to
have a parent who is incarcerated (Kjellstrand & Eddy, 2011). Kjellstrand
and Eddy discussed inequity:

> When broken down by racial and ethnic background, the current study
> revealed a disproportionate amount of children from African American,
> Native American, and Hispanic backgrounds had experienced parental
> incarceration during their first 10 years … 9.1% for Caucasian, 25% of
> African American, 30% for Native American, and 18.2% for Hispanic
> children experienced parental incarceration during their childhood.
> (Kjellstrand & Eddy, 2011, p. 32)

Although from 2000–2009, incarceration rates for African Americans
decreased, there is still a larger population of African American men and
women who are incarcerated (Mauer, 2013). During this time, White women
rose 48.4%, possibly due to prescription drug arrests, and Hispanic women
increased by 75% in prisons, which mirrors the increase of Hispanics in the
United States population.

Family Literacy Initiatives

Due to the growing population of incarcerated parents, prisons have
increased their effort to develop parenting programs designed to teach

incarcerated parents how to build and maintain healthy relationships with their children (Loper & Tuerk, 2006). The implementation of these family literacy initiatives began in the U.S. in the 1990s (Nutbrown et al., 2019). According to Blumberg and Griffin:

> Research has demonstrated that parents' involvement with their children's educational activities, particularly reading, translates into increased interest and, ultimately, achievement in school. For incarcerated parents, reading programs provide an opportunity to re-establish parental roles, reassure the children of their continued love, and encourage the children's reading behavior.
>
> (Blumberg & Griffin, 2013, p. 265)

Some prisons nationally and internationally afford various supportive services and programs for children to interact with their parents who are incarcerated. Many facilities offer programs where a parent reads a book while audio or video recorded, and then the recording is then sent to the child (Hoffmann et al., 2010). For example, the *Oklahoma Messages Project* filmed parents reading age-appropriate books to their children and then sent a hard copy of the book and the video to the children. This project aimed to lessen the effect of parental incarceration on the child and help to increase family connections and literacy skills. This digitally distributed reading program resulted in 62 % of incarcerated parents feeling that they built a stronger relationship with their children, and 44% of the participating children improved in literacy and academic skills (McLeod et al., 2021). Additionally, the *Read to Your Child/Grandchild* (RYCG) program was implemented in Pennsylvania to increase relationships between children and incarcerated parents and support family literacy development through a shared reading program. This included video recordings of parents/grandparents reading a book to their child and creating a scrapbook with personal notes, photos, and letters to give to the children (Prins et al., 2020). In Florida, the *Reading Family Ties: Face to Face* program allows incarcerated mothers to have weekly visits via video conferencing in which they would read books aloud with their children (Bartlett, 2000). The implementation of these family literacy programs leads to implications for our current education system. Local school districts and teachers should consider utilizing video conferences and distributing literacy materials that incarcerated parents can work on or read with the children when they visit.

Teachers' Support and Care

Teachers must first acquire an awareness of their students' circumstances, then they need to know their needs (Reimer, 2019). The teachers can support the students' needs through cultivating a caring and empathetic environment and providing interventions. When working with any child, it is important to consider the many aspects of their lives, including their home environment and relationships inside and outside the classroom. This begins by listening carefully to students and providing a safe space in which they can share their experiences (Morgan et al., 2013; Wiseman et al., 2019; Wissman & Wiseman, 2011). Noddings (1992) emphasizes the need for care in the education system, and true care is not simply creating a warm and fuzzy feeling, but instead, caring implies doing the best for individuals in our care. Sitler (2009) advocates for an approach to learning that requires greater attention to viewing the learner as a whole person with physical, emotional, and cognitive needs. Due to the stress and emphasis on high-stakes testing, care of the whole child can often be overlooked. Teachers must take the time to get to know their students to determine who they are, where they come from, and what needs they may have to genuine care for and provide the necessary support (Reimer, 2019).

When working with children affected by incarceration, it is important for teachers to challenge their own attitudes and bias toward incarceration. CPI are often stigmatized by both peers and teachers (Warren et al., 2019). Dallaire, Ciccone, and Wilson (2010) found teachers often lowered their standards for students who had incarcerated parents, which can be incredibly harmful to students' academic and social development (Rossen, 2011). Teachers can offer flexibility and understanding without lowering standards or viewing students as unable to academically and behaviorally succeed (Rossen, 2011). It is important to hold all students to high expectations and reframe judgments about the child's behavior. Instead of viewing a child negatively, teachers must view certain negative behaviors as indicators that the child's needs are not being met (Sitler, 2009).

Parents who are incarcerated are also often stigmatized. Therefore, it is important to consider attitudes toward parents who are incarcerated and work with them in a non-judgmental way, "recognizing that the child's parent is still their parent regardless of what they have been convicted of" (Morgan et al., 2013, p. 205). As a teacher, it is important to dismiss judgment when a parent is unable to attend conferences, answer phone calls, or sign important documents (de Guzman et al., 2018; Wiseman et al., 2019). Instead, we suggest building connections with all caregivers of the child and finding ways to engage the family. The key to supporting CPI is to foster a relationship with their caregivers (Nesmith & Ruhland, 2008). Teachers must consider ways to build connections with the caregiver, who is home with the child, as well as extending communication with the parent who is incarcerated; this often requires being open and flexible to meet the needs of the family. Rossen (2011) suggests teachers consistently share positive feedback with the child's caregivers, what is being taught in the classroom, and how caregivers can assist the child at home. Teachers can also implement opportunities for students to create artwork, write letters, or send classwork or projects to their parents to increase the connection between the child and parent (Morgan et al., 2013).

In addition to building family engagement and connections, teachers should consider collaborating with all stakeholders. Besides the child's caregivers, stakeholders may include teachers, guidance counselors, social workers, correctional officers, and any adult who might play a role in the child's life (Warren et al., 2019). Teachers can advocate for their students by connecting the child with other adults who might provide additional support. Guidance counselors and school psychologists have experience working with children who have experienced trauma; therefore, they may have valuable resources and knowledge to bolster classroom activities and build positive mentorships. Teachers should also utilize their school social workers' expertise to establish partnerships between the child and families and outside agencies that might offer ways to accommodate the families' needs (Morgan et al., 2013).

We argue teachers should also consider how to cultivate an empathetic learning environment in the classroom. Sitler (2009) suggests establishing peer mentors in the classroom as an approach to improve social engagement and academic needs, as well as develop positive peer relationships. It is also imperative to facilitate opportunities for emotional outlets, such as art, music, physical activities, and expressive writing (Sitler, 2009). Walker et al. (2022) describe how reflective journaling and writing activities can positively facilitate catharsis and healing. Through children's literature, teachers can raise awareness and develop empathy with other students with discussions and implement activities that promote internal reflection and expression.

Bibliotherapy is also an exceptional way to cultivate an empathetic learning environment where students feel safe to share and can learn from each other (see Chapter 2 for more information on bibliotherapy). When children read books that include characters who look like them or have similar experiences as them, they begin to identify with the literature or peek into the lives of their fellow classmates (Bishop, 1990). When children are educated on the incarceration of their parents, they are given more freedom to speak about their experiences and connect with others who share similar experiences, which in turn can help them cope with the situation (Nesmith & Ruhland, 2008). Walker et al. (2022) suggests bibliotherapeutic activities promote catharsis and healing and allow students to form their own vision for resiliency and empowerment. Using children's literature to facilitate open-ended discussions about parental identities is a powerful intervention tool that allows children to express their emotions and feel that they are seen and heard (Cryer-Coupet et al., 2021). Educators have a unique opportunity and responsibility to bolster the social, emotional, and academic needs of CPI. By building relationships, considering personal bias, engaging with all stakeholders, and cultivating an empathetic learning environment, teachers can support children who are affected by parental incarceration.

Methods for Book Selection

In this section, we describe the selection criteria for how we selected the multicultural children's literature to support CPI.

Selection Criteria

Jessica (third author) conducted a focused search of literature to build a recommended core list of timely books related to family incarceration to enhance classroom collections. Initial selection criteria included award-winning English-language contemporary children's fiction literature published from 2012 onward, suitable for kindergarten to 5th grade aged youth, and depicting families experiencing incarceration.

Search Strategy

To conduct the search, Jessica utilized the Children's Literature Comprehensive Database (CLCD), a leading resource for librarians and educators seeking unbiased information on a vast collection of diverse books. Over three-million titles are indexed in CLCD, with comprehensive metadata noting grade and age level, genre category (fiction/non-fiction), Lexile and AR scores, and publisher information. Particularly helpful to this search is the inclusion of abstracts, reviews from over 50 noted professional sources, and indication of national and international award recognition (CLCD, n.d.). She used the following advanced search options within the database:

- Subject field: incarceration OR jail OR prison.
- Grade Limit: Kindergarten; 1st, 2nd, 3rd, 4th, or 5th.
- Category: Fiction.
- Audience: Children and YA only.
- Publication date: 2012–2022.
- Awards and Honors: Winners or Honors.
- Award Winners Only.

Initial Results and Refinement

The initial search resulted in 90 potential books for consideration. Jessica then further narrowed that pool by manually reviewing each book's record for appropriateness to the search. In addition to excluding clearly irrelevant titles outside of the established search criteria, we decided to remove titles related to prisoner-of-war [POW] camps at this time in addition to fantasy stories, such as those depicting child spies attempting prison escapes. After this thorough review, 18 potential books remained.

To organize information on each remaining book, Jessica developed a spreadsheet, noting the following: Title, Author/Illustrator, Publication Date, Age Range, Abstract/Review, Awards, other tagged subjects, which family member was incarcerated, what type of carceral institution, and location information. We then obtained these 18 books via interlibrary loan at the university and from the local public library system.

After we obtained the books, we developed this rubric based on previous published articles that evaluated children's literature (Al-Hazza & Bucher, 2008; Bennett et al., 2021; Bishop, 1990; Gunn et al., 2015; Gunn et al., 2021). Three of the authors then read the books and rated them based on this rubric.

Recommend Children's Literature

Based on the results of the rubric, we recommend the following children's literature (see Table 15.3) to open classroom conversations to support CPI and to develop empathy and understanding with their peers.

Table 15.2. Evaluating books that represent families members who have been incarcerated rubric.

Criteria	1–3 (1 = poor; 2 = meets some of the criteria; 3 = excellent)
Culturally Pluralistic Theme	The book fosters the idea that incarceration impacts families in multi-faceted ways. Founded upon tenets of social justice the book portrays relationships between individuals who are incarcerated.
Positively Portrayed Characters	The characters accurately define concepts of struggles for justice appropriate to specific families. The literature avoids stereotypes associated with individuals who have been incarcerated.
Setting in U.S.	While the book may contain historical or cultural perspectives from other countries, the main setting of the book is in the U.S., and the setting takes place or discusses of U.S. correctional facilities/institutions.
Authentic Illustrations	Illustrations complement the book and represent diverse populations.
Strong Plot and Characterization	The book has a strong plot and effective characterization for reader's enjoyment of the story. The piece of literature is well written and of high quality in regard to theme, plot, setting, and characters. Will children enjoy this book?
Reader's Cultural Consciousness	The story components has the potential to provide "windows and/or mirrors" and the power to positively shape his or her cultural consciousness about families who have a member(s) who have been incarcerated.

Table 15.3 Recommended pieces multicultural literature for elementary aged classrooms.

Book Information	Summary
Title: *Knock Knock: My Dad's Dream for Me* **Author and Illustrator:** Daniel Beaty (Author), Bryan Collier (Illustrator) **Awards:** *Coretta Scott King Award; Boston Globe-Horn Book Honors; Marion Vannett Ridgway Honors* **Grade Level Band:** K-3	**Summary:** A little boy shares a daily morning "knock knock" ritual with this father, until one day those knocks do not come. The boy questions what his father's absence means. He writes a letter asking his father to come home and receives a response full of love and support. The exact nature of the father's incarceration is left open, allowing the young reader who is experiencing absence or loss to picture themselves within the story.
Title: *Far Apart, Close in Heart: Being A Family When a Loved One is Incarcerated* **Author and Illustrator:** Becky Birtha (Author), Maja Kastelic (Illustrator) **Awards:** *Kirkus Reviews Best Books Award* **Grade Level Band:** K-3	**Summary:** This book follows multiple child characters who each have incarcerated parents. The story taps into and validates various emotions a child may feel when a parent is incarcerated: fear, anger, loneliness, or sadness. Young readers are reminded that overcoming these feelings is possible, things can get better again, and they are not alone. Helpful tips for staying connected with an incarcerated parent, as well as being true to your own feelings are shared.
Title: *Milo Imagines the World* **Author and Illustrator:** Matt de la Peña (Author), Christian Robinson (Illustrator) **Awards:** *Kirkus Reviews Best Book Award; Boston Globe-Horn Book Honors; Publishers Weekly Best Book of the Year; ALA Notable Children's Book* **Grade Level Band:** K-3	**Summary:** Milo rides the subway with his older sister to an unnamed destination, illustrating the imagined lives of the people around him as he travels. Once he reaches his stop, Milo notices another young rider is headed to the same destination – the visiting room of an incarceration facility where Milo will visit his mother. Milo suddenly realizes you cannot know everything about some's life just by looking at them.
Title: *Missing Daddy* **Author and Illustrator:** Mariame Kaba (Author), Bria Royal (Illustrator) **Awards:** *Center for the Study of Multicultural Children's Literature Best Books; Chicago Public Library's Best of the Best Books 2019* **Grade Level Band:** K-2	**Summary:** A little girl misses her father, who is away in prison. She shares how his absence impacts her life and reflects on the joy she has when she can visit him at the prison. Despite the distance, the child and her father are still able to maintain their bonds of love. Throughout the story, other adults affirm and support the child's feelings.

Book Information	Summary
Title: *Let the Children March* **Author and Illustrator:** Monica Clark-Robinson (Author), Frank Morrison (Illustrator) **Awards:** *Choices Awards; ILA Children's and Young Adults' Book Award* **Grade Level Band:** K-6	**Summary:** In 1963 Birmingham, Alabama, thousands of African American children volunteered to march for their civil rights after hearing Dr. Martin Luther King Jr. speak. Many of these children and their family members were incarcerated due to these efforts. This book is a fictionalized account of a true historical moment, which may allow for expanded conversations about the complexity of incarceration, social justice, and civil rights.
Title: *Ruby on the Outside* **Author:** Nora Raleigh Baskin **Awards:** *Cooperative Children's Book Council Choices Awards; Notable Books for a Global Society; Book Page Children's Top Pick* **Grade Level Band:** 3–8	**Summary:** Rising sixth grader Ruby has never had a best friend, nor shared her deepest secret – her mother is in prison. Ruby lives with her aunt and visits her mother every weekend. Ruby makes a new friend and wonders if it is finally safe to share her secret. At the same time, Ruby is becoming more curious about what led to her mother's incarceration and seeks answers, along the way finding healing and acceptance.
Title: *All Rise for the Honorable Perry T. Cook'* **Author:** Leslie Connor **Awards:** *Best Children's Books of the Year; New York Public Library's 100 Titles for Reading and Sharing; Goodreads Choice Awards* **Grade Level Band:** 3–8	**Summary:** Eleven-year-old Perry has a happy, yet unconventional life. Since birth he has lived at the minimum-security prison where his mom has been incarcerated, alongside her fellow incarcerated individuals and prison staff. Authorities take notice and place him into foster care. Perry seeks answers about his mother's crimes in hopes they will be reunited sooner. Throughout, he tells the stories of his other incarcerated friends to show that incarceration is just one aspect of their lives.
Title: *From the Desk of Zoe Washington* **Author and Illustrator:** Janae Marks **Awards:** *Top 10 First Novels for youth, Best Children's Books, 2020; Heartland Books Recommendations for Lifelong Readers- Excellence in Young Adult Literature* **Grade Level Band:** 5	**Summary:** Zoe Washington wants to show her parents how responsible she is in order to enter the Kids Bake Challenge on National TV! However, her plans are interrupted when she receives a birthday card from her father in prison who she has never met. He has never contacted her......or has he? Zoe, challenged to understand different perspectives surrounding her father's case, enlists the help of the Innocent Project to clear his name.

Book Information	Summary
Title: *Land of Cranes* **Author and Illustrator:** Aida Salzadaar **Awards:** *Americas Award for Children's and Young Adult Literature, Jane Addams Book Award, John and Patricia Beatty Award,* **Grade Level Band:** 3–5	**Summary:** Betita, a nine-year-old girl, and her family left Mexico to escape the cartel wars and moved to California. Her father tells her stories of her Aztec ancestors who came from the land of cranes. Her father is arrested and deported back to Mexico, and then soon after, she and her pregnant mom are placed in a family detention center. Betita writes picture poetry to reflect and express her feelings. *This book offers a place for discussion around a different type of imprisonment.

Reflection Questions

1. Examine biases you might have about individuals who are incarcerated. How would that affect how you teach students who have a parent in prison? How would you make sure you were supporting that student?
2. Choose one of the suggested children's literature and develop a set of questions you might ask to facilitate a discussion in your class.
3. Describe how you would create a safe and caring environment to support a student with a parent in prison.
4. Visit at least three of the different resources and determine how you could or why you wouldn't incorporate it into your classroom.

Additional Resources

App

- Sesame Street Incarceration App: www.sesamestreet.org/apps

Podcasts

- Advocating for Children of Incarcerated Parents (Episode 23): www.britannica.com/podcasts/raising-curious-learners/raising-curious-learners-conversation-with-Ebony-Underwood
- How to Support Pupils Affected by Imprisonment: https://open.spotify.com/episode/4JkojDNnlhWHiyOjpwgCQO?si=jkMqEqddSqu7fZIF4Z8G4Q&context=spotify%3Ashow%3A6QVuC4nXF5Xdm9VRMPTVrr&nd=1

Videos

- School Staff: Supporting Youth with Incarcerated Parents: https://youth.gov/youth-topics/children-of-incarcerated-parents/federal-tools-resources/tools-school-staff
- Sesame Street: Little Children, Big Challenges: Incarceration - Animation: Visiting Dad in Prison: www.youtube.com/watch?v=I3sf7O5mrIY
- Dallaire: How to help children with incarcerated parents: www.youtube.com/watch?v=MbTP4o4nQGs

Websites

- Tips to Support Children When a Parent is in Prison: www.healthychildren.org/English/healthy-living/emotional-wellness/Building-Resilience/Pages/Tips-to-Support-Children-When-a-Parent-is-in-Prison.aspx
- Tip Sheet for teachers: https://youth.gov/youth-topics/children-of-incarcerated-parents/federal-tools-resources/tip-sheet-teachers
- Children of Incarcerated Parents—Presentations: https://youth.gov/youth-topics/children-of-incarcerated-parents/presentations
- We Are Not Collateral Consequences: Children of Incarcerated Parents: https://thenext100.org/we-are-not-collateral-consequences-children-of-incarcerated-parents/?gclid=Cj0KCQiAk4aOBhCTARIsAFWFP9Esq_ub5tKri9Gh3vsoAzD4VgzcWnavXUfE82i9-SP6tQgTOQfGLhUaAqY1EALw_wcB
- Creating Inclusive Schools: How to Support Students with Incarcerated Parents: https://teach.com/resources/counseling-students-incarcerated-parents/

References

Al-Hazza, T., & Bucher, K. T. (2008). Building Arab Americans' cultural identity and acceptance with children's literature. *The Reading Teacher, 62*(3), 210–219.

Annie E. Casey Foundation. (2022, March). Children who had a parent who was ever incarcerated by race and ethnicity in the United States. https://datacenter.kidscount.org/data/bar/9734-children-who-had-a-parent-who-was-ever-incarcerated-by-race-and-ethnicity?loc=1&loct=1#1/any/false/1696/10,11,9,12,1,13/18996.

Bartlett, R. (2000). Helping inmate moms keep in touch: Prison programs encourage ties with children. *Corrections Today, 62*, 102–104.

Bennett, S. V., Gunn, A. A., van Beynen, K., & Morton, M. L. (2021). Religiously diverse multicultural literature for early childhood. *Early Childhood Education Journal.* https://doi.org/10.1007/s10643-021-01180-7.

Bishop, R. S. (1990). Windows, mirrors, and sliding glass doors. *Perspectives, 6*(3), ix–xi.

Blumberg, D. M., & Griffin, D. A. (2013). Family connections: The importance of prison reading programs for incarcerated parents and their children. *Journal of Offender Rehabilitation, 52* (4), 254–269.

CLCD. (n.d.). About CLCD. www.clcd.com/#/universal/aboutus.

Cryer-Coupet, Q. R., Wiseman, A. M., Atkinson, A. A., Gibson, S., & Hoo, A. M. (2021). Teaching note—drawn together: Collaboration between social work and education to address family trauma. *Journal of Social Work Education*, 57 (4), 817–824.

Dallaire, D. H., Ciccone, A., & Wilson, L. C. (2010). Teachers' experiences with and expectations of children with incarcerated parents. *Journal of Applied Developmental Psychology*, 31 (4), 281–290.

de Guzman, M. R., Brown, J., & Edwards, C. (2018). Introduction to parenting from afar and the reconfiguration of family across distance. https://digitalcommons.unl.edu/famconfacpub/220.

Gramlich, (2021). America's incarceration rate falls to the lowest since 1995. www.pewresearch.org/fact-tank/2021/08/16/americas-incarceration-rate-lowest-since-1995/.

Gunn, A., Bennett, S.V., & Morton, M. L. (Winter, 2015). Culturally responsive literacy pedagogy: Using children's literature to discuss topics of religious diversity. *Florida Reading Journal*, 49(1), 17–24.

Gunn, A. A., & Bennett, S. V., van Beynen, K. (2021). Talking about religious diversity: Using multicultural literature as a tool. *Social Studies and the Young Learner*, 33(1), 10–16.

Hoffmann, H. C., Byrd, A. L., & Kightlinger, A. M. (2010). Prison programs and services for incarcerated parents and their underage children: Results from a national survey of correctional facilities. *The Prison Journal*, 90(4), 397–416.

Kjellstrand, J. M., & Eddy, J. M. (2011). Parental incarceration during childhood, family, context, and youth problem behavior across adolescence. *Journal of Rehabilitation*, 50(1), 18–35. https://doi.org/10.1080/10509674.2011.536720.

Loper, A. B., & Tuerk, E. H. (2006). Parenting programs for incarcerated parents: Current research and future directions. *Criminal Justice Policy Review*, 17(4), 407–427.

Love, B. L. (2019). *We want to do more than survive: Abolitionist teaching and the pursuit of educational freedom*. Beacon Press.

Martin, E. (2017). Hidden consequences: The impact of incarceration on dependent children. www.ojp.gov/pdffiles1/nij/250349.pdf.

Mauer, M. (2013). The changing racial dynamics of women's incarceration. www.sentencingproject.org/publications/the-changing-racial-dynamics-of-womens-incarceration/.

McLeod, D. A., B. Pharris, A., Marcus-Mendoza, S., Winkles, R. A., Chapman, R., & Fuller, C. (2021). Reducing trauma from behind bars: Enhancing parent-child attachment through a digitally distributed reading program. *The Prison Journal*, 101(5), 575–590.

Morgan, J., Leeson, C., & Carter Dillon, R. (2013). How can schools support children with a parent in prison? *Pastoral Care in Education*, 31(3), 199–210.

Muth, B., Sturtevant, E., & Pannozzo, G. (2017). Performance and beliefs: Two assessments of literacy learners in prison part 1. *The Journal of Correctional Education*, 68(1), 71.

Nesmith, A., & Ruhland, E. (2008). Children of incarcerated parents: Challenges and resiliency, in their own words. *Children and Youth Services Review*, 30(10), 1119–1130.

Noddings, N. (1992). *The challenge to care in school: An alternative approach to education*. Teachers College Press.

Nutbrown, C., Clough, P., Stammers, L., Emblin, N., & Alston-Smith, S. (2019). Family literacy in prisons: fathers' engagement with their young children. *Research Papers in Education*, 34(2), 169–191.

Pochlmann-Tynan, J., & Turney, K. (2021). A development perspective on children with incarcerated parents. *Child Development Perspectives*, 15(1), 3–11.

Prins, E., Stickel, T., & Kaiper-Marquez, A. (2020). Incarcerated fathers' experiences in the read to your child/grandchild program: Supporting children's literacy, learning, and education. *Journal of Prison Education and Reentry*, 6(2), 168–188.

Reimer, V. P. (2019). Hidden children: Using children's literature to develop understanding and empathy toward children of incarcerated parents. *Language and Literacy*, 21(1), 98–121.

Rossen, E. (2011). Supporting students with incarcerated parents. *Principal Leadership*, 12(3), 12–16.

Sitler, H. C. (2009). Teaching with awareness: The hidden effects of trauma on learning. *The Clearing House: A Journal of Educational Strategies, Issues and Ideas*, 82(3), 119–124.

Sykes, B. L., & Pettit, B. (2014). Mass incarceration, family complexity, and the reproduction of childhood disadvantage. *The Annals of the American Academy of Political and Social Science*, 654, 127–149.

Thompson, H. A. (2010). Why mass incarceration matters: Rethinking crisis, decline, and transformation in postwar American history. *The Journal of American History*, 97, 703–734.

Turney, K. (2019). Understanding the needs of children with incarcerated parents: What educators should know. *American Educator*, 43(2), 22–28.

Walker, S. L., Connery, C., Blackson, G. N., Divine, T. F., Walker, T. D., Williams, B., & Bartel, K. (2020). Developing resilience in youth with incarcerated parents. *Journal of Correctional Education*, 71(2), 37–56.

Warren, J. M., Coker, G. L., Collins, M. L. (2019). Children of incarcerated parents: Considerations for professional school counselors. *The Professional Counselor*, 9(3), 185–199.

Wiseman, A. M., Atkinson, A. A., & Vehabovic, N. (2019). "Mom, when are you coming home?": Family literacy for parents who are addicted, incarcerated, and/or homeless. *Language Arts*, 97(1), 36–41.

Wissman, K. K., & Wiseman, A. M. (2011). "That's my worst nightmare": poetry and trauma in the middle school classroom. *Pedagogies: An International Journal*, 6(3), 234–249.

Childrens Literature Cited

Baskin, N. R. (2015). *Ruby on the outside*. Simon & Schuster.

Birtha, B. (2017). *Far apart, close in heart: Being a family when a loved one is incarcerated*. Albert Whitman & Company.

Clark-Robinson, M. (2018). *Let the children march*. Houghton Mifflin Harcourt.

Connor, L. (2016). *All rise for the Honorable Perry T. Cook*. HarperCollins.

Daniel, B. (2013). *Knock knock: My dad's dream for me*. Little, Brown and Company.

De la Peña, M. (2021). *Milo imagines the world*. G. P. Putnam's Sons Books.

Kaba, M. (2019). *Missing daddy*. Haymarket Books.

Marks, J. (2020). *From the desk of Zoe Washington*. HarperCollins.

Salzadaar, A. (2020). *Land of Cranes*. Scholastic Press.

Appendix: Foundational Teaching Tips

1. Children with a parent who is incarcerated might have serious emotional and mental challenges. A teacher should first read the children's literature and possibly seek an expert in the field to discuss the best ways to approach the classroom conversation around the book.
2. After reading the piece of literature, it is always important to create a safe and comfortable environment where the child can respond in other ways such as writing or drawing. The child might not be ready to share verbally with the teacher or classmates.
3. As the teacher, you should think about how different children might respond to the characters who are in prison. You should develop questions to ask before, during, and after reading to facilitate comprehension and empathy from the children.

Index

Note: *Italic* page numbers refer to figures and **Bold** page numbers refer to tables respectively.